Under Magnolia

CROWN PUBLISHERS
NEW YORK

Under Magnolia

A SOUTHERN MEMOIR

Frances Mayes

Copyright © 2014 by Frances Mayes

All rights reserved.
Published in the United States by Crown Publishers, an imprint of the
Crown Publishing Group, a division of Random House LLC,
a Penguin Random House Company, New York.
www.crownpublishing.com

CROWN and the Crown colophon are registered trademarks
of Random House LLC

Library of Congress Cataloging-in-Publication Data
Mayes, Frances.
    Under magnolia: a southern memoir/Frances Mayes.
      pages cm
1. Mayes, Frances. 2. Authors, American—20th century—Biography. 3. Authors,
American—21st century—Biography. I. Title.
    PS3563.A956Z46 2014
    811'.54—dc23
    [B]   2013042448

ISBN 978-0-307-88591-3
eISBN 978-0-307-88593-7

Printed in the United States of America

Book design by Elizabeth Rendfleisch
Photographs courtesy of the author
Jacket design by Elena Giavaldi
Jacket photographs: (magnolia) Georg Dionysius Ehret/Getty; (tree) The Granger
Collection, NYC. All rights reserved; (plant) ullstein bild/The Granger Collection,
NYC. All rights reserved; (map) Historic Map Works LLC/Getty Images;
(stamp) Georgia Brown Thrasher and Charokee Rose © 1982 United States Postal
Service. All rights reserved. Used with permission; (young Frances, Frances's mother,
Frances's father, house) courtesy of the author

10 9 8 7 6 5 4 3 2 1

First Edition

for my daughter, Ashley

Memory believes before knowing remembers. Believes longer than recollects, longer than knowing even wonders.

WILLIAM FAULKNER, *LIGHT IN AUGUST*

CONTENTS

Contents

Under Magnolia

PREFACE

A Grape Leaf from Faulkner's Arbor

At a few times in my life, I've not been aware that I've just stepped onto a large X.

Change might not be on my mind. Why change? I've always admired lives that flourish in place. The taproot reaches all the way to the aquifer, the leaves bud, flourish, fall, and grow again. I like generations following one another in the same house, where lamplight falls through the windows in squares of light on the snow, and somebody's height chart still marks the kitchen doorway. But there I stand on the X, not knowing it's time to leap, when, really, I'd only meant to pause. In Oxford, Mississippi, one chance weekend, the last thing I expected was a life-changing epiphany.

Looking up at a white southern manse with the requisite rocking chairs and hanging ferns on the porch, I ratcheted my carry-on bag up the steps and rang the bell.

"Is this all right? Everything decent is full because of the football game," the woman who gave me a lift had explained.

Decent, she said. You hear that word all the time in the South: *a decent person, a decent meal, a decent amount of time, that's decent of you.* I don't recall hearing the word often at home in California. As she drove away, I waved and her car picked up speed.

A shutter hangs slightly askew, and from paint-encrusted windows white flakes scatter on the porch floor. *Lead-based.* If I pressed a screwdriver into the sill, I'd find rot. Now, standing on the other side of a screen door, I'm biting the side of my forefinger, as I do when I'm nervous. But why should I be nervous? A memory flashes of my mother dropping me off at camp, gunning the Oldsmobile out of there as soon as my trunk of summer clothes was unloaded.

No one is on the other side of the door, but on a table I find a note: "WELCOME! You'll find number three at the top of the stairs on the left." The hallway smells familiar. Pound cake? A toasted slice smeared with butter, my preferred snack when I was a southern child.

A four-poster bed with a nubby white bedspread almost entirely fills the square room. Crocheted doilies adorn scuffed bedside tables; a fake bouquet fails to brighten the chest of drawers. There's a smell, not bad but not good, no, not good. Pine-scented disinfectant, worn-out shoes, and certainly a mattress someone has sweat-soaked during August naps. Speckles of blue mildew border the shower curtain. Dust motes. A thousand memories suddenly free-fall through me.

. . .

I've long since cut the tie that binds. I left the South a million years ago. And I'm midway into a book tour, a celebratory trip; this will be only a short hiatus before my reading at Oxford's famous Square Books. For two weeks, I've been traveling—the exhilaration of events in bookstores, jaunts on everything from supersized flying mastodons to kite-sized flap-a-doodles, sumptuous feasts, even the late-night minibar dinners, have been fun, plus the constant joy of new places. My energy even overpowers the chronic sleeplessness that keeps me rotating on the sheets until my skin feels rope-burned.

Ah, it's the quiet old house that throws me back inside the globe. Shake it and golden dust falls down over the fairies. The high ceilings, the graceful proportions of the room, the trapped time—that's it, a room where a newborn squalled and a reprobate uncle slept it off and a woman sat monogramming pillowcases in the rocker. When I was eleven and stayed overnight at my grandfather's house, I'd sleep in the square pale green bedroom where my grandmother spent her illness before she died. Mother Mayes rested in a slipper chair by the window. The coils of her shimmering silver hair sprung close to her pink scalp. I caught a faint, rank odor: her flowered, flounced gowns—talcum, yes, Fleur de Rocaille perfume, rice pudding, starch, rose lotion, a back smell of pee-pee. In the glass by her bed, her false teeth seemed to smile.

My heart booms. It's damned hot, even though October is half over.

. . .

When I left the South at age twenty-two, the force that pushed me west was as powerful as the magnet that held me. For years when I went back home to visit, I broke out in hives. The insides of my arms erupted in the same place as when I had severe poison ivy at thirteen as a junior bridesmaid at my sister Nancy's wedding. My mother was annoyed. *Keep your disgusting arms close to your sides.* The weepy yellow seepage stained the pink tulle dress.

Powerful juju, I say aloud.

My cell phone has no signal. In the hall I find a house phone and call a taxi. After a hundred rings, a woman answers. She covers the phone with her hand and I hear her yell, "Can you go get this lady?" I wait on the porch with my bag. The ancient man who pulls up in a dilapidated car takes me to a motel near downtown. I need neutral ground. Not Tara Redux.

Good luck—they do have one last tragic little room. At least I can walk out to a restaurant, instead of eating a package of cheese crackers for dinner. At least I see no giant oaks spreading their bony fingers outside the window, no hedges of arching bridal wreath, no rectangular panes of gossamer light on polished heart-pine floors. Just a shaky wall heater that sounds as if it's flying to Atlanta, and a maroon bedspread covering thousands of nights of unspeakable acts. The carpet resembles matted hair.

Late in the afternoon, I walk into town and am stunned by the human scale and harmony of glossy white and redbrick nineteenth-century buildings, some with upstairs porches called so charmingly in the South "piazzas." Shaded streets complete the natural complement of architecture that does not dwarf but, instead, extends the excellent proposition that the body will live well in this space. Under the protection of the sun-spangled leafy canopy, I feel suddenly buoyant. The verdurous air sends me reeling back to my Georgia hometown's trees: crape myrtle, oak, palm, longleaf pine, magnolia, pecan, sycamore. Roller-skating on bumpy, root-torn sidewalks, in and out of shade, down the street as though down a green chute, I knew the blitheful cool, then—what a shock of difference—the sliding into light. The sun could melt a bar of gold. In Fitzgerald, so much green—that's how we saved ourselves from the burning eye of God.

The great white courthouse presides, a promise of justice that so long eluded this handsome square. William Faulkner called the courthouse "musing, brooding, symbolic and ponderable." *Ponderable,* yes, much to ponder. How could only twelve thousand people in this small kingdom need so much legal help? The names on small swaying signs—Chaffin, Clisby, Fondren, Percy, Mason, Hatcher—seem like authors' striving attempts to brand their characters as memorable. One shingle says Landon Tallesin Calder, a name Faulkner easily could have made up. Where's that drugstore where he checked out mysteries from the lending library? The department store window looks like pre-WWII families still shop there. Overalls, green jumpers, undershirts, kneesocks. *Kneesocks.* Inside, I buy a pair of black sneakers because my flats feel like tightened vises around my heels. I've pricked both blisters with the needle from a hotel sewing kit I found in my luggage. I run my hand over stacks of coarse plaid wool shirts—hunting season is starting, a thought I've not had in decades. Not my father, but someone will be bringing home passels of doves for a luckless woman to pluck and stack in mounds of mauve pink flesh. Those downy feathers rising in the air. Many's the time I've bitten buckshot.

Thinking of dinner, I start to notice how many inviting restaurants enliven the streets. I'll love the updated hushpuppies with mint and crab and the pork tenderloin with pecan crust. But surely some old place still slings out fried pies heavy enough to sink a rowboat, peppery smothered quail, cheese grits, and smoky barbecue. Ah, that's what I want. All of that.

Like Cortona, my best beloved Tuscan hill town, Oxford invites you in, makes you a participant in the repetition and variation of its particular themes. As in Piazza Signorelli, you're a star in the cast as you step into the daily play. Your breathing slows, your shoulders push back. All the proprioceptors agree: This is how a town should be built. But unlike any Italian town, here the green air under massive trees dislodges my senses: world in a jar. You may stroll in this vast terrarium, or so I felt growing up in a one-mile-square town in south Georgia. One reason I felt immediately at home in Tuscany was that certain strong currents of life reminded me of the South. The warmth of people and their astonishing generosity felt so familiar, and I knew well that identical *y'all come* hospitality. "It's unhealthy to eat alone," our neighbor in Italy told us early on. "We're cooking every night so come on over." I learned that the attitudes toward food were not an external custom, but, as in the South, a big cultural clue about how people weave together their lives.

A faint church bell sounds and a bright-eyed terrier joins my walk. Although no bells tolled, in Fitzgerald we had the Tuscan sense of *campanilismo,* the bonds among those who live within the sound of their parish church bell's ringing. Those who hear the five dongs and three dings live at the center of the world; those outside of range live in *terra incognita.* We had no visible gates into Fitzgerald, but still they were there. When Southerners meet, in Mexico, Cleveland, or Sri Lanka, in a way they know each other. "Do I hear a southern accent?" the dental hygienist in San Francisco asks as she gouges. She stops. It is as if we have gone to the same college or survived an earthquake together. "I'm only from Louisville," she admits, "but my mother is from Chapel Hill."

The complex interconnections of family and friends, the real caring for one another, the incessant talk, emphasis on ancestors, the raucous humor, the appreciation of the bizarre, the storytelling, the fatalism, the visiting, the grand occasions—in both Tuscany and the South these traits offer an elaborate continuity for solitary individuals. Deeply fatalistic, Southerners, again like Tuscans, can be the most private people on the globe.

Tuscans are at home with the past, and when I was a child, we locals also felt that comfort. "Now, your great-grandmother

Sarah America Gray," my aunt began. She had only a small cache of stories about this "Mericky," as she was called. The half-moons of Mericky's nails repeat in mine, or so my aunt told me.

Science may discover the truth of backward time. Southerners and Tuscans already know it in their bone marrow. I can lie awake at three a.m. and imagine that I am lying awake at three a.m. in all the places I've had insomnia. I am still in that camp cabin, still on the sailboat *Primavera*, still in my old house in Somers, still in the upstairs room in Tuscany. I transport myself from bed to bed, year to year, multiply myself simultaneously until I am extant in times and places, wide awake in all of them.

You may thrive, you may never scale the slippery glass terrarium walls and fly away, and this enclosed and greenest-green world is so beautiful that you may never want to.

The dog spots a woman pushing a stroller and patters after her without another glance at me. At Square Books, pilgrimage site for readers and writers, I wander the hallowed sections, pull down *Absalom, Absalom!,* and at random place my finger on a paragraph:

> *Do you mark how the wistaria, sun-impacted on this wall here, distills and penetrates this room ... That is the substance of remembering—sense, sight, smell: the muscles with which we see and hear and feel—not mind, not thought: there is no such thing as memory: the brain recalls just what the muscles grope for ... —Once there was ... a summer of wistaria. It was a pervading everywhere*

of wistaria (I was fourteen then) as though of all springs yet to capitu-
late condensed into one spring, one summer . . .

As children, we opened the Bible and stabbed a finger down
onto a verse that we read as a personal message from God. And
so I take out my notebook and copy Faulkner's passage. I'm loving all those colons connecting everything so nicely. *Wistaria.*
Once there was a summer of wistaria.

Soon Oxford pulls me back outside. I would like to walk for
days. I'm pressed to know: why the exuberance and melancholy
attacked me, why the abrupt heart flips, why the primal rush of
memory, why this physical magnetism that feels dangerous . . .
there is no such thing as memory: the brain recalls just what the muscles
grope for. He's nailed that. The intense physicality of being here
seems to electrify the synapses in my brain. I'm returned to my
hand reaching down into ice water to pull up a Nehi soda, my
feet avoiding the cracks that break my mother's back, my arms
feeling the hoist up the knotted rope into the pecan tree, all
extensors working, my straight spine a muscle that remembers.

The fall-touched air tastes like home. Not home as I knew it
but home behind home. Does this make sense, Mr. Faulkner?
Now why *did* you spell *wistaria* like that?

Morning is iffy. Great stony clumps of cloud seem more
likely to pour down an avalanche than the spitting rain starting
now to sting my face. Let it rain—my raincoat has a hood and
I'm taking this free day for a Faulkner quest. Let the backlit

leaves filigree against the sky. Faulkner wasn't ever a favorite of mine. In high school, I could fall into his sentences that meandered like old rivers curving back and snaking forward. Most of his characters seemed as familiar as the red clay dirt my bare feet learned to walk on, as the flat-out ornery, peculiar, unto-themselves folks I knew as the only possible world—those who might have a fake eyeball monogrammed "RG" (means *real good*, he leers), or who could go on and on about somebody swallowing a fly, or wear aqua chiffon with sneakers. My high school boyfriend lived to catch dreary-faced rockfish with poison spikes on their backs. He hardly ever snagged one, but every blue moon he hauled up an old horror with a dozen rusted hooks dangling algae from the lower jaw. These splotched creatures somehow detoured up brackish creeks from the ocean bottom, rootled the blackest pools for two hundred years, and grew two feet long.

Because when I was young, Faulkner felt so *known*, I often smacked down *Light in August* or *As I Lay Dying*, thinking *I don't want to*. What did confound me was the transcendence Faulkner could achieve, like a sudden leap of a circus lion onto the higher perch—ah, there's the magical lion face, impassive, imperial, looking down on the little ringmaster with the puny whip. The South I knew didn't transcend. I wanted out of there. No future I imagined took place below the southern fall line. "She took the first thing smoking on the runway out of here," my family is fond of remembering. But they forget; there was no runway.

. . .

Saint Peter's Cemetery would not be a bad place to lie, if one must. Among the graves rise obelisks, draped urns, broken columns, and languishing, ministering women, the everlasting symbol. The word "obelisk" originally meant *skewer*. Sacrificial bits and pieces were strung on poles for veneration. Well, we're skewered by death, aren't we? I pass some Falkners, but not the big guy who changed the spelling of the family name. One of them, his stone says, has been "borne on eagle wings" to the great beyond. Ah, the mythic South, the only swath of America not strangled by the deadly literal mind. Wandering about, I see a grave with an empty bottle of Jack Daniel's on it. Here's where I find William Cuthbert Faulkner.

The wife Estelle's stone sinks to the right. The dead here seem really dead, and bone lonely, unlike the graves in Italian cemeteries, bedecked with fresh flowers, red votive lights, and photos of the deceased. I always imagine that they must rise at night and visit among themselves, the way they used to in the piazza.

I did cry over *Absalom, Absalom!* Maybe I did like him; maybe I've taken a circuitous path to this grave.

His compatriots in death are people he must have known. Near him lies Maggie Sue Lewis. Was she a music teacher who rapped knuckles of haphazard students? Opal Miller Worthy close beside Haley Dewey Worthy, Malcolm Argyle Franklin—did they read *As I Lay Dying*? Thomas Somerville Cully—there's a Faulknerian name—then a child-sized indentation of a long-lost occupant identified as Baby Alabama.

. . .

After lunch, where the waiter tells me "Yes, people often go out to have a drink with their old friend Bill," I walk out to Faulkner's home, Rowan Oak. On the way, I pass a delectable southern-style home for sale. The sprawling clapboard house and screen porch seem to ride on a raft of azaleas that must be pink in spring. Massive shade of sycamores and oaks casts wavy subaqueous light over white boards and grass blue in shadow. My grandmother's Rook partner, Mrs. Ricker, might be inside painting camellias on white china. Or, can I see myself cutting out biscuits on the yellow Formica counter? No—writing a novel in the spare room, calmly living out the southern life that would have been mine had I not headed west, yanked by some driving instinct for the tabula rasa. Instead, all these years of my life in California I've felt happily balanced on the last crust of the United States, just before the oblivion of the Pacific.

Mrs. Ricker became a recluse. Through eyelet curtains beginning to shred, my friends and I spied on her. We saw her sitting on her oven door to keep warm. Gaunt in a white nightgown, her white hair spiked out around her face as she swiveled toward the window and her owl eyes found our three grinning faces. *Oh, Jesus H. Christ.* We scrambled out of the spirea, screaming and laughing.

The cedar-lined entrance to Rowan Oak looks Italian, though the trees have gone gangly and unkempt. Orange caution tape drapes across the drive. The waiter told me that restoration soon will begin. Since the place looks deserted, I walk in anyway. Add to my résumé: trespasser at the house of Faulkner. A black-tailed deer chewing weeds regards my approach with mild interest. Rowan Oak, a peeling, modest two-story plantation house, looks anthropomorphically alone. Concentric brickwork marks an old garden. Pick a rose for Emily? Nothing but moss grows in the beds. Of what remains of abandoned places, the garden proves to be less ephemeral than you'd think. The broadest gestures, such as the leaning brick wall, retain tenacity. Even a great camellia, or a burst of yellow irises along a drive, can endure longer than the memory of the inhabitants. From a plane, sometimes a garden's foundation architecture remains visible for centuries. A sign warns politely PLEASE DO NOT CLIMB THIS TREE. But no tree remains.

Faulkner lived here from 1930 until his death, with a long sojourn in Virginia late in his life. I wonder if he'd had it up to here by then. Behind the veil of rain, I'm more intrepid than usual. I even try the door. *He opened this door thousands of times.* Locked. I cup my hands around my face to cut the glare. Peering into the windows of William Faulkner's house! When I see the plain staircase to the second floor, suddenly his presence feels palpable. Here he stepped—barefoot, wearing boots or felt slippers up to bed. Descending in the morning, tying his robe, for a cup of what, Jack Daniel's? Ovaltine? What sustained him through all those convoluted books? He plotted chapters on one wall, writing in pencil. Did he want to look literally at *the handwriting on the wall*?

The house is flanked by a *porte cochère* and upstairs porches. They probably sweltered here in the days before AC. Any slight mosquito-laden breeze must have been welcome. In our house, the spinning blades of the attic fan drew air out of the wide hall, pulling coolness in through the windows. I could see the lift of curtains in the bedroom where my father napped and my mother rested in a satin cap to protect her hairdo. I lined up my dolls on the sills and fed them raisins to keep them cool and happy.

I wonder if there was an attic fan at Rowan Oak to bring in the muggy, delicious night scents. Nothing about the South stirs me as much as the narcotizing fragrance of the land, jasmine, ginger lilies, gardenia, and honeysuckle blending, fetid and sweet. The scent entangles with the euphonious chorus of tree frogs, and the mouthy baritone swamp frogs croaking *contrappunto*. Only here can I step outside and, by merely inhaling the air, say, "Lord God."

I was born in late March on Easter Saturday and must have inhaled from the window the particular concoction that still brings me the undeniable sensation of *home*. Is it the smell of a just-washed newborn child, or a fox among wild dog roses, or the rattler's skin shed in the woodpile? Maybe it's pinesap dropping in spring water. Lawd o' mercy, Uncle Remus, that must be the song of the South.

How many countries I've seen, and nowhere else experienced the soft balm of a southern night. Somewhere, near the heart of India, exotic lotuses, cow dung, green mango, and the silty yellow river must throw out a powerful essence of the land. Or the African veld, mixing a perfume of acacia pollen, suntoasted grass, ancient mud where animals have wallowed, and bleached bones of jackals. I don't know. I've never been there.

Faulkner made a deep place. I feel that instantly. Old mother magnolias shine in the rain, their lay-my-burden-down branches touch the ground. Did his wife, as my mother did, strain her hand to clip tough stems so the fireplace in summer was filled with great face-sized flowers? And the daughter, whose name I have forgotten, did she pick out red berries from the cones and fill the doll's dish? When the Bartrams, early horticulturists and adventurers, roamed the South, they were awed by the magnolias. The bloom spells South, primitive and elegant. What other flower is there to lie on the dark wood coffin of your father?

Out back on two arbors, grape vines still curl and twist. I pick a small leaf and carefully place it between two credit cards in my wallet. What a primitive impulse, to take something home, a talisman to remind that you once were there. As I turn back for a last look, a wave of gooseflesh runs over my arms. Ah! That's why I'm entranced. Rowan Oak looks similar to the Mayes house, built on Lee Street by my grandmother's father in Fitzgerald, Georgia. When I was growing up, the house had a wraparound porch, but after a fire, my aunt added spindly columns, thin as femurs.

I have a few hours before my talk at the bookstore. Almost no one is in the café as I sit at a table by the window and look at my notes. The waiter brings me a glass of tea so sweet my teeth throb. *The old Italian idea of place as locus of memory,* I wrote last night in the motel. Back to my notes: *Place as storehouse and generator of memory.* I knew my hometown's every twig, culvert, chimney, curb, fireplug, street sign, drain, birdcall, horn, and spigot. I have loved living in San Francisco and in Tuscany. I have been a lucky tourist enchanted for thirty years with the hedonic, aspiring city, with my *vita nuova* on the far West Coast, my face toward the unknown Pacific. I escaped to the West, as though you can be purified by a lightning strike, drink a horn of honeyed goat's milk, and walk forth wearing a laurel crown into a new life one step from oblivion.

San Francisco is the hyper-real, exciting present, constantly in formation, constantly leaving the past behind. *It's the only place to live,* I've condescended to say many times to my southern relatives, who stared back without saying *Have you lost your mind? You have no people there.* But I have my work and my lively, ambitious friends; I have my Spanish-style house with lemon trees and a glimpse of the Pacific. I have the white city with water, water everywhere, the iconic bridge crossing north to the green Marin headlands; Berkeley blanketing the east, sparkling at night, and sparkling, too, with intellectual fire; the snarl of freeways south, leading to the promised land of Palo Alto and Silicon Valley, where our futures are flashing across thousands of computer screens, and "multicultural" no longer is a self-conscious word. Truly, what's new today is old by tonight. The Bay Area—the optimistic bellwether for the country. Where what I imagine becomes what I do. Like it or not, what's happening there now will happen everywhere later.

And Italy, magic realism for me—to live in such beauty, where art is as natural as breathing, and every turn off the road leads to discovery. I bought an abandoned villa in Tuscany on impulse. Often, seemingly spontaneous acts come from a deep, unacknowledged place, and a sudden decision feels inevitable and right. One summer day, I stepped out of the car, onto a mysterious invisible X. As I looked up at a rose and gold façade and faded shutters, I said, "That's my house," as though I had known about it forever. More than two decades later, I'm still enamored with the Tuscan way of life. Although the Tuscans are thoroughly contemporary people, time runs slowly. My friends speak of Hannibal battling the Romans at the bottom of our hill, the Medici art patrons, and their own ancestors who minted money, jousted, and built houses still standing after ten centuries. Time seems alive, like a warm hive buzzing. My neighbors meet in the piazza every day to nip espressos, shop for bread, and catch up on all the momentous events that have happened since this time yesterday.

The waiter refills my glass. I am going to fly out of here on sugary caffeine. *Give me some sugar,* my father said, raising his cheek for a kiss. Add a tablespoon of sugar to tomato sauce, my mother said, to cut the acid. Such sweetness, the South. My high school love and I parked on sandy country roads to listen to Cajun music from New Orleans on the radio. We rolled down the windows for the wafts of plums, wild violets, and dusty cotton fields; the night chorus of stridulous crickets and tree frogs accompanied the music. If I mistook the drift of honeysuckle for the scent of his hands, the nectar inside the bloom for the taste of his hard mouth, then the mistake was well made. When we swam in the Oconee, the dank, tannic smell of the river rose from the slicing of our arms through the current. We would kiss behind the gardenias in my backyard, the heady, heavy scent penetrating my skin. He pressed me against the wall of the barn and we kissed and breathed in and out of each other's mouths until I almost fainted. Lack of oxygen, I see now, but I thought it was the gardenias.

My last note: *I wonder if I have the courage to reimagine the place I fled.* A large question starts to form. X marks the spot.

Where is the red diary I began to keep when I was nine? For each day, five lines. Why was "I'll Fly Away" my favorite song? In the moments before he left the South, Willie Morris wrote that he always felt *some easing of a great burden . . . as if some old grievance had suddenly fallen away.* Yes, I know that lift, which I've experienced so strongly that the force itself seemed to raise the plane off the steaming asphalt. *Get. Me. Out. Of here.*

And now, this sweet succor of air.

After the reading and dinner, walking back to the motel, I suddenly think, *All my memories of California are portable.* This place is not. Previously, I thought that was a good thing, like the writer who said that his subjects were his home. Well, that's a bleak, disconnected idea. I roamed. I flew away to Italy and made a home. The South always stayed resolutely in place, as resolute as my uncle's grave, which has carved under his name the letters "MPDSHW." "What in the name of glory does that stand for?" my mother asked when she saw the stone put in place. Aunt Hazel whimpered, "My precious darling sweet husband Wilfred."

And there he remains. Flipping through my notebook, I read something I copied: *What thou lov'st well shall not be reft from thee / What thou lov'st well is thy true heritage.* Thanks, Ezra Pound, you could have chiseled that onto the palm of my hand. *Reft*—I underscore the word.

My husband, Ed, is thousands of miles away. It's seven in the morning in Italy, his best writing time. A rational hour, he says. Here, it's midnight. Now I've spilled water on my notebook but still can read a quote from Eudora Welty I copied today: *The boat came breasting out of the mist and in they stepped. All new things in life were meant to come like that.* Ed is probably awake. The phone rings and rings in his study where a hook-nosed portrait of Dante looms over the desk. Before he answers I'm preparing to say, "I want to move back to the South."

LOOKING TOWARD HOME

Bees swarm inside a giant boxwood near the kitchen door. Hundreds of them. The whole bush hums. As I pass, four golden furry ones zoom out and dive around my face. As soon as the weather warmed, a six-foot black snake adopted the front porch for its shady naps. Proprietarily, it coils on a chair, and sometimes slinks behind the cushion, which can be startling if you happen to take a break in late afternoon with a glass of tea and a book. Late one night when guests were leaving, we found it draped around the doorknob, dangling a long tail. I lifted it with a broom handle and flung it onto the grass.

Owls belong to no peaceable kingdom. In the wee hours, I hear their solemn oboe notes, often followed by terrible shrieks as they pounce on their prey.

Often we see foxes, delicate does with fawns, rabbits, coyotes, and a charming young skunk, still mostly white, who sashays across the front lawn. And birds. Are we living in a giant aviary? Even I, with a violent phobia, am enchanted by the darts of bluebirds and finches among the hedges, and by the individual songs. One repeats "T-shirt, T-shirt, T-shirt"; another simply chirps "Birds-birds-birds-birds." Looking into layers of spring green, I recall that the etymology of "paradise" means *walled garden*. Not walled, this one still feels Edenic. I would not be surprised to see Adam and Eve cavorting naked in the meadow.

We live in a plain, two-story pale yellow Federal house, a former tavern and inn on the Eno River in Hillsborough, North Carolina. Built on the burned foundations of a 1770 structure, the house dates from 1806. Thomas Jefferson was president; Lewis and Clark prowled the Northwest; the Napoleonic Wars raged, and Beethoven wrote his fourth symphony—none of which was of immediate concern to the farmers who hauled their grain to the gristmill and stopped in for a pint of ale, or, if the river flooded, an overnight at Coach House. The inn section had only two bedrooms so they must have slept piled up like puppies. I imagine fleas and snoring and sweat and couplings with the serving girl and corn husk mattresses full of weevils—not the genteel South of family portraits, canopied beds, and silver dresser sets. I doubt if the inn had slaves, so at least there's not that haunting. The place became Chatwood in the 1950s, when the bird-watcher owners found that chats (a kind of thrush) stopped there on their migrations. They also planted a complex and extensive garden, which I am trying to revive.

The basement feels just like home to possums, snakes, and

mice. Because an air-conditioning vent mistakenly opens there, their lairs stay nice and cool all summer. All the rooms in the house are warm, honey-colored heart pine. Read: dark. Every system needs work. To the old house, another even older house was attached in the 1930s. The twenty-inch-wide floorboards glow as though they have light inside them. Where one house meets the other, it's fine downstairs, but upstairs the two parts link via a tiny room where there is a toilet. You must go through this toilet closet to get from one bedroom to the other. Now that's beyond funky and will have to go, thank you very much, National Historic Register. I like the way the house sometimes creaks in the night, as though we are on an old schooner plying the high seas.

Two years after my impulsive Mississippi-midnight call to Ed, we disentangled ourselves from California and moved. Ed already was thinking of a change. Ever since graduate school in Virginia, he's loved the mellow southern winter, the humane pace, and the sweet green beauty of the land. Like me, he even likes the soul-melting heat of July. My daughter, new Ph.D. in hand, divorced, and with a child, wanted a fresh start. Long story short, we picked up and headed south.

I always have visited my good friends in Chapel Hill—Anne, close to me since Randolph-Macon Woman's College days, and her family. When I was invited to start a furniture collection in High Point, we began to travel more frequently to North Carolina. Ed researched universities, cultural life, and the proximity to a good airport, so when friends asked why we were moving to "the dropping-off place," we mentioned those attributes, plus the four distinct seasons. But, really, such an uprooting is instinctual. Time to rebel. Internal gears began to grind, propelling you forward—then you invent the reasons.

My ties with California had been fraying for a while. I loved my university life, and my department encouraged experimentation; we never bogged down into the dangerous repetition of teaching the same play or novel thirty times. But the teaching load was tough. Until I was department chair, I taught four intense graduate courses each semester. One Christmas Eve, as I was sitting down to dinner with my family and friends, a student called. "I've got to read you what I just wrote. I think it's my best." I refrained from saying, "Do you know it's eight o'clock on Christmas Eve?" I listened to several long stanzas. At the table, my family and guests banged their glasses and groaned, but, really, I was touched that he felt free to call, and I liked his poem. There's little to compare with the privilege of mentoring those who strike out into the wilderness of a creative life. But after many years, my own writing became limited to the summer break.

After my first book of prose, *Under the Tuscan Sun,* unexpectedly took off with a life of its own, I had just barely enough financial stability to take a chance and quit my job. Should I? I decided to step off that X, gamble on my writing, and give up secure tenure. When in doubt, I reasoned, fly. I'd taught for twenty-three years. Time for the new.

I was surprised when the intense bonds with most of my col-
leagues faded quickly. Twenty-three years and it was as if we'd
been on a cruise ship together, had seen the islands, danced at
midnight, and weathered some mighty storms. Back on shore,
scrawled email addresses on menus are quickly lost in a stack of
maps and receipts.

Our friends lived all over the Bay Area. We drove an hour
to get together. Many of them didn't know one another, therefore we never belonged to a tribe. Hardly ever did I run into
friends by chance. When cars stalled in traffic on the bridge, I
thought of the Loma Prieta earthquake of 1989; I imagined the
cables starting to sway back and forth, my car sailing through
the air and into the water below. My list lengthened: reservations weeks in advance to the hot restaurants, long lines for
movies, more traffic. I'd lived with those things for years and
they didn't bother me, then suddenly they did. Blame it on
Tuscany. Living in a place with an intense sense of community
made me want that all the time. Blame it on the bad fairy who
prophesied at my birth: You will be restless.

San Francisco changed from being the place of my best op-
portunities, the *only* place I could live in America, the most
beautiful city, to being *always cold*. Soothing cool fog became
dreary. (Now I often long for bracing sea air, and the lowing
sound of the foghorns, and the flashes of blue-blue views, and
that flip your stomach makes when you nosedive over the crest
of forty-five-degree hills, and my worldly-wise friends, all of
whom knew we'd lost our senses when we left.)

Ed quit, too. Our time in Tuscany had activated his farm-
ing genes, and he wanted land. He mentioned a tractor. My

daughter always loved her visits to Georgia and longed for a big change. My conversion moment in Oxford reawakened a longing to breathe southern air. That felt sure and right.

Pin the tail on the donkey—if you can move anywhere, where will that be? Flying into North Carolina, we saw a sea of green. We lighted in the middle of that vast forested expanse, once again looking for home.

In the earliest stories, after the quest, the hero finds his way home. I never intended to do that, and even now I won't say it's permanent. My philosophy is *stare attento,* stay attentive, beware. I may spend my last years in a pied-à-terre in Montreal or a pink cottage in New Orleans. The most pitiable spirits in Dante's hell are those unable to move out of their assigned circle. *Stare attento*—always look for the next circle to jump to. *Mother, may I? Yes, take three butterfly twirls and one leap.* I'm back on the land I came from, and moss-draped nostalgia plays (almost) no part; the South I fled was hard to boil, hard to eat.

By returning, I just wanted to place my hand on the cool clay earth.

At Chatwood, on a rusted nail, I find a key labeled BANDING ROOM, and wonder how the ornithologist Dr. Watkins who lived here in the 1950s netted the birds, and how he secured a place name on their legs. No one who moved here after him discarded his test tubes, his small bottles of desiccated insects, or his tiny jars of thread. As for Mrs. Watkins, I'm tending her seventy-year-old garden and scouring the Internet to find replacements for her rare French roses as they die off. Many are no-name roses that she found in cemeteries and falling-down farms. From her hand-drawn maps I can see her sense of order and how she wanted to live in garden rooms. If I were inclined, I might look to glimpse her, knocking a copperhead off the brick wall, or leaning down to inhale the perfume of her Louise Odier. The house smells like a Tuscan stone church opened only for Easter. The great walnuts lining the driveway must have preceded her. Why would anyone plant them near a garden? Didn't they know that the roots seep out a noxious chemical that withers most plants within fifty feet? I don't have the heart to cut them down, and I'll guess that Mrs. Watkins didn't, either. I just hope not to meet my fate with a conk on the head by one of those little bombs.

Fragrances, wisps, fragments linger in an old place. *Ubi sunt; ubi nunc*–where are they; where now, those who came before us? Roman tomb inscriptions, and an abiding theme of poets. Under the walnut trees, I dig up the stones of a path that leads nowhere. A fallen springhouse cools no buttermilk. A pen houses no goats. An allée of rusty cedars approaches no house. There's no water to reflect your face in the bottom of the old well. Faintly visible on the attic door: Wesley's office. In a closet, a handmade hanger holds no coat. In the woods, my neighbor shows me a tombstone. Malley, age twelve now for fifty years, fell from the gristmill window, landing on rocks near the waterwheel. Daffodils bloom in loud clumps. Beside him, his mother's grave is unmarked. Did she plant the bulbs? She died of grief, a suicide. The dog leaps into the pond and emerges, shaking off water.

These discoveries of the memory of the land at Chatwood started to work as memory prompts for my early history, long pushed aside. (Yes, even repressed.) As I walk the path skirting the gristmill, through woods and across the cornfield, an outbreak of quartz, a clutch of blue bachelor's buttons, a hunter's hut, a swath of lupine, even a buzzard eating carrion, can arouse a hundred images from my past. Turn the kaleidoscope a quarter inch and shards of memory rearrange and shift, bright as ever.

Simultaneously, the present merges with the heady rush of memory sensations. I'm worrying about getting a tick. What looks like wild kale sprouts along the edge of the field, and, oh, poison ivy crawling up the pine tree. Daisies, Queen Anne's lace, pretty yellow weeds—if I'd brought scissors, I could take home a bouquet.

The stream I step across on mossy stones surges toward the pond that falls toward the mill. Water still rushes where the wheel last turned. Four turtles line up on a log, ready to dive.

BY MY LIGHTS

When we moved from California to North Carolina, I found in a box, unopened for many years, a cache of true primary material—childhood diaries, high school scrapbooks, a reading log, letters, and photographs. How solemn I look at thirteen in a white evening dress, dancing with Clifton MacDuffie. Wrist corsages gone to powder smear the brittle pages. A childish handwriting turns into a prim cursive. My father in *his* chair—so ordinary, just reading the newspaper. In the red diary with a lock, I endlessly obsess on possible romances. *I really like Monroe. And Jeff thinks I like him.* And often, *I'm not sure who to like.* Then I come upon *My daddy died today. That sounds cold blooded. I don't know what to say.* The words are plain in this little diary. Odd that so much chaotic memory is banked up behind them.

What was it really like down in the belly of the beast so long ago?

In another box, I faced a stack of student poems, teaching

evaluations, mission statements I once spent weeks writing, and copies of letters to the dean when I was department chair–call the shredder service! Finally I unearthed a folder, also from the 1990s, of autobiographical pieces that I wrote and then stowed away. Not that I could forget them.

Growing up in Fitzgerald, I lived in an intense microcosm, where your neighbor knows what you're going to do even before you do, where you can recognize a family gene pool by the lift of an eyebrow, or the length of a neck, or a way of walking. What is said, what is left to the imagination, what is denied, withheld, exaggerated–all these secretive, inverted things informed my childhood. Writing the stories that I found in the box, I remember being particularly fascinated by secrets kept in order to protect someone from who *you* are. That protection, sharpest knife in the drawer, I absorbed as naturally as a southern accent. At that time, I was curious to hold up to the light glimpses of the family that I had so efficiently fled. We were remote–back behind nowhere–when I was growing up, but even so, enormous social change was about to crumble foundations. Who were we, way far South? "We're south of everywhere," my mother used to lament.

What I'd aimed for was an homage to the place and people I sprang from. When I first read creation myths in anthropology class, I identified with the story of the deity who slapped into shape humans from local mud.

Writing those pieces, I'd fallen in love with prose. Each day was like holding on to a horse that bolted the barn. I wanted the southern *words* I'd missed in California. Teeninny, cussed out, pray tell, cut the light, mash that bug, hired out, greased light-ning, yo-ho, dogtrot, snake boots, done did, doodly-squat, belle-hood, fixing to, take ahold, chirrun, barking mad, young'uns, hie, I swan. I wanted to glue on my notebook the silty creeks, the drifts of Queen Anne's lace, the brackish water in ponds covered with hyacinths, the crape myrtle's dusty pink flowers that felt like the skin on my grandmother's neck. Memory—a rebel force, a synesthesia that storms the senses. At age ten, as I'm weaving a hat from palmetto fronds, our cook Willie Bell says, "Flies can fly right through the blue in stained glass," just as a deer outside the window touched his tongue to the ends of wet pine needles. Memory—like that.

Names of people came back: Fussie, Son Junior, Hannibal, Buddy Man, Halloween, Cusetta Mix, Dimple Harden, Dy-namite, and my all-time favorite, Sugar Marie Jo Harriet. All southern writers have to be drawn to the eccentric language of the South, the rhythmic loops of the narrative, wild metaphors and hyperbole, larger-than-life figures in local legends, the still-alive folktale pattern of telling three incidents in order to illus-trate a point. Writing reminded me of archery at camp: the hard pullback on the string, the dead level aim, the propulsion of the release, the *thunk* of contact with the straw-stuffed target, even the sting on my left inner arm if I had not the proper rotation.

Back then, when I published a few pieces in literary maga-zines, no one in the Mayes clan was enthusiastic, to say the very least.

My good girl training was long and rigorous. I have a small family. Did I want a rift? No. I shoved the essays into a folder; I moved them to "archive" on my computer files. I went back to writing poetry and buried the collection I called *Under Magnolia*. Anytime I felt the impulse to start my southern opus again, I instead headed for a movie or a new Thai restaurant. I'd go jogging or read a novel until the impulse faded. I wrote books of poetry, a college textbook. I was busy with my teaching, busy, busy, raising a daughter and squeezing writing into the cracks.

Did my relatives fear *Peyton Place* with a drawl and a plateful of grits? I stalled as I internalized their voices. I admired my friend Molly Giles, who, when asked how she could write frankly about her family, quickly replied, "Well, that's what God gave them to me for." Parents should be careful, we agreed—they may be raising a writer in the house. Little Sissie mentally takes notes as the father yanks down the draperies and the mother weeps and rolls her hair on orange juice cans.

My California-bred daughter loved the family stories, and said, "You *must* write about them." She always has been fascinated by the South, by the talk, talk, talk, the symphonic movements of conversations that diverge and go back and pick up, reach denouement, and continue to crescendo.

When she was four at a family wedding reception, she asked, "How do you learn to talk without saying anything?"

"It's an art," I replied.

I buried my stories; I bought the abandoned Villa Bramasole in Tuscany and made a life there. Out of my new love, I wrote another kind of memoir, *Under the Tuscan Sun,* and then went on to write other books.

Under that ancient sun, under the native magnolia grandiflora: As in many Renaissance paintings, beneath the Virgin's spread blue cloak people gather close and life is lived under that providence. I think there's always a spread cloak.

Now I find the stack of chapters I called *Under Magnolia.* Why, after many years, even open these flowered folders? *Dare alla luce,* the Tuscans say at the birth of a baby, to give to the light.

On several of these brilliant spring evenings, I've sat in the garden reading about an instantly familiar girl in Fitzgerald, Georgia. What if she'd seen a flash, at fifteen, of herself years hence, reading on a garden bench, evening rays raking the meadow where coral poppies face the sun? Would she know instinctively that the older self only appears calm, that she still feels the instinct to light out for the next episode? But she would not be interested. She'd rather see herself—how? She has no idea.

Under Magnolia

A SILVER GLOBE IN THE GARDEN

As I open a book that I once pulled from the ashes of my grand-parents' house, the dusty, mildewed scent catapults me to their back hallway.

Through the double door, made of tiny mullioned panes, I see the entrance hall waver, a quivering of claret and sunlight from the front door. Wafting from the kitchen, the smell of chicken smothered in cream and pepper until it's falling off the bone. I'm playing an ancient wind-up record left over from when my father was a boy; "K-K-K-Katy" crackles in my ear. Through my grandmother's open bedroom door, I glimpse chintz dust ruffles, hatboxes, the slender oval mirror over the dressing table, where she leans, and I see her dab the fluffy puff between her legs.

That's it: brief cloud of bath powder, grinding consonant K-K-K-Katy (*I'll be waiting at the k-k-k-kitchen door*), warped light throwing rainbows back through the door. And I wonder, always, why do such fragments remain forever engraved, when, surely, significant ones are lost? The kitchen fragrance, no mystery. For who, ever, could forget Fanny's smothered chicken?

An early memory of my father: He opens his buff hunting coat, and in all the small interior pockets, doves' heads droop. He and his friends Bascom and Royce break out the bourbon. From my room in the back of the house, right off the kitchen, I see through the keyhole (keyholes are a large part of childhood) the doves he's killed piled on the counter, and someone's hand cleaning a shotgun barrel with a dishrag. The terrible plop-ploop sound of feathers being plucked makes me bury my face under the pillow. When his friends go, my father stays at the table with his tumbler of bourbon. I'm reading with a flashlight under the covers. My specialty is orphans on islands where houses have trapdoors into secret passageways that lead to the sea. Rowboats, menace, treasure, and no parents in the story. As the water darkens and danger grows, I hear my father talking to himself. When I quietly crack the door, I see his head in his hands, his bloodstained coat hung on a hook. Very late, he hits the wall with his fist, and says over and over, "Beastly, Christly, beastly, Christly." I put the palm of my hand over the spot where he is pounding with his fist and feel the vibration all the way up my arm. I press my nose to the window screen and look out at the still backyard.

A tea olive tree grows outside my bedroom window, its scent airy, spicy, and I prefer it to the dizzy perfume of the gardenias and magnolias that rule the neighborhood. Tough ovoid leaves scrape the screen; the tiny flower clusters are fit only for dollhouse bouquets. Then the back door slams and the car screeches out the driveway.

My father's parents live two blocks away. I like to gaze into the silver globe under the giant oak in their backyard. My face looks distorted and moony, especially when I cross my eyes and stick out my tongue. In the mirrored sphere, the yard curves back, foregrounded with oak branches like enormous claws. On the latticed back porch, my grandmother Mayes washes a bowl of peaches with her maid, Fanny Brown. Mother Mayes's hair is as silvery as the garden globe, and her crepey skin so white she's almost blue. She looks as though she might dissolve or disappear—her pale eyes always seem fixed on somewhere just beyond me.

Late in the afternoon, she puts up her bare feet on an ottoman. With the lamp haloing her hair, she's ethereal, but then I see crude, tough yellow corns on the last two toes of each foot. They're translucent in the lamp's glow, as she relaxes with *The Upper Room,* a church book of devotional reading, open on her lap.

Dove heads, tea olive, silver globe, bowl of peaches, church books. Images are the pegs holding down memory's billowing tent. From them, I try to figure out who my people were and where we lived, what they did and what they could have done.

South Georgia, where I was born, may look to a stranger speeding down I-75 like lonesome country where you can drive for miles without seeing more than a canebrake rattlesnake cross the road. At the city limits of our town a sign said IF YOU LIVED HERE YOU'D BE HOME NOW. The logic is irrefutable. Thin roads shimmering in the heat lead into Fitzgerald from Ocilla, Mystic, Lulaville, Osierfield, Pinetta, Waterloo, Land's Crossing, Bowen's Mill, and Irwinville, where Jefferson Davis was captured by the Yankees. Then, no I-75 existed.

To those whose ribs were formed from red clay, the place is complex, exhilarating, charged, various: mighty brown rivers to float along, horizons drawn with an indigo pen, impossibly tall longleaf pines, virulent racism (then, and not all erased now), the heat that makes your heart beat thickly against your chest, the self-satisfaction of those of us who have always lived there, tornadoes twirling in a purple sky, the word "repent" nailed to trees. A place of continuous contradiction, a box with a false bottom. A black rag doll becomes a white doll when I turn her upside down. I jump onto soft green moss behind the cotton mill and sink into sewage. Daddy in his white suit fishes me out, shouting curses. I'm born knowing that the place itself runs through me like rain soaking into sand.

We are fabric people, as others are the Miwok people, circus people, lost people. In the cotton mill—my father's business—the light is gray because lint catches in the screened windows. Oily black machines, gigantic strung looms as beautiful as harps, their shuttles pulled by lean women. Bins to climb and then dive from into piled raw cotton. In the tin cup of the scale over the bin I ride, the needle jerking between fifty and fifty-five pounds, then fly out, the landing not as gentle as I expect.

Rayon is softer, and squeaks as I fall in. But to fly, actually, as in dreams. A natural act, as later I would swing out over the spring on vines at night, dropping into cold black water below, crawl up the slippery bank, grabbing roots, then swing out again and again for that moment of falling. Water moccasins, thick as my leg, thirty-pound rockfish with primitive snouts, even crocodiles lived in these deep streams I dove into, pushing my fist into the icy "boils," that bubbling force at the bottom.

While my father ran the cotton mill and hunted birds, my mother gathered, and created perfect bridge luncheons, with the aid of our cook Willie Bell. The house pulsated with cleanliness. My two sisters were both in college by the time I was eight, but I stayed in my room at the back of the house instead of moving into theirs. Often I riffled through their scrapbooks and high school notebooks in their closet, and tried on their left-behind dresses that had more flounces than mine, and the flowery scent of White Shoulders lingering in the tucks and pleats.

I loved the square brick Carnegie library, the quiet that engulfs you as you gently close the door, the globe to spin and stop, with a finger on Brazil or China, the cold light in the high windows in winter, the way the bookcases jut out to make little rooms, my yellow card with due-date stamps, the brass return slot, the desk where presides the librarian, who looks like a large squirrel. Before kindergarten, my sisters showed me the low bookcase for my age. I moved year by year to a different section of the back room. So much later, I may cross the threshold into the main library where I can check out only two, then four books.

Other literature was mail order. I never had seen a real bookstore. We had Book of the Month. We subscribed to *Harper's Bazaar,* for copying dresses, *Reader's Digest,* required for school, and, for some reason, *Arizona Highways.*

Fitzgerald, where I might have lived forever, was as rigidly hierarchical as England. We had our aristocracy, with dukes, bar sinisters, jokers, local duchesses in black Cadillacs, many earls, and, of course, ladies, ladies, ladies, many of them always in waiting. Everything and everyone had a place and everything and everyone was in it. It was a cloying, marvelous, mysterious, and obnoxious world, as I later came to know, but fate placed me there and, although the house was not lilting, I was *happy as the grass was green.*

We were not normal. We lived next door to normal people, so I knew what normal was. The father worked for the state agriculture department, the mother gave a perm called a "Toni" to her sisters and friends, and they laughed and had fun as they breathed in ammonia fumes. Their boy sang in the choir, and the daughter, Jeannie, with wild hair, was my playmate. We found house-paint cans in the barn and brushed black and white enamel over each other. Our irate mothers scoured us with kerosene, and Jeannie seemed to be lifted in the jaws of her mother like a kitten and taken home. Her father built a swing set with a pair of rings that we learned to grip, push off into a somersault, vault up on our feet, and hang upside down. On the swings we could pump so high we'd almost flip over the top. He took us to farms in his truck and we sat in back eating raw peanuts we'd pulled from the ground. They tasted like dirt. Jeannie and I made hideouts in the vacant lot next to her house, elaborate setups of pallets and cardboard boxes, with tin doll dishes and stolen kitchen knives. We sat on a pile of sour grass weed poring over the Sears, Roebuck catalog. *What would you choose if you could choose anything on this page?* After pelting rains, our walls sagged. On Christmas mornings, she and I ran back and forth between our houses, looking at what Santa left, long before anyone awoke. We strung tin cans with string between our bedrooms, but never could hear a thing. Her mother, Matrel, had lively sisters named Pearl, Ruby, and Jewel. Her uncle always called us "Coosaster Jane," which we thought was German he'd learned in the war. She called her daddy "Pappy." He was strong, redheaded, and sweet. I wonder why I did not envy them. I think small children may have no imagination for a life that is not their own lot.

Other families were happy, too. "The Greeks" were happy even though their daughter Calliope had polio and had to walk with crutches and go to Warm Springs and lie in an iron lung, that awful water heater turned on its side. The Lanes were happy even though the father drove a potato chip truck for endless hours and the delicate mother had a problem so that their bathroom was stacked to the ceiling with sanitary napkin boxes. I was in awe over how they pampered Rose Ann. My best friend, Edna Lula, was the only child in the perfect family. She was doted on and prettily plump; their house had beds with warm dips in the middle like nests, and French doors that opened onto a long porch with a swing. Happy mother and daddy who called her by a nickname left over from baby talk. I could not be at her house enough. There, I fell under their bountiful love. They thought I was funny. They called me by my family nickname, Bud. There was no chink. Ribbon candy always filled the same dish on the sideboard. We licked peach ice cream off the wooden beater, loved pouring the rock salt slush out of the churn. They were admiring, told jokes, hugged; their garden fish pool had a statue of a naked boy, clean water coming out of his thing, landing on the old goldfish in the murk. There was a baby grand piano. My friend plunked out "Song of the Volga Boatman," and "Blest Be the Tie That Binds." Church not only Sunday morning but the evening service, too. (I drew the line at that.)

My mother and her friends laid swatches of fabric over sofas. They carried samples of peach, ivory, teal, and cream paint in their purses. They contemplated the recovered wing chair with the attention surgeons give to incisions. Pale peach is a good color, a lasting color; it never looks as if the chair has just been done. You never want the chair to appear just done. There are fine points: double welting, never tacks except on leather. The act of attention was intense and disciplined. The house must have a sense of itself. Greens and blues will fool you; you don't remember shades as well as you think.

My mother wants color and polish and devotion. She wants the linens ironed and the windows clean. Fabric, stitching, tatting, piecing into designs, interfacing for durability and form.

Her friend Grace can see a dress on someone in Atlanta, go home, and cut the pattern out of newspaper. The methods are sound: hem by picking up the stitch, doubling back for it then going forward, around a circle, as in writing—the piercing bright words, the tension of the thread.

The network of women existed in a world as private as purdah. Among themselves, my mother's friends were brutally frank, raucous, and never oblivious to compromise. Talk was of *should*, of standards, local gossip, and, at least five times a day, of how each person looked. Judging every nuance of appearance was part of our chromosomal makeup. They went out as if disguised by veils. Appearance. And feigned innocence, the vise that keeps women "girls" well into their sixties.

A generality may have a use, as does a bludgeon, but it obliterates what is of particular use by oversimplifying. Nothing has been dealt this blow so much as the southern woman, black and white. The power behind the throne, iron hand in velvet glove, she endured (what else could she do?), belle of three counties, a little vixen, *she's like a member of the family*, a great lady, ad infinitum, ad nauseam, and all evidence to the contrary notwithstanding.

Every mother I knew could cook like the devil. There's their *jouissance*, that fine, forgotten-in-English word. Pressed chicken, brown sugar muffins, quail (smothered), Sally Lunn bread, grits with cheese, a spectrum of pies with lemon meringue as the lowest, and black bottom as the epitome. Lane Cake (which no Northerner could ever hope to emulate in this life or the next), and key lime when Mr. Bernhardt got in the Key West limes at his fruit stand. No matter what. Unconditionally, we will cook, from restorative broths to nutmeg custards to grand heroic meals.

The splendid matriarchs with power in the open were rare birds. And always endangered. More common is the third-rate power, manipulation. We learned it as we learned cartwheels and the multiplication table. I had my daddy wrapped around my little finger when I was five because I was "a pistol," his "sweetheart and buddy." We knew Scarlett could get Rhett back. "Blink your eyes slowly as you look up at a boy," my mother instructs. "Don't swim so much. You'll get ugly muscles." "Let *him* win the match."

For what we later came to call "role models" of independent living, there were just the old maid ticket takers at the theater, the librarian with the gray bun, and the McCall sisters, who looked like twin bulldogs and taught first and third grades. "You must suffer for beauty," my mother says as she curls my sister's hair so tight her eyes are drawn sideways. "You'll end up like *them*." "Your brains are showing," she tells me, as she smooths her eyebrows. "You'll have teaching to fall back on," she says later. Much of it took, like a big vaccination scab, leaving me well marked.

To be a woman was to own nightgowns softer than a peachblow. Beneath the batiste and the trim of eyelet and smocking is the smear of blood, armpits smelling of dry herbs and resin, a feather of hair, the sex like a patch of moss in the dark. To be a woman was to know the rooster foot is good for thickening, the cooter foot good in soup. If you scald claws until the tough skin and talons slip off, then you've got something.

Listening to women—playing bridge, shelling peas, visiting the dressmaker—those who were dead seemed present. Listening from just out of sight, I could imagine the person evoked to be rounding the corner, about to call out, instead of staring up for many years at the underside of a coffin lid shut by the Brothers Paulk. Talk, talk. Words as tactile as pebbles and bits of broken glass. Georgia has a fine, enunciated, lyrical gentry speech, a harsh, chopped-rock cracker speech, and the cane-syrup-rich deep black speech, with good stories from all.

An ancient black babysitter tells me stories about the "brownies" who could fly to Africa. "Now, you're a brownie," she says, "you just don't know it." The story thrills but scares me. Her smoky whites of eyes and little white tufts of hair stand out in the dim bedtime light. "You go to sleep, Brownie, or the brownies will take you off to Africa." The other storyteller is the tubercular doctor next door, who sits me on his bony knees and tells me of a mythic eagle who grabs curly headed babies in its talons and flies. A soaring eagle, he gestures, meanwhile spitting brown juices that spatter on my legs. *It'll take you into the North!* I am afraid of catching TB but too polite to wipe off my leg. Craggy, old yellowed eyes, a big suit he seemed to flap around in: He is the eagle.

. . .

Fitzgerald was ordered, one of the few planned towns in the country. Veterans from the North and South, who gathered in 1895, long after the War Between the States, devised a perfect grid with straight streets. Intersecting Central and Main streets are each two lanes wide, with islands of oaks and palms. On the grid, you could not be lost. When my grandfather was mayor, he named the town "the Colony City" because it was colonized by aging Confederate and Union soldiers looking for their balm in Gilead down in the southern pines. As in other colonies, the news seemed distant.

The streets running east and west are named after southern shrubs and trees: Jessamine, Cypress, Lemon, Pine, Magnolia; north and south streets are named for generals of the war: Lee, Grant, Johnston, Jackson, Sheridan, Longstreet, Sherman. The four borders are battleships: Monitor, Merrimac, Roanoke, and Sultana. The islands of palms, azaleas, and gardenias relieve the grid. Thirty feet of amaryllis my mother planted when I was small bloomed for decades on the island across from the Methodist church. Even the cemetery comes out of war memory. Named Evergreen, after the one at Gettysburg, the cemetery, both in terrain and design, recalls the gory battle where more than fifty thousand died. Our dead, too, lie in plots lining Emmitsburg Road, Seminary Ridge Road, Little Round Top Lane, Taneytown Road. Many of the soldier/settlers must have fought at Gettysburg and survived. Thirty years after the battle, the geography of the fallen was still on their minds.

As in most southern small towns, the black people lived around the edges in small, usually unpainted houses. At the

Grand Theatre, a "colored" entrance led those patrons up to the balcony. In the dark, fear of getting caught must have kept them from dropping things on us. Two water fountains stood side by side at the gas station: Colored and White. They had their own grammar and high schools. Separate but equal, we were told. A thriving Jewish community owned the clothing and shoe stores. How did they journey to Fitz from Odessa, Romania, and Poland? As far as I can find, no history exists that tells how Abe Kruger from Russia made his way to tiny Fitzgerald, Georgia, across the globe, in 1911. He left a substantial amount in his will to buy Christmas presents for poor children. What had been the Methodist Episcopal church when my father attended as a boy became a synagogue for all the Jews across south Georgia. Sometimes when something astonished my father, he said, "Well, that beats the Jews." His tone was one of admiration. A community cordiality existed; I'm not sure there was social mixing among the grown-ups but the few children were not singled out for anything negative, as far as I know. I played with the three Kaminski boys, all of whom were fun, in the vacant lot between my grandfather's house and theirs. They were rich and their mother, with long hair and shawls, seemed exotic.

When my mother redecorates my room, she inadvertently gives me a new place to hide. In the corner space left when she placed the twin beds at right angles, she had a cabinet built, so that for each bed's head, there was a place for a reading lamp. Below, she had a door built into the cabinet for extra storage. If I pull the bed away, I can squeeze inside, reach out, and almost realign the bed. The door has to stay open a crack so that I can plug in my toy stove. Inside, the space measures about three feet by three feet. I can sit up on a folded blanket among my games and dolls and collections.

Uncle Wilfred saves his Antonio y Cleopatra cigar boxes for me and I leave them open in the sun until most of the pungent smell evaporates. I keep blue, amethyst, and green broken glass in one, arrowheads, buttons, beads, and rocks in others. In shoeboxes, I save paper dolls with costumes from around the world, and also postcards, seashells, and the tiny train cars I make from matchboxes.

For hours, for years, I hide, reading by flashlight. Through books I learn of other galaxies where girls drive convertibles and solve mysteries, and live in the Alps and eat fresh cheese. The first poem I learn is "The Land of Counterpane" from a book by Robert Louis Stevenson. I'm enthralled by the cozy pastel scene of the boy playing with soldiers when he was sick in bed, and by the closing line "the pleasant land of counterpane." I figure out that the word means *bedspread*.

I have enough sense not to light candles. When my mother calls, I don't come out. My stove is supposed to cook when its lightbulb heats up. Into a small frying pan I break an egg. For a long time, two or three chapters, nothing happens, then the edges begin to curdle. After another few chapters, the enclosed lightbulb begins to smell hot and nothing more happens to the egg. Finally, my mother raps her knuckles on the top. "Come out of there right this minute. You could suffocate in there." Yes, well, I could suffocate out of here, too.

. . .

In my hideouts, I thrived. Without my protective coloring, I felt fully exposed to my wild parents. Every night was chaos. They shouted and slammed doors, roaring off in the car in the middle of the night. They acted out every bad play they invented. Dingbat fights began with the whereabouts of keys and bills. At bedrock, I sensed that my parents loved each other. I still feel that was true, still never have broken their code of relentless ornery behavior, the determination to stay in motion, spiders, continuing to spin out the same tensile thread.

Memory is capricious. I can look back and see decadence, old bigots, the constant racial slurs, the bores, the wild cards, the bighearted, the family album of alcoholics, the saints, the old aunt propped in a chair saying only "da-da," the slow-motion suicides, but at four, six, ten, they loomed, powerful, not as types but as themselves. Among them, logic takes wing. There's Aunt Hazel, whose soot-black hair left a shadowy print on cushions, telling me that she had to gather her twenty beaux to the front porch of Daddy Jack's house to announce her selection of the one to marry. I glance over at Wilfred, *numero uno,* with the enormous wart on the side of his nose, as he nods over the Sunday paper. More helpfully, she tells me, out of lifelong idleness, "Never learn to type. If you learn, you'll have to do it."

"And no cooking," she adds.

Years later my friend with the perfect family wrote me, "I would not have you believe that we were not happy." She's still puzzling out the moment her father shot himself at his office.

That act still snags in my memory, a log fallen in a river that catches debris. No way to reconcile Paul in his armchair, teasing us, and Paul lifting the gun to his temple. Another friend came home from school to discover his mother in the kitchen, bullet through the mouth. Gingerbread on the counter and teeth stuck in the ceiling. I'm stuck on that image, too, and the barbed notion that seeming years of perfection perpetually will be mocked. What did all that good father's gentleness mean? Why did we churn all that ice cream? Mystery. The seven veils, the eleven subjects for writing, the ten thousand things. There were other suicides, too, among them my other best friend's mother—another gun to the head out on the patio—but a story can sustain only so many examples. My mother claimed that Fitzgerald had the highest suicide rate in the country. "And no wonder," she added.

Memory is a swarm. What is stunning is how little remains when the swarm flies away. Henri Bergson is right; if the industrial revolution had not happened, we could find logical ABC reasons to explain whatever happened instead. I could trace the threads leading me as easily to the Peace Corps in Africa as to the country club in Birmingham where, in college, the waiters Country and Becautious served us Cuba libres. I could find my way to an off-Broadway Ibsen rehearsal as well as to radio station WBHB in Fitzgerald, where the Story Lady read every evening to the children in the heart of the heart of Dixie. I would like to have the silent areas of my cortex stimulated so that I could discover more, follow the canaliculi's secret paths toward truth.

The mildewed, scarred book I found in the back hall of my grandparents' house is *The Face of a Nation*, excerpts from the writings of Thomas Wolfe. On page 97, someone from a long time ago—my father?—has marked a sentence from a passage entitled "Destiny": *Each of us is all the sums he has not counted: subtract us into nakedness and night again, and you shall see begin in Crete four thousand years ago the love that ended yesterday in Texas.*

I think I must tap into ferrous earth and pull out red core samples.

TALKING BACK

On the frontispiece of this memory book, I'd envisioned a drawing of a white goat pulling a painted cart. A long-haired goat brushed to shine, with a garland of violets around its ears. True red cart with wooden wheels. In a yellow-flowered sundress, I am standing in it: a little charioteer of Delphi, only this is down in Georgia where the flat pine country begins to go swampy. That was my desire, the goat I would name my own secret name, *Nicole*. I liked looking into the eyes of a goat, that black bar for a pupil. Did it see in blocks, like looking through a crack in the wall? Silky hair to comb and braid, marble knobs that slowly turn into curving horns.

But I had no training in getting what was unavailable to the imaginations of parents who thought of dolls as presents, and so I did not obtain my goat to prance me through the streets. With logic of their own, they gave me a green parakeet named Tweedle. They thought my fear of birds was silly and I should get over it. When my mother put her finger in the cage and said, "Pretty boy, pretty boy," the bird went crazy, all wings, turning over the water and lid of seed. My request gave Daddy an idea. He gave a goat and cart to the little boy in the mill village who lived next to his office. Robbie Gray. I'll remember his name.

Daddy asked him, not me, to help hand down the Thanksgiving turkeys. Like me, he was seven. He stood, snaggletoothed and shorn, beside Daddy in the back of a truck piled high with frozen birds as the mill workers stepped forward one by one. "How about a big one for Mattie?" Daddy said. He was careful to say each person's name. Robbie lifted one to him and Daddy said, "Now you all have a big Thanksgiving." I was standing by the truck door, not supposed to get dirty, Daddy said, but it was just one more time when I was the third girl and not a boy.

I wanted to be a child, but, instead, I was "Successfully disguised to myself as a child," as James Agee described himself. I knew from stories and friends the concept of childhood. Magic and fairies and castles and the family going on cozy trips in the car, over the river and through the woods. Picnics at the beach, and all-day sings, and dinner-on-the-grounds reunions, and holding hands around the table for silent prayers, a little electric squeeze traveling around the circle. I wanted to be a read-to child with a bedtime and warm milk and snow days. But the lavish events of reality constantly undercut the power of Oz dreams and animals that talked at midnight in tiny books. Plus, we had no snow.

My parents, powerful, slapdash, weary of children, continued to lead unexamined lives. The brakes simply were gone.
Nothing to do except face each other. Southern Comfort, re-
criminations, and if onlys.

The house was short on closets. Mine was in the hall. My row
of shirts and dresses and pile of shoes were squeezed in with the
linen, my father's hunting guns, a shelf of medicines (I loved the
deep blue Milk of Magnesia bottle), boxes of Mother's old love
letters up top, and, on a hook, the ragbag sewn from a navy bedspread my uncle brought home from the war he spent docked in
San Francisco. I closed the closet door, pulled open the draw-
string, and crawled in. I settled in the corner and turned on my
flashlight to read while my parents in the kitchen laughed those
HA! false laughs, broke glasses, and droned on. At some hour,
one of them would weep.

At his worst my father ripped open his white shirt, buttons
popping off, and carried his loaded rifle through the house aim-
ing at lamps or windows. "Not a one of you appreciates me," he
shouted. He was getting a sloping belly. His scar, an exploded
star from when he was shot, shone on his side, front and back.
The bullet, meant for my grandfather, had gone straight through
his body and hit the wall, and he'd lived. Even so, he was in the
hospital a long time and had to be carried on a stretcher to the
trial. I was in the back of the courtroom on the colored side
with Willie Bell. He rose up on his elbow and pointed his finger
at Willis Barnes. My father was a hero. He'd jumped in front of

my grandfather when a mill worker came to their office waving a pistol and shouting he'd get that bastard. Barnes referred to Daddy Jack—"the Cap'n," the big boss, my grandfather—whom my father saved. Barnes's immediate bosses, Joe Peacock and J. H. Clark, were killed outside the office. Everyone left the trial excited, saying Barnes would fry. My father: bullet in the gut from three feet. Later we dug it out of the wall with an ice pick and placed it upright on his desk.

First memory: a man at the back door is saying, *I have real bad news,* sweat is dripping off his face, *Garbert's shot,* noise from my mother, I run to her room behind her, I'm jumping on the canopied bed while she cries, she's pulling out drawers looking for a handkerchief, *Now, he's all right,* the man says, *they think,* patting her shoulder, I'm jumping higher, I'm not allowed, *They think he saved old man Mayes,* the bed slats dislodge and the mattress collapses. My mother lunges for me.

Many traveled to Reidsville for the event, but my family did not witness Willis Barnes's electrocution. From kindergarten through high school, Donette, the murderer's daughter, was in my class. We played together at recess. Sometimes she'd spit on me.

After Daddy recovered, if I heard him in the hall or banging the toilet lid in the bathroom, I clicked off my flashlight and crouched still on the worn-out towels and torn sheets in the ragbag until he wandered away. My toes curled against the butt of his smooth, polished gun in the corner.

. . .

Restless and bored, my parents drove us at least once a month to the beach at Fernandina. We could stay at the Seaside Inn anytime because my father gave them the drapery material (Tung Shan, which he invented) for the whole hotel. Whatever else they were, my parents would give anyone anything. At Fernandina they behaved better; they smoldered rather than blazed. I heard them as a drone through the wall, while I sat cross-legged on my bed reading and eating oyster crackers softened by sea air.

A hot day. I open their door to say I'm going down to the beach. My parents are sleeping on twin beds. My mother's gown twists around her legs, the spongy pouf of her stomach rising and falling, the tiny scar on her nose. A soured towel smell, the frosted gin bottles. My father in his boxer shorts is frowning, his eyes roving back and forth under the pale lids veined blue like a film of oil over water. His arm is flung out toward my mother's and hers is also, but they are not touching. I run down the hall and out. I can't wait to roll down the dunes, chase sandpipers, run after fluffs of foam.

On the beach I expand. Running fast, I feel bursts of pure energy. If out early, I sometimes find a sea turtle making her way back to the water after laying eggs. I step up on the barnacled back, my arms out for balance. At the edge of the waves, I jump off, give her a push from behind, and watch her slowly move toward deep water, feeling the thrilling, powerful rush through my shoulders and down my back and legs.

I look back at the hotel and see my parents at the window.

Why is she awake so early? I wave but she must be looking farther out to sea; my father must have his eye on the sunrise. They're vague shapes behind rusting screened windows a long time ago.

Reading on the seawall one afternoon, I see two jets heading for each other over the ocean. They will crash! I drop my book and I'm shouting NO, as they explode into each other. Broken metal falls slowly to the sea and a body flies up in the air, then falls. I run inside. They don't believe me. "You are reading too many books. Your imagination is running away with you." At dinner, the TV over the bar announces the crash. The pilots ejected safely. "Well, what are the chances of that?" Daddy brags to Pops, the hotel owner. "My little Bud saw the whole thing. Isn't she sharp as a tack?"

My mother in sparkling white met my father at a dance at the Lee-Grant Hotel. She was down from Georgia State College for Women, ready to dazzle. Already she had a boyfriend, Max, who flew low over the campus scattering red roses for her. Those are his letters on the closet shelf—he who went out rabbit hunting when he heard she'd married, and shot himself in the heart.

On the night my parents met, my father was recently up from a mysterious year in a wheelchair. He did nothing but raise white doves. When he was expelled from high school for pushing a teacher downstairs, he was sent to Riverside Military Academy. Things didn't go well there, either. He'd come home sick with rheumatoid arthritis to stare for a year at the sky and to train birds to come back to him. Then, somehow, he's out of

the wheelchair and well, which makes no sense. But now he drives up to the hotel in a cream-colored convertible with a horn that plays a tune.

Hair black as tarmac and the eyes I've seen in the photographs of snow leopards. He's learning the saxophone. The orchestra is playing "The Darktown Strutters' Ball," and he asks Harvey Jay, "Who's the new girl in white?" They dance, her hand is light on his neck, they walk out on the long porch facing Central Avenue lined with magnolias, and the legend ends there, fades out into the heavy fragrance, darkness, and the fu-

ture. I've never heard a recording of "The Darktown Strutters' Ball," only one of my parents humming it in odd moments, wearing a deep groove in my memory. *I'll be down to get you in a taxi honey;* and in such a small town no taxi ever was. From their framed photographs, they stare directly at me. Often, I stare back. *Like that,* I say, I'd like to have met you *like that.*

Time sputters. And as W. H. Auden's refrain goes, *Time will say nothing but I told you so.* I thought, with luck, the gypsies who parked their squalid trailer behind the gas station would steal me and I would disappear *without a trace*. My parents, those stars, proclaimed a daily misery to the heavens and the rains, a face-to-face, hand-to-hand combat. Border wars. Territorial disputes. Manifest destiny. Why did my mother court trouble? Why did my father carouse? I found the pink pop-apart pearls on the floor of his Oldsmobile. They were tacky. When I answered the telephone, a woman laughed and hung up. She didn't sound like anyone we would know. I said many things to myself by the age of seven. *If I ever get out of here, I will never select unhappiness.* When the plate of unhappiness is passed around and more and more is offered, I'll say no thank you, no. But they wanted seconds, thirds.

At school I could fall into being a child. Now and then a fact sticks: the capital of Afghanistan, vitamin C prevents scurvy, slavery was "a good idea" at the time, times change. My country was represented in the corner by the mended flag; there is only one way to fold it, like a note you throw across the room, and only one way to raise it and Monroe Fletcher was chosen. For the rest, chalk sounds on the board gave the teacher the creeps, and she crossed her legs in dust-colored support stockings, and told dull stories of her vacation to Vero Beach when she left her bag in the car and came back four hours later and no one had touched it: *People are basically decent.* The desk with initials cut deep. Cards with holes, and numbers turn to faces when sewn right with yarn. At recess, I love taking out the coil of rope.

Double time, red pepper, hot stitches, and: "Mother, Mother, I feel sick, call for the doctor, quick quick quick. Mother, Mother, will I die? Yes, my child but do not cry. How many cars will be at my funeral? One, two, three . . ."

Negro houses surround the playground on three sides. Washwomen scrubbing pots of clothes under the pecan trees, spreading towels over bushes to dry, folding sheets on the sloping porches. In one of the leaning houses a fortune-teller lives and big cars pull up and white women go in. Could one be the voice on the telephone? *Why don't Negro children have to go to school every day? Because they don't need to know. You do.* Grade to grade, I worked my way around the playground. Hopscotch, jump rope, red rover, jungle gym: the cardinal points. Outside I was a wholehearted child, under the watchful playground duty of Miss Pope, Miss Hattaway, Mrs. Gurganus, Mrs. Bailey, and Miss McCall, who'd been, once, to Mexico and wore a red felt jacket embroidered with sombreros and cacti for the seven years I was in grammar school. It always caught my eye. *Lamentable,* my mother said. In third grade, she was wearing it the day Gill C. Tucker said to her: *You look like a bulldog,* and she said, *Would you say that again?,* and he didn't have the sense to shut up. We were all thrilled, and he said straight up, *You look like a bulldog,* and she told him to get out of her class and she started to cry and said we'd have to excuse her but she wasn't used to putting up with white trash. She hoped none of us ever would be rude, crude, and socially unacceptable like that. Gill C.–the possibility of open rebellion. Gill C., truth teller, a horse running into fire.

Because my family was overwhelming, the small self-conscious pains of ordinary childhood never bothered me. I could take the hooked stick and fish for the window shade ring in the hot classroom with everyone staring while I aimed and missed and let the shade fly up and hit the ceiling until everyone laughed and Miss Hattaway got furious. The fury of teachers never impressed me. I envied Jane Floyd's total blush when she was embarrassed. I rarely was. I felt bad for Joan Appleton's face while she had a "fainting fit" with her tongue out. The teacher got a spoon out of her desk drawer. I held down Joan's arms, skinnier than mine, and saw her fascinated face in its privacy and twisting. It seemed she let some anger out—anger I might have, too—then she was limp. She wet her pants, too, but never cried when she woke up—just let herself be led to the nurse's room. I pretended to be simple. At the fair, picked up, swung by the farmer square dancing, I was not a smiling rag doll, but stiff as wire, face pressed under his arm and him hahooing, moonshine breath. I thought of kicking and did not, rode it out, only made a face when he put me down. My English was only as far as a lisp of bad words said to the mirror.

In summer, the transfer to Highlands Camp, a two-week interruption to the sound and fury of my house. Camp was tall pines and good girls, willow twig armchairs and wisteria. We bathed in cold water, rubbed archery blisters with balm, learned to post. The girls shared a streak of DNA, a litany of running off at the mouth, screaming giggles. I'm in a skit. I'm a planter with nothing to do for months of winter. "Accompany me to Paris," I say in fake French.

I've escaped. My new friend from Marietta has a golden retriever at home and her father is a pediatrician and I don't know what that is. She plays voluntaries on the cello and says the word should have an apostrophe in front of it but people are too ignorant to know that. I've never seen a cello, with or without the apostrophe. We have only the baby grand at Daddy Jack's, with one broken key that I plunk over and over until someone shouts *Stop that*. She wants an English saddle, will get one. Plump and slow, she farts when she runs. In the woods I hide notes in boxes: *If you ever find this please write to me*. I'm out of the mess and rattling of home. There are those who care about apostrophes. Then there's my father turning over the table during a game of penny ante, pulling down the chintz draperies. Some fathers care for *babies*.

I see an opening I've seen only in books.

On the final night of camp, with candlelight and the girls all in white with linked arms singing, "Thy sunshine is fairest, my summer-time home," I'm suddenly homesick for somewhere, not there, but somewhere. *"My Highlands calls me wherever I roam. . . ."* Four hundred girls in pressed shirts and shorts, everyone waiting for Mrs. Sykes to give out the achievement awards. Everyone anticipating. I arrange the blank on my face. High Dive. Beauty Queen. Progress. Equitation. Archery. Best Camper. . . . This is long after I arrived and the counselor jerked me aside after fifteen minutes, said I had the wrong attitude, was cheeky, a troublemaker, and I'd have to clean my

plate whether I liked it or not. Now the girls, running up to
the podium one after another claiming a bit of glory. Tennis.
Crafts. (My beaded moccasins are very nice.) And at the very
end my name is called, a special award announced, *For Learning
to Eat the Crust of Bread.*

Within my family, I could not be a child. But wait, my parents regarded me as smart and adorable. "She's the cleverest
little thing you've ever seen," they'd tell anyone. Praise was for
the wrong things, often, but it was plentiful. I was showered
with a feeling of immense (if inappropriate) possibilities. *You
are going to grow up to be Miss America! You have a memory like an
elephant! You can have anything in the world you want—just tell me
what you want and you can have it! You could float down the Nile
covered with flowers!* No one was strong on realism; inexplica-
bly, the strong suit was family pride. *Never forget you're a Mayes.*
Looking around, I could see no possible reason to do anything
else but try my best to do exactly that. Sometimes, when my
mother was angry, she'd say, "Marry a Hungarian peasant. The
blood's all shot in this line." I felt bad for my new cousin when
he was named the Fourth because his father, the Third, banged
on our back door drunk and shouting at least once a week, and
his sweet mother, who once was Miss University of Georgia,
had sugar diabetes and hands that trembled when she lit a cigarette. Because she knew I loved German chocolate cake, she
baked them on Saturdays, while the Third sat by the shortwave
Stromberg-Carlson, listening to static and foreign voices, star-

ing at the cover that flipped up to show a map of the world time zones and frequency bands. He twitched in his leather wing chair and said when I walked by, "Well, you think you're something don't you, Miss Priss? Well *I* am a graduate of Georgia Tech." Adults could do anything. Anything.

My ally was Willie Bell. She had worked for us since before I was born. It was not a cozy, member-of-the-family, Aunt Jemima, *Gone with the Wind* Mammy thing. I was not clasped to her soft bosom for darky lullabies. She was skinny, anyway, and she and I simply knew we were in it together. She for her twenty dollars a week (*We pay more than anyone in town.*) and I for the duration of childhood. "Just run out and play, try not to pay them any mind, they all crazy," she'd say, not looking up from the stove.

She offered me not sympathy, but a steady point of view. One sass at the table and out I had to go to pick my privet switch in the yard. As I stalked through the kitchen, Willie Bell shook her head. "When are you going to learn?" she said quietly. "Just don't talk back."

My mother switched until my legs bled, frowning and working her lips. My father read the paper, looking bored. If I cried he'd say, "Cry and I'll give you something to cry about," or "Cry louder! Can't you cry louder? I can't even hear you."

Usually they were too busy between themselves—jets over the ocean—to notice what I did. I began to drive the car at nine and they never knew. Once, I ran away. I stayed in a culvert all night, just a block from home. When I returned, blank and tired the next morning, I felt grimly triumphant. I expected the state patrol, my mother properly distraught, my father taking vows never to act up again. No one had noticed that I was missing.

I was unguided, rebellious, solitary, a prankster, at war. No side to take. I taught myself the bull's-eye with arrows. I could disappear in the tops of trees. I walked to school every day past the Spotted Pig restaurant, down the pig trail, through the Blue and Gray Park, past poor houses, sidewalk graffiti (only one word, relentlessly repeated), cottages draped with peavine. Lonely, rowdy, I knew everything (like all children) and pretended to know nothing. I reported to the flat streets. I passed Mrs. Drummond every day, her huge bulk in the rocker behind the lard cans of geraniums lining her porch. Her daughter, Emma Sue, worked at the Pig and brought home leftover chicken-fried minute steak. I know because Judy Pike and I combed the alleys and pulled things out of trash cans. We held up bloody sanitary napkins, odd balloons like squashed jellyfish, bills demanding payment, the tinfoil and remains of the old steaks. As I walked home every day, I smiled a sweet six-year-old smile at Mrs. Drummond, who said, "How you today, little Missy?" Like policemen are said to understand crime and are trained to respond with a shot—they're closer to crime, in their fastest blood—so was I to innocence. A girl in a blue-checked pinafore skipping home. *The apple of her daddy's eye.* Mrs. Drummond had a brass vase made out of a bomb her son brought home from Germany. *In bad taste.* She weighed at least three hundred pounds, all steak. Her false teeth were whiter than Chiclets. One day, on my way home, a spot of warm blood blown by the wind landed on my blouse. From where? An angel with a halo, a bird, a body going to heaven? I could not be sure.

COLORING

When I look in the mirror for the scar, I can't see it. But I run my finger above my upper lip and I feel a slight ridge. So much lost to sight remains for the touch. What is stranger than memory, that selects a certain day to remain vivid, when thousands of others are totally lost?

That morning, the first thing I said was, "I won't go to Willie Bell's."

"Now hush. She'll hear you. Think of someone other than yourself." Years from then, when I heard "The walls have ears" in history class, no one had to explain it to me. In my childhood, someone always was almost within earshot, about to hear the truth, from which, of course, they must be protected. My mother tips the Shalimar bottle and dabs the glass stopper behind her ears and on her wrist pulses. Willie Bell comes in to

50

tell her Mrs. Parrott doesn't like to be late and she better hurry. Willie Bell looks down at me.

"What ails you? You look pouty."

"I don't like school. Julie Sykes is the teacher's pet."

"That's not true." My mother brushes her hair back and opens her lipstick. Because of the way she twirls the tube, it's shaped like one of the Monopoly "men," like the top of a circus tent. "Miss Goff told me you were adorable. She said you were in 'A' group. Put that lip in; I could ride to town on it."

Soon I would be in the first-grade classroom with all the letters of the alphabet cut out of colored construction paper and tacked around the blackboard. There I can watch the clock's long minute hand click and jump from one line to the next, see time pass between the numbers. At recess I'd play red light. "I like school," I say softly.

"There, I knowed you did all along." Willie Bell pulls up my socks and ties my sash for the third time. Mother, still in a peach satin and lace slip, snatches her soft buff-colored suit out of the closet and quickly dresses.

On mornings when Mother started dressing before I went to school, I knew what was up. She'd stand at the mirror, clip on square topaz earrings, pat two triangles of rouge on her cheekbones then rub them in with fast little upward motions. I begged to go to Macon, too, thought of Morrison's cafeteria next to Davison's where we shopped, of the green plastic trays sliding along shiny tracks. Rows of red Jell-O cut in cubes, cream pies with banana slices, an enormous roast beef, and stainless steel boxes of steaming, limp vegetables. I could take two desserts without her noticing until the end of the line when it was too late. She went three or four times a year on major shopping expeditions. My father, who later would find bills hidden among the tablecloths in the sideboard, was never told until after the fact. He'd come home from work, pull in behind her car still ticking from the fast ninety-mile drive. He held his hand above the hot hood, seeming to count the bugs splattered on the windshield.

Last time in Davison's, I threw a tantrum for a little white dog that played a song when you wound him up. I'd never seen anything like that and had to have it. She said no. I hit the floor, kicked and rolled. My mother grabbed my hand and, squeezing until the birthstone ring cut into my fingers, pulled me along the floor. "I want it! I want it!" Sitting on the floor of her bedroom, I almost hear my shouts and I smile a little. My mother slips on her alligator pumps. What will she bring me? A full skirt with wide rickrack to twirl in, patent leather shoes with a button on the side strap, a white angora sweater? I think of Willie Bell's, chickens scratching under the porch, and how dark it is beyond her screen door with its balls of cotton stuck on with bobby pins to catch the flies. Even from there the smell of boiling turnip greens smacks you in the face.

After the two-thirty bell, I want to play on the swings but I'm supposed to go straight home. I can feel how cold the blue bars of the jungle gym would be if I stopped to climb. The janitor, Mr. Fountain, rakes leaves into a ring of small piles. He has a dozen children and a wife with wonky eyes, and they live in one room. He leans on his rake, watching the sycamore leaves catch, smolder. The air fills with eye-stinging smoke. I wave my painting of my own handprint, with many ruby and emerald rings drawn on the fingers. Julie Sykes skips across the playground toward her mother's car. Her dress is too short and I see her ugly underwear. Her mother has something wrong and won't go anywhere except to drive Julie because she might pee-pee on herself. My mother picks me up sometimes, but usually she is busy. The Magnolia Garden Club has to replant the parks that went to weeds during the war. They have luncheons to plan the flowers. They play bridge constantly.

I run across Blue and Gray Park (named for the uniforms of both sides in the real war), passing the Northern marker near the street and the Confederate one close to the creek. Once I saw a Negro man in the sour grass, spitting on the Confederate stone.

From a block away, Willie Bell recognizes the triangle of my red skirt running under the pine trees and begins to wave. She's ready to go. She has changed from her uniform into a skirt and a sweater set that used to be my mother's. "We're going by a viewing on the way. Now if you're good—and you know what good means—we'll get you a drink afterwards."

"What viewing?"

"There's nothing for you to pay no mind to. My auntie"— she pronounced it *ont-ee*—"passed away and she's up at George Riggs's. I want to pay respects."

"Do what?"

"It just means good-bye. Her funeral's tomorrow. She was my daddy's baby sister. You knowed Auntie, she worked for the

Earlys." We turned down Sherman. Willie Bell walked fast toward colored town.

"Was Sherman a Southern or Northern, Willie Bell?" The town of Fitzgerald was a refuge for both sides.

"I don't know. That was too long ago but we're almost there. I want you real quiet. It's disrespectful to the dead to make noise." She opens a door under a flaking sign that says NEARER MY GOD TO THEE. An oily man in a suit with white lines on the pants looms in the dim light. The smell of roses feels so heavy it's as if we've stepped inside a flower. Pink shades on hanging lamps make the room glow like inside a shell. I see racks and wreathes of flowers. "You stay right here till I get back, you hear?"

I hunch down on the red rug between the feet of a coatrack. I understand dead. People die all the time. I'd just seen a hump of clay at the cemetery with a pot of purple plastic tulips. Mother said how cheap that was of Mrs. Parker, him not dead two months. In the flower room, I see Willie Bell talking to two old women. All around them are roses, carnations, bows sprinkled with sequins, and big gold flowers like my sisters wear to football games. Waves of scent roll out of the room every time the front door opens. The old women come out. Leaning on one another, they almost step on my outstretched legs. The shriveled woman has a handkerchief pressed to her nose and her cheeks are streaked with tears. As they leave they sign in a book on a stand. God and Santa Claus write down everything you do in a book then look you up when you get up to heaven and when you send your Christmas list. I stand up and walk to the doorway. The man in the suit slowly walks over to me with his hands behind his back. He leans over. I don't like his stuck-together mustache. It curls down around fat pink lips that look like a plucked dove. He smiles a big gold smile at me. I see a long box up on a table draped with a shiny pink skirt. "I expect you better wait over here. You just wait pretty." The fat man goes to the door to greet someone and I slip around the corner and quietly into the flower room. Willie Bell's kneeling, her face in her hands. Everything's swagged like a puppet show. There's another smell now, the same as the back of my mother's closet where the old shoes get mildew on the insides and the summer dresses crush together with their stale perfume. I look in the box.

Auntie Gray. But her face doesn't look like polished wood anymore. It's the color of rust and she has on her little gold glasses even though her eyes are closed. Is she really dead? In the tiny space between her lips she might, secretly, still be breathing. Her hands are folded over her stomach like Daddy Jack's when he naps. Suddenly I have to go to the bathroom. I cross my legs to hold it. I reach out and put my hand on Auntie's. She's hard as a candle. I try to lift up the hand but it's frozen like the frog I found in a bucket. Auntie sometimes stopped by to see Willie Bell. She'd pour her coffee into the saucer then pour it back into the cup. Then, she was just one of the maids who walked home down Lemon toward colored town every afternoon. Now she looks so important with purple crepe dress and lace collar. She had a soft cackle of a laugh; now her fingernails are the greenish color of old bruises and her hair lies

in flat crimps around her face. Still, like a doll of herself. Someone behind me breathes fast and I turn, expecting the owner.
It is a man with a hat in his hands. He looks at Auntie, not me.
His lips begin working but I hear no sound. His eyes are popped
out and cloudy like a dead catfish's eyes. Swallowing down the
sound my throat suddenly wants to make, I run back to the
other room, hunch against the coats again.

Willie Bell comes out walking fast. She reaches over me for
her sweater. "You were good—you can be good when you try.
Let's go get you that drink." I jump out into the hard winter
light. Everything looks the same: the mean little stores and men
in overalls leaning along the walls, pale sun that looks as if
it shines through white tissue paper. I want to ask Willie Bell
something. What? And Willie Bell has her shoulders hunched
up, her big lips stuck out. I don't ask anything. I turn two cartwheels on the sidewalk, not caring if my panties show, and wipe
the mud on my skirt.

In Lester's, Willie Bell unknots her handkerchief and takes
out the change Mother gave her for me. I open the drink box
and look down at the bottles standing in the dark cold water. I
fish out an orange Nehi from all the RC Colas. "Who's that you
got, Willie Bell, one of Cap'n Jack's granbabies?" Lester had a
wad of something in his jaw. "Just the spit of her old man, ain't
she?"

"She's like her Mama some, too."

"Yessir, I guess nobody will have to show the bobcat's chil'
how to spring," he says, laughing.

"I'll bring the bottle back tomorrow." Willie Bell snaps her
purse shut, cutting off further talk.

. . .

"You play outside awhile. I got thangs I need to do." Willie Bell gave me a big spoon and a pail. "Find some worms. We're going fishing tomorrow." I did not want to find worms. We'd been given tin compacts at school. We had to put our own "specimen" in it for hookworm tests. When the results came back, Arnold and Lucy were sent to the nurse and we all knew they had worms. Willie Bell said they didn't need a nurse; worms will be driven out if you eat chinaberries.

I run to the fence and look for Tat. There she is on the side of her house waving a stick. Willie Bell, changed into a wash dress, bangs the back door. She starts up the fire for boiling dirty clothes in an iron pot. Willie Bell told me that Tat plants sweet potatoes in the dark of the moon. Shame weed spreads out from her one-stump step to the edge of the corrugated clay road.

Stabbing the forked stick against hard ground, she rises up on her dewclaws and douses for water, but the willow shakes wherever she points.

Tat's hair twists into a bulb and a red rag winds around her head. Thin as a hoe, she works herself around the packed dirt yard. Squawking mad or mouthing silent words to a few frizzle chickens. Then she walks backward, sweeping away her own footprints with a broom made of palmetto fronds. Tat's feet: big as a man's.

Tat is dark as longleaf pine bark, dark as slash and burn fields. (My mother, white as Wonder bread. My mother has vanishing creams.)

Tat never shut up. God must have grown tired of that harangue, though sometimes God shouted back through her own mouth then shook her by the teeth. She raised sand. She humped glory. She buried candles in the four corners of the yard. She grabbled in the dirt with her bare nails, digging fast like a dog. Odd: Her legs were orange as a heron's.

Willie Bell went in the kitchen to make pork gravy and corn bread for supper. Shucking corn, snapping beans, clanging the black skillet she called "spider." Willie Bell paid no mind to Tat, her everyday background music. They lived side by side in small wood houses. Willie Bell, a one-person domestic industry, all action. Willie Bell, biding her time. Tat raving to the stars and trees, crazed, her brain on fire.

Sometimes she'd look up and in a suddenly sane voice call "Frankie!" as though someone were stepping over the ditch toward her, someone wonderful from a long time ago just alighting from a convertible. No one was there, but the startled wonder and joy in her voice made me look and look again. Who was Frankie? That's my mother's name, but Tat didn't mean her—didn't even know her.

To tat was something I was supposed to learn, the tiny edging on tea towels. My mother liked piecework. She trimmed my dolls' panties and gowns. That takes patience. My hands wouldn't. I snapped the balled-up thread. She monogrammed hand towels. Fussbox Tat didn't decorate anything. I could see inside her bare shack: silvered boards, wallpaper made from Sunday comics, calendar Jesus looking straight through the room and out at corn stubble fields and a big sky.

. . .

Tat's shifts were sudden, like streak lightning, or St. Elmo's fire in the swamp. She cut loose. I was attracted. She shouted all the bad words, a thrill. I wished my aunt Hazel could hear; she'd turn to butter. My grandmother who only seemed to say the same nice sentences over and over—she would croak if she knew what I heard. Turkeyfucker. Shitass. Fuckface. I did not even let my lips form the words—felt that if they passed into sound I would be ruined. But her other language she really let rip. (Was it a long holdover from Fante or Bantu, taught by a slave grandmother?) Was it God's own? Sometimes in a dream I expect to hear that language again: Tat's whooping *o*'s and *l*'s, rising and falling to a growling whisper. Tat's voice rolled and sped, seemed to catch me later in the dark when I couldn't sleep. She gave herself to the small scorpion roaming her brain. At night in bed, her face zoomed close to mine then pulled back fast, crying. I never imagined terrible haints and night monsters since I knew one so plainly by daylight.

Finally evening cooled. She sat on the stump, dipped a little snuff, pulled the rag off her head, and cursed to the ground. "Sons of bitches, bastards, motherfuckers, all of them mother-fuckers. Jesus knows you. He DIED for you. YOOUUUU."

Where was my mother? Not that I wanted to go home, but I didn't want to stay at Willie Bell's either. When my mother was mad she could start to rant. Not like Tat but closer to Tat than to her usual self. Tat was what happened if you let yourself look in a certain direction. Had my mother looked? At Bible school they said the smallest seed, placed under a dead man's tongue, could grow into the tree that made the cross. Here's Tat in a dirt yard baying like a bird dog. What words should be spoken? What should never be said?

Was Tat always that way? Willie Bell said so. "Long gone," she said, rotating her finger beside her temple. "Lun-a-tic." Tat spit and foamed, never noticed me hanging on the wire fence getting rust on my smocked blouse. She drew X's in the dirt. All she had was an old hinny tied to a bush. He looked as if I could push him over. Mule or donkey I didn't know, but I licked my thumb, pressed it to my palm, then stamped my palm with my fist for good luck. When it whickered and whinnied, she stared at the sky. Anger bolted her to the ground. "The wicked gonna perish from the earth. The wicked KNOW who they are." Her words almost sparked. Then she'd get the gift of tongues and shout in her own secret language. Sometimes a string of drool roped down from the corner of her mouth and I'd laugh, then duck, afraid she'd turn her wild eyes on me. Willie Bell, relentlessly calm, shook her head with disgust so I did, too. She took my hand and led me into the house.

I follow Willie Bell through her dark living room into the kitchen. From her paper sack she takes out a new coloring book and a thirty-two-color box of crayons. She sits me at the white porcelain table, and then turns on the iron. The kitchen has two other tables instead of counters and Willie Bell covered them in red oilcloth and stapled it underneath the tops. Over the drainboard hangs a picture of Jesus with his eyes rolled back, and three iron pots swinging from nails. I like the things Willie Bell has—the straight chairs with pony skin bottoms and the cigar box of forks stamped with U.S. NAVY. Her plates are each a different bright color.

While the iron heats, Willie Bell sits down. "What are you going to color me? You color me a pretty picture and I'll hang it there by the door so's I see it every time I go out."

I study the pages and select a colt looking down at a daisy in a meadow. I begin to zigzag two shades of green crayon over the grass. Willie Bell takes a droopy black dress off the back of the door and holds it up to the window. "I've got to get this dress ready to go to the funeral." She dips a corner of a rag into the pot on the stove and rubs at the sleeve.

"What are you doing?"

"I clean off spots with coffee. You can't wash this kinda material." When she irons, the scorched smell of sweat rises in a steam around the iron. I remember the flowery mildew smell around Auntie.

"Where is Auntie?" I make dark blue loops for the sky.

"Why, you know, she's laying out at Riggs's."

I put my face down on the cool porcelain. I keep coloring slowly. "I saw her, too."

"What? Yo' mama ain't going to like that one bit."

"I won't tell her. I wanted to see. What *happened* to her?"

Willie Bell pushed back my hair. "Sugar, she had a seizure, a fit; she's just gone, that's all."

"Did she go to heaven?"

"Yes, they says so." I wait for her to say more but she goes back to the iron and carefully presses the piqué collar. *What's a seizure,* I wonder, *something like an enormous hand shaking you?* I imagine Auntie walking down Lemon and a bony hand coming out of the pecan trees and shaking her to death. Could a seizure happen anytime? I run my tongue around my mouth, counting my teeth to myself.

Outside the window I see the wooden shed over the well. I remember Mother reading me a story out of the *Atlanta Journal* about a little girl who fell down an old well in a vacant lot. If I go running in any field, the ground could collapse; I could fall, fall, fall, splash into black water and no one would hear me scream. If I tried to climb up the sides, the way I shinnied up doorframes, I would slide back down the slimy stones. I remember Willie Bell has a well, too. "Can't we get a drink from the well? I'm thirsty again."

Willie Bell slides the cover off and I lean over and see my face, small as a nickel, way down in the water. The bucket goes down on a rope, tips and slips under water, then Willie Bell cranks it up, dips in a gourd, and pours a drink into a jelly glass. I hold up the glass and see little specks swimming. Just as I am about to ask Willie Bell why it doesn't taste like faucet water, a rooster comes out of a row of dry corn. He flexes his wings and lifts up on his claws. Every instinct I have turns me toward Willie Bell but she is taking sheets off the line, just out of reach. The rooster gives a low, broken cackle. I raise my arms with a little cry just as he squawks and flies at my face. Pecks and flaps. Willie Bell lets go of the sheets. In one motion she kicks the rooster hard and jerks me away. The rooster, suddenly indifferent, ruffles his feathers and struts around the house. Willie Bell slings a clod after him.

A thin line of red drops darkens my red skirt, as in summer when I got nosebleeds that wouldn't stop until Willie Bell held cold scissors against my back. Willie Bell lifts me on the kitchen table and swabs my face with water. I stare into her brown face as she paints the cut with a cold wand of iodine. She looks as though it hurts her, too. She frowns and makes little clicking noises. "Lord, Lord." I kick at the table legs as the medicine burns into my cheek. Sudden stings of pain force my tears. I burrow against Willie Bell's arm. "You cry all you want to." Willie Bell holds me on her lap, rocking me back and forth. The rooster seems to fly at me over and over. The hard, beady eyes and the hooks of his feet. I think I never can get away from the feeling of his feathers all over my body and I am right. I curl as small as I can, crying until I stop and my chest feels tight with no more tears. Something dense and heavy, like a stone growing inside, keeps me still.

At six o'clock, the blare of the Oldsmobile horn. As I open my eyes I see Willie Bell's black dress still draped over the ironing board. My hair sticks to my forehead. Willie Bell buttons my sweater and hands me the crayons and coloring book in a paper sack. "You can finish tomorrow. Now run on, yo' mama's waitin'."

I climb in the backseat. My mother looks at me through the mirror, then turns around, her smile disappearing as she sees my face. I watch her mouth move into an O. "What on earth happened to you? You look awful."

"A rooster pecked me and scratched me."

"You were teasing him?"

"I was not. You always . . ." I run my finger over the rough welt that is now my face.

"Always what?"

I don't answer. I don't know what I even started to say.

"Well, look in the pink bag on the floor and you'll feel better." I find the bag among the other boxes and sacks. Before I see it, I feel the white musical puppy with blue velvet under his ears. I wind him and put him to my ear. He smells new and I can hear the little mechanical purr under the sound of the music.

"Mammy, did you know Auntie died?"

"Um-hum. That was sad, wasn't it?"

"I was scared of that rooster."

"Awful. Wasn't Willie Bell looking after you?"

"Yes, but she couldn't help it. He was too fast. He shook me in his beak."

"That's not so, but I just hope it doesn't leave a scar." I see my mother's eyes in the rearview mirror.

"Is so." She is looking straight ahead at Roanoke Drive. Even in the dusky light her eyes are blankly clear, almost like the blind beggar I saw on the sidewalk the last time I went shopping in Macon. He sold a cup of yellow pencils, his milky blue eyes tipped up toward heaven. But my mother looks soft, too, especially with the rusty-colored foxes around her neck. I over-wind the new dog and he plays his song double time all the way home.

ISLANDS IN SUMMER

Many primitive charms must be worked in solitude. On the island I slipped out early to walk the beach washed clean of footprints. My father taught me about the beach at sunrise. All the years I was small, he often would wake me up and say, "Come on, Bud, let's go to the beach." At this hour it's easy to see why these are called the Golden Isles of Georgia. The first peach-cream rays slide over the water and strike the sand first, lighting the beach as if from underneath. We pick up sand dollars together and line up our collection along the driveway wall. I tell my father the little bones that rattle inside are doves of Jesus's because I saw that on a Legend of the Sand Dollar postcard, but he says nonsense, sand dollars are real money that mermaids use. When I break one open, the "doves" that fall out look like my baby teeth that I've saved in a ring box at home.

They've warned me not to go in the ocean alone. The undertow pulls even in shallow water. My father was sucked under as a boy. He said he knew not to fight, not to try to get back by paddling against a current stronger than man or beast. *When a current pulls you out, swim sideways, parallel to the beach, gradually angle in, and let the current help you.* Since I know that, of course I swim alone. I am nine and I've had lessons. I can sidestroke all day. I'm a cold-blooded animal and walk into the water at dawn with little shock, ride waves in until my fingertips shrivel, then cartwheel dry. By the time the wobbling gold orb hoists out of the water, I'm on the beach wrapped in a towel with my knees against my chest, every ugly hair on my arms standing straight up, my teeth chattering though the air is soft and my skin powdery with salt. I like to stare out at the straight line of blue ink horizon. How could they ever have believed the earth was flat? Why couldn't they see the ocean water would drain off the edge? Where could the tide go when it went out? Someday I will live here alone and have my own boat and sail out exactly to that line where the ocean and sky meet. I will have candles and a bunk bed and a two-piece bathing suit. *So very vulgar to show the navel,* my mother says.

Sometimes Willie Bell comes out to find me and swears she will tell if I do this one more time. On the island she doesn't wear the black or white uniforms she wears at our house in Fitzgerald. Here, she's in a pressed red plaid dress, with short sleeves that point, and sandals. We're the only ones up and I walk back to the kitchen with her. She makes me a piece of oven toast—I don't like toaster toast—and a soft fried egg because I will dip my toast into the yellow with lots of salt and pepper and she will eat the white.

We love St. Simons, Sea Island, and Jekyll. *Summer* is here, less than three hours from home, on this string of barrier isles, ocean on one side, marsh on the other. We stay sometimes on St. Simon's, sometimes on Sea Island. Jammed with my mother, sisters, and Willie Bell (my father and the dog traveled in a separate car with a driver), along with a month's supply of clothes, games, cheese straws, fudge, and beach towels, we cross the rickety bridge from Brunswick to St. Simons and I see the marsh grasses waving, sense suddenly the land not earth, not water, but both, with the grass moving in time with the tide and the sulfur-laden wind. Then it comes to mind, the poem I'd just been required to learn by heart in third grade:

As the marsh-hen secretly builds on the watery sod,
Behold I will build me a nest on the greatness of God:
I will fly in the greatness of God as the marsh-hen flies
In the freedom that fills all the space 'twixt the marsh and the skies

The jolt of connection. "Look—the marshes of Glynn. We had a poem about them," I shout. No one seems impressed. They're talking about the reek of the paper mills. But I experience a pure surge of joy. After that, I have a new sense, like taste and smell.

We pull into the driveway of a long brick house with a breezeway and a little house out back for Willie Bell. My mother jumps out of the car, holds out her arms wide enough to embrace the summer.

. . .

By noon, the island sings with heat. Cicadas hum like high-power wires, and air rising off the road wavers so that what I walk toward is real but looks like a mirage. The tree frogs won't shut up, either. We love the ocean, all of us. On weekends, Daddy catches the sunrise. Mother takes long walks down the beach, scudding her soles to smooth away calluses. As she swings out her leg to slenderize her thighs, her toes sketch arcs in the sand. My two sisters, home from college for the summer, slather themselves with oil and lie on beach towels for hours. They don't want straps to show, don't want red noses; they run splashing and screaming in the ocean to cool off, then baste themselves again. Their burnished gold gleaming bodies radiate the dense smell of coconut and salt and hot sand, the smell of summer. I don't tan. I burn and freckle like a quail egg. I love the warm powdery sand sifting through my fingers, the drip castles I build at the edge of the water.

In the afternoon heat when there is nothing to do I take pictures. My mother thinks I should rest so I won't get polio, but I never will. I snap a lizard asleep on a leaf, my dog Tish asleep under a bush, my sandals on the slate steps, my sisters coming in from the beach laughing together. In the lens of my Brownie, I center Barbara and Nancy in hourglass bathing suits. Briefly they pose in fifth position, their bare feet tender on the oyster shell driveway. They squint and smile over my shoulder, impatient.

They are older, with clothes on their minds and boyfriends. What they do not want is me pestering them. In my not-boredom but lack of available activity, I eavesdrop from their closet, hunching down among the Capezios and crinolines piled on the floor.

They talk and talk about beach parties, Ralph from Augusta, the local lifeguard, Neil. "Who is that girl visiting the Addisons? She was about to pop out of that corny gypsy blouse. I don't know what her reputation in Macon is, but . . ." Whatever the revelation I wait for, it never comes. When I become annoyed with hiding, inevitably I make a noise.

Nancy, ironing a skirt, flings open the door, shouting, "What are you doing? This is the limit!" I race around her, leaping to the twin bed next to the wall. I bounce higher and higher, my fingertips smudging the ceiling, until her shouting reaches a crescendo. Barbara stares into the dressing table mirror. "Just don't pay any attention to her. She's just trying to attract attention. Spoiled brat, brat, brat." Barbara smooths Aquamarine Lotion on her legs.

"Meow, Meow," I call, louder and louder.

"Would you shut up? Now."

"Make me. Make me."

Nancy carefully turns her skirt, spreading the eyelet flounce as flat as she can against the board. "Get off. That's a new bedspread!"

I keep catcalling louder and louder. "Try and make me!"

Nancy bangs down the iron on the metal holder. She lunges for me as I leap back onto the pillow. Her foot catches in the twisted cord and the hot iron falls, browns into the carpet. She grabs my ankle, pulls me down. Suddenly we smell the singed animal odor of burning wool. Barbara jerks the iron from the scorched triangle in the pale blue rug and I bounce one more time. "You did it, you did it. Ya ya ya ya Ya ya."

"You little . . ."

As I run out I see Nancy giving me the finger and Barbara rubbing a washrag on the rug. Nothing came up. She just streaked old makeup across the burn.

They didn't bother to tell on me since my parents never listened anyway. Certainly, Willie Bell wouldn't tell. She got the fingernail scissors and snipped away the tip ends of the rug fibers. In the soft pile, the slightly shorter threads hardly were noticeable. She always knew a solution.

Willie Bell looked like Nefertiti. When our third-grade class did the unit on Egypt, I first saw the famous profile and recognized Willie Bell's, without her gold-rimmed glasses. She must be a descendant of the distant queen, the genes for that flat sloped forehead and chiseled cheekbones spinning along the DNA of generations of royalty, then slaves, and finally manifesting again with force in Willie Bell Smith. Her grandmother was a slave. I knew her as a child-sized, ancient gray woman with hair tied in colored strips like kite tails. It seemed impossible that she'd once been something as exotic as a slave. I didn't know when or where Willie Bell was born. We measured her age only in how long she'd been with us, six years, eight, eleven. Out of the many years she worked for us, I remember her most sharply on the island because there I first saw her as separate from us and felt the first inkling that there was something wrong between the races.

• • •

The light on the islands is white, reflecting off the white sand dunes and oyster shell roads that can shred your feet. In late evening, after a long twilight, the sky darkens quickly, like a room someone walks out of while holding up a lantern. Even after the fringed tops of pines disappear into the dark, the bright sand holds down the light that suffuses the air with soft silver. Sky and ocean disappear into each other. Twisted coastal oaks draped with Spanish moss make the landscape doleful or romantic, depending on one's frame of mind. In *The Mind of the South*, W. J. Cash maintained that the blue air, softening all edges, gave us our ambiguous ways of seeing things. And yes, it is as easy to imagine the early settlers vanishing into time as to imagine them raising houses, greeting Chief Tomochichi, and planting pot herbs and fruit trees: debtors—altruistic James Oglethorpe called them "the worthy poor"—hauled out of English jails and sent to paradise to start a silk trade.

Walking with Willie Bell around the tabby remains of Oglethorpe's settlement, I stood looking at the site of the baker's house, just an outline of crushed shell, and imagined the oven, women walking under the oaks to get their bread, the fragrant smell as they stood at the door. I thought *I'm walking here just as they walked, just as I walk they walked*. That was my first inkling of how the past pounces: Once they were here so I can be here thinking of the fragrance of their bread.

Minding me, Willie Bell was allowed on the beach but did not wear a bathing suit. She sits in a low chair at the tide line, her feet close enough that the waves run over them. My swirly blue beach ball looks like a world globe and I like the particular rubbery *ping* when I bounce it to her. She throws it into the waves and I splash out to grab it before the undertow does. She smokes and buries the butts in wet sand.

In the quincunx of family, my parents—never one of the girls—take turns at center position. On the island, I can step out of the thrall of that pattern and it's Willie Bell who centers my memory.

She lived out back in the brick cottage with a dressing table made from a treadle sewing machine base, a maple sofa printed with American eagles, and bright yellow walls from the same paint can as the kitchen in the main house. Between the twin beds was a night table for the white Philco and a cranberry red lamp made of bumpy glass. Now I see that she left her family to go to the island with us. Did she like that? Her old mother with rheumatism took care of Willie Bell's adopted daughter, Carol. (Willie Bell asked me and I named her after one of my friends. Was that way of naming a leftover custom from slave times? Later I named Willie Bell's son Robert Nelson Smith after Lord Horatio Nelson.) Willie Bell's mother ate big spoonfuls of damp red clay. Did she coax Carol to try some? Willie Bell's husband kept working for my father at the mill.

Willie Bell takes me crabbing on Saturdays. We buy chunks of rotten meat at the grocery and take crab baskets to a bridge so low it almost touches the black marsh water when an occasional car passes. We lean over the rail for hours pulling in crabs. Mother will be so pleased; she never has enough crabs, shrimp, or flounder at home. Willie Bell picks them up by the pincers and throws them in a croker sack. Over and over I ask, "How can you eat crabs when they eat rotten meat?" She'd answer, "Just don't think that way." Then I'd wonder, how do you have a choice in how to think when the smelly hunk of meat lies in the bottom of the crab box?

Willie Bell met Kitty, the maid who came from Detroit with some people who made Fords up there. Kitty wasn't crabbing for her employers, only out walking. "They can *buy*, honey," she explained. I think Willie Bell never had met anyone of her own color from the North. Kitty's employers had a lot more money than we ever dreamed of, and her world must have sounded impossible to Willie Bell.

I met the Detroit people's daughter, Alicia, at the Cloister Hotel pool. When I went to her house for lunch we sat in a baronial dining room, and Kitty in white brought out two little tuna sandwiches on Merita toast, and Cokes. I thought it was amazing that someone so rich ate tuna fish, which I was too picky to touch since it smelled bad and came out of a can. When Alicia's parents invited mine, my father refused to go because they were "nigger-rich" and "How can anyone live in Detroit?" My mother said they lived outside it and they were very nice. She was determined to meet interesting people. The ritual Sunday dinners, bridge games, gossip—the same days repeating endlessly in Fitzgerald—were not what she had in mind. "Not everyone is stuck in the backwaters of Georgia," she'd remind him.

"Well, why do you think they'd want to meet countrified people from these backwaters?" he argued back. He was always a good defense. In the large argument, the meta-argument of their life together, he knew she had to be defensive. He knew, too, that many people would like to meet my mother. He'd wanted to look at her for the rest of his life when he met her. Aunt Hazel said that when they met, she'd never seen two people so much in love. Though who knew what happened to that.

Out of town, my mother became what she thought of as herself. This self charmed everyone. The clothes she bought in Atlanta or had copied from magazines were gorgeous. She carried herself as if our name meant something, though its radius of influence was about ten miles of backwoods at most. "Anyway," she'd insist to him, "there are some fascinating people here. I met a newspaper writer from Chicago. His wife had a purple birthmark on her back. Wonder if he saw it before they married? Really dark like raspberry juice. She had on a suit with a low back. She must not care. He smoked those little black cigarettes. And an old woman is studying slave songs and dances, writing them down for the future." My father drains his drink. That would be his idea of nothing to do and all day to do it. "There's a writer," she continues, even though he is not going to discuss it further. "You know that big Spanish house with the red tile roof right down the road? The one with the bent pines and the white stucco wall?"

He rolls his eyes back and shakes his head.

"Eugene O'Neill lives there." She heard this from the newspaperman who said O'Neill was a famous writer with a strong sense of family. "His plays have been on Broadway." (My ears pointed when I overheard that—a writer. I wanted to write books, too, and didn't know writers lived anywhere except in remote Irish castles.) "They named the house 'Casa Genotta'—for Gene and Carlotta. Her name's Carlotta." My father heads for the gin cabinet. "Don't you know who Eugene O'Neill is?" she asks.

"No."

"Well, if you don't know, I'm not going to be the one to tell you." Soon they'd go out.

I didn't know the word "racism." Black/white polarity was the God-given order of things. My fingers are poised over the keyboard: impossible to relive that state of mind, impossible to convey how remote we were from the great movements beginning to grind tectonic plates under our feet. My part of the South was decades off; we were metaphorically in an Irish castle or a hut on windswept moors. When Daddy asked the yardman to dance a jig for us, I felt embarrassed for both, but with no clear idea why. Drew, the yardman, and my father had little exchanges they went through on meeting. One stemmed from the time Drew first asked for employment at the mill, and my father filled out an application. When he asked Drew's middle name, Drew replied "none," and my father understood him to say "Nome." So, on greeting ever after, he always says, "Drew who?" and Drew replies, "Drew NOME Hill, Cap'n, Drew NOME Hill," and laughs. Drew could lift the proverbial bale of cotton on his shoulder. He was blue eyed, a "high yellow," enormously strong. He could have mashed my father into the ground with his fist. I remember him later, crying at my father's funeral, telling me how good the Cap'n always was to him, how he'd lost the best friend he had. My father, all generosity, all meanness, all enigma. Is it possible that the little name game, so obviously demeaning, did not seem so to them? When I found out Drew was afraid of the evil eye, my ritual with him was to close one eye and stare hard at him with the other. I chased him around the yard, with him begging me not to put the evil eye on him. Was he serious? Or indulging these peculiar white folks? I liked Drew. I teased anyone, black or white. As soon as I started school, I began giving Willie Bell grades on food. At the end of every meal, I pronounced "A," or "C-." That these were adults and I was a patronizing, tormenting child I did not then see; it took me a long time to invent the idea of justice.

Willie Bell was unfailingly kind in her sangfroid way. From her arrival at seven a.m. until she left for afternoon rest, the house was a better place to be. My father was gone, which helped, and I was at home with Mother and Willie Bell–if only it could stay like that. They planned the menu, straightened the house. Mother went to the beach while Willie Bell washed underwear or vacuumed. If Mother shopped, she honked when she got back and they unloaded the groceries and started dinner. The orderly world of The House, my favorite game, metaphor, reality. I set up a parallel house in the breakfast room, laid my dolls on the corn silk as Willie Bell shucked, ironed my doll dresses as Willie Bell ironed, cooked on the toy electric stove as Willie Bell cooked. I always had the father away at a war. The black face of the reversible doll lay head to head with the bisque face of the doll that belonged to my mother when she was a child. All I knew on the subject of race was the Sunday school song "Red and yellow, black and white / They are precious in His sight / Jesus loves the little children of the world." I mixed the song up with "Autumn leaves are now falling / Red and yellow and brown / Autumn leaves are now falling / See them tumbling down."

If this sounds too archaic to believe, believe me. When I went to Nicaragua a couple of years before the revolution, my friend there picked me up in his big green Mercedes. I'd known him as a poet in Princeton; he'd gone home and become the secretary to Somoza, something like a prime minister. As we rolled through the streets I had glimpses of poor—very poor—people parting in the streets to let the rude chauffeur's horn through. I was alarmed. "Why aren't they throwing rocks at us?" was the first question I asked in that country. My friend answered, "Because they don't know to."

Willie Bell didn't "know to," either, though soon she'd learn a stronger approach than rocks. Within her range of action, she felt lucky to go to the beach, or so she told me. I think she enjoyed her mornings with my mother, who was never a prima donna and would crack crabs, rinse out bathing suits, shell lady peas, and wash the salty windows. They laughed and gossiped. As at home, on Sea Island Willie Bell soon knew everything through the maids' grapevine.

My mother would have stayed forever. Sea Island suited her essential sense of life: a tropical island of perpetual vacation from the reality of her daily life. Sometimes days were too long for me and I wished we were at Uncle Mark's house near Daytona Beach, where there was a Ferris wheel and boardwalk and a shop where a parrot on a string cursed while I bought a cherry snow cone. My sisters liked the St. Simons lifeguards who came over at night and played canasta and bridge. I spied from behind the sofa. Later, they'd go to the beach to look for loggerhead turtle eggs. At Sea Island there was no one to play with. Alicia was prissy and wanted only to dress and undress her dolls. She did not like to get wet.

I wrote my name and address on squares of paper and put them in pickle jars. On one I quickly added *I am a prisoner. Save me.* I asked Daddy to give them to shrimp boat fishermen to take out to sea. I never had answers from Nassau or England, as I hoped. My sisters found boys and took off on the backs of scooters. Everyone at Sea Island seemed old. All there was to do besides play on the beach was to swim at the Cloister pool and order club sandwiches and ginger ale out under the umbrellas. The pages of *Anne of Green Gables* and *Freddy Goes to Florida* stuck together in the humidity and developed small green speckles.

On Saturday nights my parents dress up and go to the Cloister or the King and Prince bar. I have to go to dinner, too, all scratchy in organdy pinafore over sunburn, the food hidden under pale sauces, and old men, mostly belly, talking about what kind of season the Bulldogs might have and ol' Harry giving them hell in Washington. I think Truman looks like a parakeet. I eat all the grapes out of the finger bowls. After dinner a band plays "I'll Dance at Your Wedding," "Some Enchanted Evening," which was my mother's theme song, and "Rum and Coca-Cola," and Mother dances with all the men and Daddy goes off somewhere until he comes back with that mean expression on his face, the half-curl smile you could think was pleasant unless you knew him. Then he wants to go home and she won't and I press my ankles together, waiting, hoping they won't erupt among all the nice people. At home, a few drinks. Something broken. They shout names, push each other around. Their routine and it never ceased to terrify.

Once she wouldn't give him the keys when he wanted to roar off somewhere at two in the morning. They chased around the house like two dogs. I was the only one who could calm my father. The absurdity of a sixty-pound human as a peacemaker got through even to him. When I stood in the doorway, sometimes he could not go on. "Hey, Bud, how're you doing?" His voice shifts to sweet. He rubs my hair back off my forehead and I smile up at him. Though I might want to throw boiling water in their faces, I would instead stand there in my flowered seersucker nightgown, forcing my eyes to look as blue as possible. To react naturally would make me like them; I had to be smarter. They were trapped on a small grid. (Thanks to my parents, I sometimes recognize small grids when I get on them.) I never heard the word "divorce" pass between them. I'd known only one "broken home." The mother worked in the dime store; the father took off for Jacksonville, Florida, and sent the two boys drugstore cards signed "Love, Daddy" on their birthdays. Divorce happened to those who were not very nice. We had love, much love, but it was scumbled. On the island, late at night, often I ran to Willie Bell.

Willie Bell likes looking at magazines. She keeps a little fan turned on her feet. That famous profile. Turning pages, she drinks Coke, and the red lamp sheds a glow on her dark brown sugar skin. In bed with her hair down, she looks different. By day she wears her hair in a bun and wet plum lipstick. Seeing her like this seems strange. I always see her ironing or cooking. Here she stretches out, the covers kicked back, her shoulders bare. She smells of rose oil. Both of her incisors are mostly gold. She has big lips and a delicate but work-strong body. If someone ever hands her a tennis racket, she'll whack the ball right over the net. She wears an old gown of my mother's. When I ask why the soles of her feet are white, she says, "The Lord dipped the African people in the dark to protect them from the sun. Their feet are white because he held them from the ankles."

"Then why aren't the tops white, too?"

"You'll have to ask Him."

When I asked if I could stay with her, she never had to ask why. I looked out Willie Bell's front window at my parents in the kitchen, watching their gestures and faces as they slung drinks and leaned forward, hands on hips, to taunt each other. Willie

Bell rarely remarked on them. How could she refrain? She was wise. A slip from me about anything she said would be expensive. For no reason, sometimes my father would call her in the middle of the night and fire her. He got these crazes. The next day my mother would apologize and say "You know how he gets." Yes, Willie Bell knew. Since her husband was slow and much older, probably a liability at the mill, she was not going to disagree with anything.

Late, after the pyrotechnics were over, I'd hear Willie Bell's soft snore. The tide, at its lowest, dragged back through the deep coquina shells, a sound like someone stepping on fine broken glass. This sound, and Willie Bell's breathing. I'd lie awake listening as long as I could. The fan on the dresser looked like a small black face slowly shaking its head in the dark.

Beyond the tabby wall behind Willie Bell's cottage, waist-high palmettos began. I am forbidden beyond the wall because quicksand could swallow me if I misstepped. I look down as I run, not only for quicksand but for coral snakes. I'd seen many moccasins, greasy blue, moving the way a hose moves when you cut off the spray at the nozzle. I didn't know other poisonous snakes but I imagined the bright twist of body in the white sand, like the delicate coral necklace in my mother's jewelry box suddenly come to life. *If one bites your finger, you have to have your finger cut off quickly or you'll die.* What if one bites your stomach? *You'd never know what hit you.* Palmettos slash against my legs. I run fast.

When I stop the sand is cool. I sift handfuls over my feet.
Where is the big red woodpecker called Lord God? I sit still,
hoping I will hear one of the small island deer clattering toward
me through the knife-sharp leaves. If I am still as a bush for
a long time, a deer might come and rub its face against mine,
even lie down beside me and let me rub its speckled side. The
deer might think I am one of them and I could step quietly with
her toward the marsh grass.

In the palmetto jungle I imagine myself living like the Swiss
Family Robinson, making bowls from shells, a roof from palmetto, fashioning a scoop out of a gourd, catching rainwater
on the tip of my tongue from oak leaves. Tarzan and Jane live
somewhere in here. I have no idea how small the island is or
that it's owned by a corporation, which blocks Jews, much less
riffraff like the shipwrecked. As I walk back home, I search the
shrubs for parrot nests. Low in the palmetto I find a small nest
made of dune grass and twigs. Three mottled blue eggs. I run
all the way home. When I see my father's car pulling in the
driveway, I cut over to the far side of the yard.

My mother sits at the kitchen table, polishing her nails poppy
red. She hears the heavy crunch of tires on the oyster-shell drive
and looks up to see the white curve of Daddy's fender turning
in. Already Friday again. She screws the top on the polish and
spreads out her fingers to dry. She sees him, his thin scissor legs
swinging out of the Oldsmobile, his rumpled seersucker suit,
the way he holds his head slightly to one side. He wipes his face
with a handkerchief and turns toward the ocean for the relief of
a sea breeze. There is none. Unconsciously, he places his hand

over his side where the bullet hit him. The island air is so thick it seems to congeal as he breathes.

He kisses her forehead. She glances at the stove clock. She could set it by his arrival each week. She can repeat without asking his answers about the week he just spent at home in Fitzgerald, but they go through the script anyway. She thinks of Oscar, the severely retarded neighbor at home, always asking the temperature. She'd made up temperatures every day for years, as though it ever had changed for him in his thirty years or ever would. She might bring up buying a house at Sea Island, but Daddy always says renting is costing him buckets of dollars and nobody notices and does she think he's made out of money? Enough never will be enough, he says. I linger, looking at them facing off for the weekend. Her hair streaked blond from the sun, him holding up the frosted bottle to the window to see how much is left.

I quietly let myself in the breezeway door. In my room, I hide the egg in a thumb of my white gloves in the top drawer, cover it with the other glove and wrap them in two handkerchiefs to keep the egg warm until it hatches. Every day I slowly slide out the drawer expecting a small bird with green jungle eyes to look out at me.

Willie Bell meets other maids easily and begins to go out with them on Saturday nights and Mondays. They go to the colored beach and to juke joints in Brunswick. I see her fastening her garter belt and slipping into sling-back shoes. Putting something from a little pot on her eyes. They darken, almond shaped, more like Nefertiti's than ever. Ten years later, when she leaves us for a new life in Chicago, my mother is sure Kitty first put ideas in Willie Bell's head. By then Orval Faubus is banging the school door in Little Rock, and waves of blacks are heading north, but my family blames Willie Bell's departure on Kitty's gold charm bracelet and high shrieking laugh that always dropped off when my parents came into the room.

Now, I still go back to the Georgia islands. I try to imagine my parents there, content and old, the parties and drinking over. Did they never want to stay home and play mah-jongg, make an omelet, and read? Who they really were remains unknowable, one of those "solve this or lose your life" riddles. Was it getting married in the Depression, furtively running away in the middle of the night, that started them off on this endless restlessness? I wonder if she ever tried to find another man on these summer trips. I certainly would have. Someone elegant from the North with graying temples and a bankroll. Her longing for a fuller life was a constant. As far as I know she never took a positive step to get it. Because of her beauty, because her own father adored her, because so many wanted to marry her, because, because, she continued to expect the life she was promised simply would materialize out of very thin air.

I see them with all their good qualities at the forefront. There they are on the breezeway, magically come to their senses and putting together Legos with a rapt grandchild. Normal. They garden and go to movies and Daddy helps clean up after dinner. They'd be bird-watchers, counting egrets over the marsh at evening, gathering signatures on a petition to protect the turtles. Ha, imagine that.

The good trick of memory: I imagine them any way I want. Willie Bell remains in the little brick house. She's looking at an old *McCall's* magazine. If I run to the door she'll look up and say, "Come on in and sit but you'll have to entertain yourself 'cause I'm all out of chat."

Jekyll Island was deserted when I was a child. Robber barons bought the island in 1896 and built vacation mansions. When they abandoned them during the difficult World War II years, the government closed the island.

From St. Simons, we could motor over there, my sister Nancy, her boyfriend Neil, and I. We cross the marshes of Glynn, going around Jekyll to the ocean side because we aren't supposed to land. This is where the illegal ship *The Wanderer* once anchored and let off the last load of slaves in the United States. The houses are enormous, larger than the fanciest ones at Sea Island. Somehow Nancy and Neil disappear behind a tree swagged with moss. The breaking waves emphasize an absolute quiet. Algae long since has invaded the swimming pools half-full of froggy water. The delicate green embroidery of resurrection fern covers live oak limbs. Stone urns and naked nymphs holding baskets of fruit startle me as I wander through the overgrown grounds. Up on stone terraces French doors swing and bang, disturbing only chameleons sunning on the steps. I go in a long room and from a black leather chaise longue pick up a letter addressed to the Cranes, the name stamped on toilets and stationery boxes at home. I take down a dusty game of Parcheesi from a bookshelf. This is better than *The Mystery at Lilac Inn* or any other book I've read.

When I tell Willie Bell about the deserted island she says she's heard from Kitty that ghosts are there, everyone knows it; everyone knows that many slaves waded into the surf at Ebo Landing and some flew back to Africa. Those who didn't sprout wings washed up on Jekyll and haunt it forever. She is holding a curling rod. She combs jelly into her hair then pulls the hot rod through the long kinks. The hot smell sizzles in the muggy air. She pulls back her hair tight and knots it at the nape. I would like to live here all year and play on Jekyll and in the palmettos. Willie Bell could take care of me. I would never miss my parents.

On the last night, my parents and I are taking the house keys back to the Cloister. My mother doesn't want to go home. Suddenly my father slams the brakes. We see a red fox ahead on the road, stopped so still it looks as if it won't move for the car to pass. "Let me out," I beg my parents. I wanted to say something softly to the fox, not words, just sounds while I moved up slowly. The fox would know me, know I meant no harm, and it would let me brush the back of my hand across its tail. All three of us stare and the fox glares straight into the headlights then slips back into the black off the edge of the road. I watch for it, not sure the two glinting eyes I see looking back at me from the dark are not my own reflecting in the car window.

As we drive by the turn to the secluded Spanish house,

Mother reminds my father that they never met the interesting writer Eugene O'Neill. "You've got it all wrong," he tells her. "They don't even live on the island anymore. The bartender at the Cloister told me he was a miserable drunk and she was some Chiquita banana with a made-up name, who didn't have the sense to come in out of the rain. He sat up there writing nonsense when it was so hot he had to sit on a bath towel and keep blotters under his hands so the ink didn't run away in the sweat. Must have been a damn fool not to think of that when he bought the place. A damn fool Yankee."

Never one to allow the last word, she retorted, "Well he's an important writer with a sense of family."

The low white wall pulls fast by my eyes like X-ray film pulled over a light.

WATERING

Noon burns the whole town into stillness. My house is dark against the heat, the heavy draperies closed. In the dining room the one air conditioner labors and sweats. I lie under it in my camp shorts and a stiff shirt printed with birds. I am home from camp, home from the island. What's left but the burned-up end of summer? I've finished the books my sister brought me from Athens, where she goes to college, and I am half through the long row of worn-out orange books from the library. The librarian, Miss Peetrie, gives a star for every book I read and after every ten I may have a free ice-cream cone at the Central Pharmacy. I want to win the Best Reader Prize for the summer— ten tickets to the Grand Theatre. *The Chinese Twins, The Mexican Twins, Anne of Avonlea, A Girl of the Limberlost.* I sip Coca-Cola through the glass straw Grandmother Mayes used once when she was in the hospital. Mother has gone to bed with a splitting headache and my sisters, packing for college, stay in their room, too hot to talk, playing "How High the Moon" over and over on the record player. I keep one ear tuned in case they play the forbidden "Gloomy Sunday," which causes sane, nice people to commit suicide and has been banned from WBHB.

After I snap shut *The Mexican Twins,* I change into my bathing suit. The attic fan sucks in the hot air, lifting the organdy curtains with the illusion of coolness. Mother does not look up. She's in her slip, propped up on pillows flicking through the pages of *House and Garden.* Her finger runs around her monogram on the turned-down sheet, FMD, thick as bird bones. On my way outside I see two women dressed like bats and my mother studying the caption under their picture.

At first the water runs hot from the nozzle, then suddenly cold. I make it rain, waving the hose in arcs. With the fine spray I spray a doll-sized rainbow just above the grass. Then Daddy comes home. The deep idleness he slices into, turning into the driveway in the gray car big as a cloud. He steps out in his sharp white suit. I have to squint to look at him.

Willie Bell knows just what he wants and comes right out with the gin on ice and the little saucer of mint and lime because he likes to choose between them. He walks slowly to his chair in the backyard.

I cool the welts on my legs and dance the water off the soles of my feet, which the bubbled tar on Lemon Street harden every summer. The woolly red suit, almost too little, crawls up beyond the suntan line on my legs.

"Well, what did you do today?" he says as he passes me without stopping.

"Nothing."

In the shade of the pecan tree, he sits in a sling chair reading the *Atlanta Journal,* avoiding the house. I swing the nozzle in figure eights, sprinkling the bachelor's buttons, the short yellow flowers full of bugs, the larkspurs, my favorites, and the St. Augustine grass so dark green at the end of summer.

"You're spattering me," he complains. Drops bead on his shoes. He looks up, as if waiting.

I drive a leaf across the grass with the spray. As I hit the tree, little bullets of water pelt the back of his striped canvas chair.

"Did you hear what I said?" He crumples the paper in his lap. When he's mad he has no lips. "Go away," he shouts. "You're driving me crazy."

I stand still. The crystal drops hang for a long moment in the air. Then, as if from far in the future, some sure instinct pulls me. I turn on him the hard spurt.

His hands spread in the air, paper dissolving on his chest. The glass falling. He leaps up, never taller. The bull eyes, the chair turning over.

I drop the hose and it snakes back and forth between us, wild now with such a good idea. He lunges for my shoulder. I dangle from his hands like a puppet unstrung. I rattle and rattle.

In my room I sit in the middle of the bed with the memory of his white knuckles. My legs are crisscrossed with more red switch marks. Willie Bell, quiet as a spider, brings in juice and a ham biscuit on a tray. "Oh, Miss Frances. Oh, Lord," and she is gone.

The screen door bangs and from my window I see Mother fresh in a pink sundress, crossing the lawn. Has Willie Bell told her? She walks among flickering green shadows. Between the trees comes the red sunset. From the back she looks young like my sisters, ready to go somewhere. But she starts the sprinkler, steps back, and watches it throw its slow fistfuls of water to the grass. She is small against the old gardenia bush with its untouchable flowers.

My eyes scan my room. The yellow rows of mystery books, the conch shell I found in Fernandina, the walking doll brought from Atlanta, my private notebook, the long vine trailing down from the sweet potato in a glass of water. Slowly, I start the list of what's mine.

NAMESAKE

After school I walked to the hospital where Mother Mayes was about to die. Ever since the operation a month ago, when they'd taken a look and simply sewn her up, everyone kept telling her she was coming along fine but Mother and Aunt Mary Helen already had picked out the ash gray crepe dress she would wear in the coffin. My mother said at supper that Mother Mayes was "eaten up" and it was a miracle she still hung on. Too mean to die was her opinion. Mother Mayes had no intention of dying. She had reservations for the month of June at White Springs, Florida, down on the Suwannee River. The sulfur water always restored her. Every year she met my aunt Hazel there for several weeks. They sat on the long hotel porch in wicker rockers or on the round porch above the springs. Just breathing, apparently, was enough. They didn't actually go in the water. I liked to dive there, deep into the bottomless, roiling black water. The sulfur smell drenched my skin, even when I dried off, and I felt I'd dived down close to hell.

I was warned not to say anything to let Mother Mayes know. But how could she not know already? She was sixty-six years old, so old, and now she never wanted any of her favorite Russell Stover candies anymore.

On my way up to see her, I stopped by the nursery on the first floor. As I came in the maternity hallway, the doors at the end swung open and I saw the delivery room: the orderly mopping the floor, the table with straps like reins hanging off the middle and stirrups hooked onto the end. Horrible to think of my own mother straddled there when my sisters and I were born. Birth was sickening. I didn't like the idea of being in someone's stomach and of my two sisters having occupied the same territory before me. Disgusting that everyone came alive that way. No wonder someone thought up a stork. I stared at the wheeled table covered with a sheet outside the door. Through the nursery windows I saw Mrs. Sams in a straight chair reading *Good Housekeeping*. The six tiny beds of yellowed iron were made up without a wrinkle. No babies. It looked like photos of places farther south in the tropics where big-bellied children died of malaria. Which bed did I sleep in eleven years ago when I was born? My sisters were home polishing their patent leather shoes with Vaseline, trying on their Easter dresses, probably coming to terms with a new baby arriving home soon. When he heard the bad news that another girl had arrived, my father went on a three-day tear. He wanted a son to name for his brother and my mother's father. MDM, for Mark Davis Mayes, was embroidered on the baby clothes I later discovered in the cedar chest.

I breathed on the glass and with my finger wrote my initials in cursive, FEM, the first three letters of "female."

I took the stairs two at a time. Mother Mayes would ask the same things she asked every visit. How is school? Fine. How's that cocker spaniel, what's his name? Tish. Fine. Are you helping your mother? Yes, ma'am. I cheered myself by thinking of the chocolates, the boxes and boxes Mother Mayes's Rook Club friends always brought, along with handfuls of cabbage roses wrapped in wet paper towels. I'd picked the candied almonds from all of them. Jordan almonds, she called them. I loved the colors, like chalk pastels, all tooth-cracking hard.

I pulled at the heavy door at the top of the stairs. It always resisted as if it were sucked closed, then it suddenly popped open and a breeze of cotton and sharp vinegary smells rushed out. I raised myself on tiptoe at the desk. "Is Mother Mayes awake?" I asked Mrs. McNeill.

"Well, here's Frances Elizabeth. Now I know it's Tuesday. Yes, she's awake, honey. You just go right on down there. Your aunt Hazel's already been and gone." Mrs. McNeill shook her head. "Poor thing can't stand to see her mother suffering so."

I walked down the green waxed hall carefully, avoiding the cracks between squares of linoleum. As I came near the closet in the middle of the long hall, I remembered Judy whispering to me in social studies, "That's where they keep the babies with funny heads, the two-headed babies the mothers donated to the hospital." I looked back. A woman in a pink apron pushed a cart of books into the next room, then the hall was empty. I opened the closet and stepped in among dusty brooms and mops in buckets of gray water. Yes, there were jars on the shelves, enormous jars with shapes in them like large pears. In three smaller jars something like seahorses curled up. I climbed over the pile of oily rags and stepped up on a box to get a closer look. The murky liquid was like that in some of the jars in the triangular room under the stairs where Mother Mayes kept the jellies, the pickled hog pears, and the green tomato pickles that sometimes turned the gray of swollen ticks. I backed out. Wasn't that a wrinkled knee, a tiny foot like a doll's on the bottom of the jar and little nickel-sized ears pressed against the glass? I looked back, just to be positive. I'd heard that someone in town "got rid of babies." There was a word for it: *aballshun,* Willie Bell said. The process involved 7UP and knitting needles. The lady in pink rattled by with her cart of books. Looking down, pretending to be examining the squares on the floor, I began hop-scotching toward room fourteen. Piccalilli, piccalilli, one, two, three, I counted out.

What if I found Mother Mayes dead? I opened the door slowly. No, there she was propped up on four pillows, her room white as an igloo except for all the flowers. More flowers! We always had roses at home. My father grew them along the cyclone fence at the mill, thousands of them, and brought them home several times a week. Someone had left Mother Mayes a corsage like the one my sister got for the Christmas dance, a purple orchid with veins of green deep in its throat. Barbara wore it on her wrist to the dance. Her arm suddenly became so beautiful balancing the dark flower on her wrist with the pale blue ribbons trailing. Mother Mayes's flowers were mostly stiff pink glads and white mums sitting up in shiny green foil among the cards that said get well, get well, get well.

"Well, it's my little girl. I thought you were Hazel for a moment. Your hair is black as soot. And how was school today, darling?" She never used to notice me or any of the grandchildren, but since she'd been sick she acted like a real Red Riding Hood grandmother. She held out her hand, as she always did. It felt too soft, cool, and boneless to me. My hands were hardened by the trapeze rings in Jeannie Walters's backyard. Mother Mayes's veins stood out like blue needlepoint threads. I stared at her hands—just like mine. I was born with old hands, thin white skin you can see right through if I hold my fingers over a flashlight. She loved rings but she wore none now, not even the aquamarine I loved or the icy chunk of diamond set up on prongs like kitten's teeth. Her fingers looked as though they were turning green. I remembered the ladyfinger pickles under the stairs.

"Did you know they have babies in jars out in the closet here?"

Mother Mayes's lips thinned to a smile that could have been drawn on her face with pencil. "Babies?"

"Yes, I saw the two-headed babies up on the shelves in big jars in the broom closet."

"Frances, that's just your imagination. Why don't you have a piece of candy?" Just my imagination. All my family said that. They always denied I saw what I said I saw if it inconvenienced them in any way. I learned early that only a slice of reality was considered real, even if what I saw should have been as plain as Stone Mountain to everyone.

"I did too! It had no toenails." I opened the padded white

box and broke into one chocolate after another, rejecting the soft pink and yellow fillings.

Mother Mayes made a gurgling noise in her chest, the same low chortling sound a pigeon makes. I looked over the little balloon puff of her stomach, out the window, and down below where Mrs. Melton, my friend Marideane's mother, was hoisting a bag of groceries from the backseat of her Studebaker. When I played there after school, Marideane and I saw rats bigger than kittens on the back porch of the hospital across the street, rats tumbling through the pails (of guts and gallbladders?) of garbage. We climbed in her fig tree and clapped, threw figs, shouted, but the rats never ran. I thought of Mother Mayes in the hospital late at night in the dark with the big brown rats running through the halls. One could jump on her white bed and run over her face. I told my parents about the rats but they said I must have been dreaming.

Mother Mayes wasn't interested in the babies. I wondered if their eyelids looked like hers, shot with purple lines. "You may not believe me . . ." I found the exact piece I wanted wrapped in silver paper. Slowly I bit into the pure caramel. "But it's true. I did see them."

Mother Mayes's face seemed to emerge from the pillow. "You must be thirsty after that long walk." She always offered water so I could drink from the curved glass straw. Once I'd said I liked it. Adults always did that; say you like one thing and they're forever forcing it on you afterward. I didn't like the glass straw all that much. I turned up one of the glasses on the towel and poured a little. What I didn't want Mother Mayes to know was that I was afraid of catching whatever she had because she was going to die. I held my breath and sucked the clear water up the straw. I never catch things, I thought. They'd showed at school the picture of an iron lung at Warm Springs. They said if we went swimming after lunch we'd get it and have to go lie in an iron lung day after day, then get braces on our legs and never swim again. So some germs can live in water. But Mother Mayes didn't have infantile paralysis; they said "eaten up." I thought of red ants and let out my breath.

Mother Mayes chortled again and sank back into the pillows. I had another piece of candy, this time just to be busy until the bubbling sound went away. "I've got to be going." A string of drool ran backward on her cheek, and her hand suddenly turned to a claw grabbing at the hem of the sheet. "I've got to do a report on the Belgian Congo." She didn't seem to hear. She rolled her head to the side and gave an ugly little grunt. I held on to the iron foot of the bed for a moment, my feet on the rung. I wanted to swing up my legs and see if I could go into a handstand, but I didn't dare. Mother Mayes had her eyes closed and a frown on her face as though she were thinking hard about something. I slowly pulled the door shut behind me.

The closet door in the hall was still open. From the window opposite it, a slash of afternoon sun angled across the hall. I wanted to see the small jars better, especially the one with something in it no larger than a peach pit. A pumpkin-shaped jar on the end was so close I almost could reach it. If only the brine, or whatever it was, were not so scummy, like old goldfish water. I shinnied up the doorframe. Three, four, eight jars in all. "How's she feeling, honey?" I dropped to the floor.

"She's fine, I guess."

Mrs. McNeill pushed my hair off my forehead. "You've got your daddy's head of hair. Where'd you get those eyes? Must be your mother's people." My mother came from Vidalia, over an hour and a half away.

On Friday, Nancy Stone came into Mrs. Bailey's class with a note while we were hearing Nancy Drew aloud. We'd started the series last year with Miss Pope, who hated every student in the fifth grade, especially on Friday, and so read Nancy Drew endlessly. We'd all become addicted. Mrs. Bailey had had a particularly bad day because Gill C. brought in a package of rubbers and tried to throw them on the girls. When Mrs. Bailey secured one she held it up and shouted at the class, "Every last one of you will sit there until I find out who brought this nasty thing in." Just at that instant the door opened and Miss Hattaway, the principal, stopped in her tracks. The wild class froze for a moment until Gill C. blew up another rubber in the back row and let the air out suddenly in a loud farting noise. When this much happened by ten o'clock, we knew we could count on an hour of *The Message in the Hollow Oak* before lunch.

Mrs. Bailey slammed down the book when Miss Hattaway's best seventh-grade student came tiptoeing in with the note. Mrs. Bailey frowned and nodded as she unfolded it. She looked up at me and I knew without being told to run home because Mother Mayes had died.

"No," Aunt Hazel said, "it won't be scary. She looks just like she's sleeping." She slid into the creamy Lincoln parked on the side of Daddy Jack and Mother Mayes's. It was rude if you didn't call on people in the coffin, even if they'd never know. "Your mother's in there now. I'll just drop you off while I run down to buy something dark for the funeral. Living in Florida, I don't really have any dark dresses."

I wasn't really afraid at all. I'd seen Willie Bell's aunt dead and Carlyle McDonald, whose belly stuck up over the edge of the coffin, and Miss Florence Petrick, the high school voice teacher. They didn't show Tom and Janet Langhorn's mother, who'd blown off the top of her head, pulled the trigger on herself with her own big toe. They couldn't make heads or tails of her. I could just imagine Mother Mayes lying there, the coffin tufted and soft like a doll bed. Hazel said she would be wearing a lilac dress, her favorite color, not the gray one Mother and Mary Helen picked out, which was too dreary for words, and would look peaceful the way she did on Sundays when she would lie down on the sofa and pull the afghan up over her feet before Fanny called us in to dinner.

I loved Hazel's car and her soft fawn-colored clothes that seemed to go with the deep leather seats and the music drifting from the backseat speakers as soon as Hazel turned the key.

"Aren't you going, Aunt Hazel . . . I mean, Hazel?" I remembered she didn't want to be called "Aunt" anymore.

"I'll go later, when there aren't so many people. This is a calling hour right now. You know, Mama and I were so close. I want to say good-bye to her all alone." Hazel glanced in the rearview mirror and smoothed her eyebrow with her little finger. The lattice fence around the backyard receded as she accelerated down Lemon Street. "You know, when Mama last came down to visit me this winter she was saying how she felt closer to me than anyone in the world. There's nothing like the love of a mother and the only daughter. Not that she didn't love your daddy and your uncle Jack and uncle Mark." Hazel's voice broke off as she reached into her handbag and fished out a handkerchief. I stared out the window at the palm trees racing by the car window. I didn't know what to say, so I leaned forward and tapped my chin with my forefinger.

On Sundays before dinner, Aunt Mary Helen and Mother and Aunt Emmy sat in the upstairs guest room and said how selfish Hazel was and how she never thought of a soul on God's green earth but herself. They said she came swanning home from Miami and expected to be waited on hand and foot. I didn't know if that was true or not. I liked it when Hazel drove up with the backseat full of dresses and Fanny baked all the things Hazel had liked when she was a girl, Marshmallow Fudge Cake and icebox cookies and Lane Cake, if it were at Christmas. And Hazel teased Daddy and my uncles. Sundays were better when she was there. Usually, when we waited for dinner, I played the wind-up player my daddy had when he was young, half listening to the conversation in the guest room. They said Hazel's husband, Wilfred, had a girlfriend in Richmond where he went on business. Lonnie Tyler saw them together in a hotel lobby when she went up for the national meeting of the United Daughters of the Confederacy. I thought that was unlikely because Wilfred was so ugly, who would have him? I played the thick records over and over. "Come, Josephine, in my flying machine" a faraway voice tinkled. I had to keep winding the Victrola or the voice would slow down to a long moan. When Hazel was at home, all the women except Mother Mayes, who rested, waited for dinner in Hazel's old room and talked about gloves and patterns and linens and parties. Hazel was always asking Mother for recipes even though she never had made a piece of toast and even had breakfast out. They tried on Hazel's new hats and admired all her dresses, pale and delicate as Miami sunrises. Later, Mary Helen would say how tacky they were and Lord, if Hazel could see herself from the rear. If Hazel saw a dress she really liked, she bought it in every color it came in. Mother said she had a warehouse in Miami just for all the things she'd bought in triplicate.

Hazel swung the big car around the palm island in the middle of the broad street and came to a stop in front of Paulk's Funeral Home, the prettiest house in town. I jumped out and before I could slam the door, Hazel pulled away.

As it turned out, Hazel was "too upset" to go to the funeral. It was because she was the only daughter, Daddy explained. Mother had another idea. "She's never even been to the funeral home. I looked at the guest book. Believe you me, she's up to something." Daddy always took Hazel's part and it made Mother furious. Hazel still called him "Boofa"—she'd tried "Beautiful" when he was born and "Boofa" ended up stuck to him all his life. Hazel was taking it badly. Just before the cars pulled up to drive us to the church, I saw her in the kitchen. She was wearing a long rose-colored robe edged with swags of crochet. I'd never seen her hair out of its chignon and it hung thin and scraggly. Everyone else, even Mary Helen, who was always late, was waiting on the porch. Wilfred kept blotting his bald head with his handkerchief. The house was too hot. I was sent back to the back porch to tell my grandparents' maid Fanny that our yardman Drew was on his way to get her. As I ran through the kitchen, Hazel was lifting a knife over the luscious chocolate cake Mother Mayes's Missionary Circle had brought over. It was the best-looking cake I ever saw. Fanny was waiting right out back. She had on her black uniform and she was leaning on the lattice wall of the back porch, a checkerboard pattern of sunlight behind her. Her face was hidden in her hands and her shoulders shook. I stopped, holding open the screen door. Fanny looked up. "This is the saddest day, sugar. You don't know how sad this day is." She didn't even tell me to close the door so the flies couldn't get in.

"Drew's coming in the truck. Mother says to get Willie Bell at our house." I jumped down the back steps, ran once through the yard, touching all four trees as I passed, and back to the front porch where Daddy Jack and the others waited. My funeral dress, dark blue moiré with a wide lace collar, weighed a ton. I just hoped none of my friends saw me wearing the ugly thing.

. . .

As soon as the slow cars pulled off, Hazel, as I now imagine that day, lifts her long robe and runs up the stairs to her mother's room. Just this morning Fanny aired it out and opened the heavy winter draperies. No one else had been in since Mama died. Hazel stops for an instant then pushes open the door as though someone were calling her in. Mama! Mama on the mantel in her wedding dress with Dad proud as a little god beside her. Mama's clock, stopped at two on the organdy scarf, and there on the dresser all the bottles of White Shoulders, Boofa's favorite perfume, and the silver brushes with the cherubs riding the waves. Hazel opens the drawer of the dressing table. Pins. A box of powder with a puff in it. Dusty rose nail polish and the familiar manicure set made of tortoiseshell. Instinctively, Hazel inspects her shell-pink crescent moons, takes the small scissors, snips off a tiny edge of her thumbnail cuticle, and brushes it to the floor. Two boxes of pills and a blue tassel bookmark. Hazel slides the drawer closed and opens the small one on the left. "Oh!" she says aloud. She reaches for the blue velvet box. The aquamarine ring. Hazel had wanted it since childhood. She slips it on her middle finger and holds her hand up to the light. For a moment, she remembers Thanksgiving when I sat on the footstool next to Mother Mayes before dinner. Mother Mayes rested with her feet up. Her corns are now as big as crocus bulbs on her little toes and her feet hurt. I was trying on her rings. I heard Mother Mayes saying "Of course, after I'm gone, you're my namesake so you can choose whatever you want except the silver. That goes to the oldest son."

"Well, this is just what I want," I said, "this and the dishes

Mrs. Beall painted." I loved the flower plates. The only way they got me to eat all my dinner was to offer extra pecan pie if I ate enough to see which flower I got on my plate. Mrs. Beall painted a different flower from Mother Mayes's yard in the center of each plate and a gold band around the edge like a wedding ring. I liked the white Cherokee rose, which climbed over my grandparents' fence from the vacant lot next door.

But Hazel shakes her head. *Mama didn't mean that, Frances is only eleven or ten, what could she do with rings besides just lose them? Mama would enjoy* my *enjoyment so much.*

Hazel's hands had never touched Ajax or dishwater. I'd heard whispers that she "had an operation right after she married so she'd never have babies." She lightly rinsed her nylons every night and hung them over a towel to dry. Everything that touched her had to be perfect, especially her hands.

She finds the tiger's-eye necklace with gold beads interspersed, a gift to Mama from Boofa. *Mama would love for me to have this,* she thinks. *She never said a thing in the hospital; she just wouldn't have upset us for the world.* Hazel rolls up the jewelry in the silk case Mama carried when she went traveling. *Oh! I should have the pearls. They'd look nicer on me than on Frankye or Mary Helen or certainly on Emmy with those awful sapphires she likes.* Quickly she unrolls the case and slips in the long loop of creamy pearls. She looks up and catches her breath. *Mama!* But how foolish—her own face centered in the oval mirror. She leans closer and lifts the corners of her eyes. Holding up the silver hand mirror, she twists her black hair into a high chignon. Shoe polish black, my mother said. Would she be blue haired and wear lavender? Already she liked flowered scarves around her neck or dresses with soft ruffled collars. I told her she looked like the queen of England in my history book with the white stiff collar on her yellow piqué. Hazel pins up a loose strand and thinks of my tangle of curls. *That child runs wild. What is Frankye thinking of? She was never that way with the older girls. It's as if she gave up by the third child. But Frances has Boofa's ways, hard as nails, and thinks when she says jump we should all say how high.* Hazel feels the aquamarine through the soft jewelry roll. She will wear it with the sea green evening dress she found at the Nifty Shop the same afternoon she looked for a dark dress to wear to the funeral. She hates dark clothes. But she had seen this swath of pale silk, what she came back to the house with—nothing for the funeral.

The funeral! That would be half through by now. *Mama.* She looks over at the high bed where she and her brothers were born. It's made up stiffly, the Martha Washington coverlet taut as if no one ever had lain there. Hazel opens Mama's closet. Her smell, the sachet pillows on the shelves and musty lingering in the sleeves and collars of the dresses. From the zippered bag, Hazel pulls out the mink stole. Mama agreed entirely with her about that. When the three boys had chipped in and bought it for her last Christmas, they'd asked Hazel if she wanted to go in on it. She told them Mama wouldn't wear it that much; it was too hot in Georgia to get the use from it. She rubs the fur against her cheek. It was much less suitable for the climate in Miami, but there are some cool nights. Mama seemed so thrilled when she opened the box from J. P. Allen's, but later she admitted to Hazel she probably couldn't wear it too often. It looks brand-new. Hazel drapes the stole around her shoulders even though the room is stifling. From the balky chest of drawers she takes peach, blue, and muted pea green cashmere sweaters. Mama has a champagne silk blouse that doesn't look too much like an old lady. Where would it be? She finds it in the top drawer. Carrying as much as she can, Hazel crosses the hall to her room. She tosses the things on the bed and pulls Mama's suitcase out from underneath. Ten of three. She packs fast, stuffing the jewelry in the elastic pockets along the sides of the bag. Just as she starts downstairs, she pauses and looks back in Mama's room. Two great arcs of soft sun curve across the bed from the big windows facing Lemon Street. Suffocating in there. *How Mama hated the heat!* On her bedside table lies a church fan with a picture on it of Jesus kneeling beside a rock. Mama's room is so full of her absence. Hazel notes the little things on the table one by one: the thimble, the neatly folded lace handkerchief, the small photograph of Mama's mother, Sarah America Gray, a fuzzy shape in white named Charlotte, Mama's long-dead sister, and now, with Mama's passing, utterly forgotten. There was Dad as a baby in England, held by a mother named Elizabeth Repton, who was shortly to die, leaving only this ugly little baby and a name that would reappear years from then in the middle of Frances's. Hazel's eyes follow the trailing vine of trumpet morning glories down the wallpaper. Idly, she pulls open the bedside table drawer and finds a scrap of notepaper with Mama's sprawling handwriting in brown ink: bell peppers, yellow thread, 2 hens, lemon, matches, squash. Hazel squeezes the list into a ball. All at once she feels a cold flare of sweat: Her mother's life is over and there is nothing left but these tiny clues. *How I hate that foreign house in Miami,* she thinks suddenly. She hits the taut bed with her fists over and over. "No, no, no, no. It's not fair. *Why* did this have to happen?" Then she notices the bedside table and pulls out the drawer; there's the ring box. Mama kept her big diamond there at night so the setting couldn't catch at threads in the embroidered sheets. Hazel opened the box and the ring flashed out rainbows over the wall. Mother Mayes had worn it ever since her mother died and they'd soaped her hand and worked the ring off because she'd grown so stout. Mother Mayes soaked it in ammonia overnight, then wore it every day.

Hazel snaps shut the box and puts it exactly where she found it. She will have to wait and see if Dad gives her that. Before she closes the drawer, she takes out the Murine and the glass eyedropper and puts them in the pocket of her robe. She must run down to pack the Lincoln now, but as she hears the cars return she will freshen her eyes with the drops that look just like tears.

All the time Hotch Dickinson delivered the eulogy, the eyes of everyone in the church fasten on the tall ivory candles around the coffin. One by one they slowly give up to the heat and droop over like the necks of swans bending toward fish under water. Most fall to the left and flicker out. A few stay lit, spattering white wax onto the burgundy carpet last winter's collection bought. The blanket of roses over the coffin turns dusky, the tight buds feathering out like heads of sleeping birds against the leaves.

I sit almost still but my dress scratches the backs of my legs and I try to inch it out from under me so my skin will be cool against the smooth white wood. It is the hottest May in memory, one of those unexpected, blistering warnings in spring of what's to come. My mother shoots me a look: *Be still.* Daddy Jack mops off his mustache of perspiration.

"I will lift mine eyes unto the hills from whence cometh my help," Rev. Dickinson says. I look out the open window, past the two shacks, past the railroad tracks, past the apartment building where Johnny Leverett lives. Not a hill in sight. I turn around in the pew. There is Miss Hattaway, the principal. I remember how to spell "principal" because my teacher said that the principal is your pal. Miss Hattaway, some pal, in the seven years I went to Third Ward School, never cracked a smile once. Way in the back I spot the dark faces, Fanny and Drew and Willie Bell sitting together. Fanny still hides her face in her hands. Over where her family always sits, Edna Lula, my best friend, waves to me. As I start to smile, Aunt Mary Helen pokes me sharply with her elbow.

I sit straight. I smell something and wish Aunt Mary Helen would move over because her green silk dress has ugly wet quarter moons under the arms.

In the funeral home car, I ride on Daddy's lap, feeling the town rather than seeing as we drive from church, up Central, down Main, left on Lemon, our street, and out Evergreen Road to the cemetery.

Daddy holds open the door and helps Daddy Jack out. Suddenly Daddy Jack's suit looks too big for him and he is looking around as if he doesn't have on his glasses but he does. Mother Mayes will be the first to lie in the family plot. Her people and Daddy Jack's are buried in North Carolina. The threshold has MAYES carved in the center. I liked the old part of the cemetery better. One iron gate gives a three-syllable squawk as you swing on it. Mother Mayes, I see, will sleep near a lamb in a nearby plot. Carved under the lamb: ASLEEP IN JESUS.

"Now what does that mean?" I whisper to Mother. I'd asked the question before. Mother squeezes my hand too hard.

"Shhh. It just means he died of diphtheria. It means that you should hush, that's all." Her answers usually involved at least one crazy link but I understood her. Rev. Dickinson stands by the hole, his big angel sleeves billowing out. The air is cooling off, mercifully. All the people from town gather around the tent, but only the family sits down in the folding chairs on a strip of carpet. Is Mother Mayes really in the coffin? I sit between Daddy and Aunt Mary Helen, who keeps checking the run she got in her stocking when she stepped out of the car. I can't see Aunt Emmy or my uncles down the row, or my two sisters, who sit on the other side of Mother. Rev. Dickinson picks up a handful of red dirt, raises both arms, and says, "Ashes to ashes, dust to dust," in a loud voice. I look up to see if that makes Daddy mad. My father's face looks out between the tent poles, toward the fields and out as far as he can look. I take his hand in mine. Mother glances down and frowns. His hand is limp, not like his face that looks as set as wax. With his right hand he wipes his cheek on both sides with his whole palm. "Don't cry," I say softly. Rev. Dickinson throws down the dirt on the clean coffin. Daddy doesn't look at the grave hole. He had come out of her and now she is inside a box. I rip off my thumbnail with my incisors.

When he finishes talking, Rev. Dickinson comes over and hugs me and says he feels close to all the Mayes family even though we don't attend church as regularly as he'd like. I swallow so hard my ears hurt. Then Mother Mayes's friend Mrs. McCarthy pulls me close to her bosom. Her eyes are funny, gray with a brown rim, eyes like a wild animal's might be. Her thin red hair looks almost pink. She even smells soft, like vetiver cologne and sweet peas. "Your Mother Mayes was a grand old gal, Frances. You got a lucky name from her." I rest my head and let myself be patted. I don't mind having Mother Mayes's name, but I would fight anyone who ever called me "Fanny," as they did her. Mother Mayes and her cook had the same name and it was embarrassing—fanny was a rear end. Many of Mother Mayes's friends called her "Fan," not so bad but almost. "She would have just loved these flowers, just be thrilled to death, oh my, thrilled to pieces." She leans down to look at a bunch of fragrant narcissi Fanny brought in a mayonnaise jar sitting among the florist wreathes. "Fan loved the wild narcissus." She straightens up slowly, a little unsteady. Her red nails dig into my shoulder for balance. "It's a beautiful world, darling; that's why we're so sad when one of us has to leave it."

As she walks to the car, I start to cry, a flash of fast tears and the hot awful rock in my throat. I don't know if I am crying for Mother Mayes or for Mrs. McCarthy, who can't see well and thinks of Mother Mayes whenever she sees the wild narcissus that springs up unasked in Fanny's yard every spring. Mother Mayes was a grand old gal, she had said. I kick up the silver tufts of leftover winter grass under the new. My parents and uncles and everyone shake hands with the same people they see every day while the man from Paulk's smokes behind the clay mound. My sisters walk off with three of their friends toward a white convertible.

For a long time, I wait in the black Cadillac. When I look out the window at the grave, I see my own reflection in the window. If I stare into my own eyes, the grave disappears. If I look at the grave, my eyes disappear. I stare at myself. *I wonder if I will be beautiful,* I thought. I jump onto the backseat and cross my legs slowly, lifting my dress just above my knee the way Hazel did. "To the opera, James," I say to the empty driver's seat. They don't come and don't come. "Why are they always so slow?" I shout aloud. I roll down the window and spit as far as I can. I pull the scab off my left knee and put it in the ashtray because it wouldn't be nice to drop it on the floor of the fancy car. *I would like to drive this,* I thought. I see Daddy helping Mrs. McCarthy to her old two-toned, humpbacked Chevrolet. He was once balled up inside Mother Mayes's stomach. How could he breathe? Now she is trapped under dirt. Children sometimes suffocated, shut in refrigerators. I kick the seat with my heels, then sigh, jerking my shoulders up and down. *When I'm grown, I'll wear only red silk.* Aunt Emmy and Mother are walking toward me, their arms around each other's waists. I don't know what I want to happen next. I trace my finger around my lips that are cool and thin, just like Mother Mayes's.

RIDDLES AND TRICKS

Other than Mother Mayes dying, late grade school anchors in memory because my friendships expanded. Sammy Dixon passed me notes, and valentines—*You must send one to everyone*—now included secret messages: *I like you*. Looking at the sixth-grade class photo, where I stand on the front row with my hands in my pockets, each child retains an intimacy. Everyone remains vivid, the clothes they wear, the fabric and color, the texture of their hair, their nails, the smells of chalk and oatmeal, pencil lead, and oranges. Their faces hold the voices I still can hear. *Be on my team; red rover, red rover send Judy right over; marshmallow roast at Kay's, sign my slam book.*

What a radical concept, that we would leave the confines of the long brick schoolhouse and travel to something educational.

Though it is early spring, the heat in the Okefenokee Swamp is as persuasive as an electric cattle prod. We're running wild

on the visitors' catwalks. I am wearing a white sailor shirt and navy denim pants with big buttons. I sketched them and had our seamstress, Mrs. Smith, make them especially for today. As soon as we're out of sight of the teacher, Edna Lula and I dab lipstick on our lips. We're with a group of our friends, all boys. The six of us climb to the top of a fire tower and look out over the swamp. As far as we see—standing black water, black tupelos, possum haw trees, and the ghostly moss-hung cypresses tapering to wisps far above their swollen trunks—the whole landscape appears to us in shades of gray. From the plank walkway, though, we see the tiny Confederate violets, sundews that can catch insects, yellow water lilies, pitcher plants where bugs drown, and the spooky Venus flytraps with jaws that snap shut. When a ranger takes us out in a flat-bottomed boat, logs suddenly rise and open their jaws. Sunning on hummocks, the alligators' enormous mouths smile, as though in a pleasant dream of an earlier epoch. In the boggy water, we pass small islands with a single tree, palms like ones in cartoons of people on deserted islands. The ranger says they are "floating" and we look at him without comprehension. How can an island with a palm tree float? He invites me to step out on one, and I stand up in the boat and leap to the island. Immediately, I feel it dip, giving under my weight. My impulse is to grab the tree but then I remember we are on the same unreliable ground. I scream and scramble back to the boat while everyone laughs.

So an island can travel, take a tree with it. The ranger says the islands are decayed leaves and sticks, forced loose by swamp gases, with the tree acting as kind of a sail. How alluring, this mysterious swamp. I see for the first time today, also, that Bill Daniel is alluring, that strange sights are alluring. The gray light's secret loveliness fills me with the sudden elation I often feel—a powerful bath of euphoria in moments like this, or for no reason at all. One alligator has a baby alligator riding on its back. I'm not sure if Bill likes me better than Marideane Melton. Probably he likes her tan skin and green eyes.

The cypress trees send up gnarly knees to breathe for them. In shops along the highway carvers sell cypress birds they've whittled, making the knobs and rings of the wood form the eyes and mouth of an owl or crane.

I know about quicksand, in which a horse and rider can go down. At Saturday movies, I've watched them sink until there's only an upraised hand seeping down, the oozy quicksand clos-

ing over the clutching fingers. The whole landscape, I see, is full of riddles and tricks. Just as I've tried to lure a rabbit to the trap with a little scent of vanilla on a cloth, the earth springs traps on us. The twister gathering into a spiral over the road will sweep through the town, lifting bathtubs and pet dogs and garages. Daddy will not let us bathe when there's lightning.

The marshy river of grass looks like land but sways in the tide. Creatures disregard their borders, too: Catfish emerge from boggy black water and walk; ibises stand all day on the backs of Brahman bulls, pecking insects out of their hides. Heron are reeds until they raise blue wings and fly. In fields where children run, old tops of wells give way and you find yourself screaming in a dry pit with spiders or scrambling up mossy walls and sliding down into the dank water. This is in the paper all the time.

If we stayed till night, we would see swamp fire zapping and hear green tree frogs' tinkling-bell chorale, but we won't. We troop back to the parking lot at four to meet the room mothers for the seventy-five-mile ride home.

Bill sits in the backseat next to Marideane, his arm resting on the window, and Jeff Hardy is on the other side of her. He's cute, too. I'm in front with the map, guiding us back to Fitzgerald, a little farther than Willacoochee and Alapaha, on up the road from Glory, Mystic, Enigma, not as far as Sunsweet or Arabi.

Equal and opposite, I experienced a different revelation in our other field trip. How did our gray-gabardine-suited teacher, who always maintained that "God's children" were "kind," "decent," "God-fearing," and "righteous," this gentle woman made of kindness, dream of taking her precious charges on a trip to hell?

I had heard the word "abattoir." When we passed an odd smell like tires burning and something else on the road to Ocilla, my mother sometimes said "abattoir." Abattoir, from the French *to fell*, regardless of the lovely sound of a garden with a glass summerhouse and purple gloxinias. I never asked what it meant. The word made a splotch of clear flat lake in my eyes, a hidden water I would find if I turned off the highway and followed the clay path back beyond leaning houses smothered in kudzu, beyond the blue tobacco fields. Abattoir—a name for a nunnery of cream-colored stones, a vine with white flowers like ghost faces; abattoir, a lethal silver knife flashing.

And so we went on the field trip. Pigs jam the stockyard we walk by. Another pen holds cows that moo and roll their eyes. A man with a prod urges the pigs one by one up a single-file ramp and into the building. Halting ones are jabbed and let out scary cries.

I've heard those sounds before because our neighbor, Dr. Griner, is a veterinarian, and when farmers pull up their loaded trucks in the alley behind his house, each pig's back legs are tied together, then it's suddenly hoisted upside down. Suspended in the garage doorway, the pig starts to shriek as Dr. Griner raises a long knife. As he hacks, I learn the word "castrate." The awful testicles accumulate in a bloody pile as the neighborhood children watch.

My shoulders rise. In the first room did the pig really swing out grunting suspended by a hook in the roof of his mouth and a glistening man with a hatchet lean out of a pulpit and smack the pig's throat? Yes, I do remember the squeal—was it educational?—and the big red spurt arching down onto the sloped floor with a drain. A coiled hose guzzled water onto the floor. Hot smell, a tin roof under broiling sun. My throat closing and freezing. I filed with the others through the high rooms where piles of tails and trotters and slabs are stacked on chunky tables and men in streaked aprons thwack and smile at us. Bucket of eyes, some open, some closed. Grinding of gristle, white knob ends of bones. My raw joints and sockets working me through the long room. As we reach the end of the assembly line, our teacher says, "If you enjoyed this, next year we can see where Jeff Davis was captured dressed up like a woman."

On the way out each of us is handed a hot dog, end of the process. Phew! Rufus Yeoman, Betty Zane, and other friends are eating theirs. I push out the door into the humidity that swallows me whole and throw mine in the bushes. That smell! Hair in an old hairbrush, rusty iron water from the faucet, it's like nothing at all but itself, something under the smell, the word: abattoir.

When I open the door to the kitchen that afternoon, my mother is making a big pan of brownies studded with pecans. I tell her about the field trip. "Pour yourself a co-cola with the brownies. And you do see what I mean?" She runs her fingers through my hair, smoothing back damp curls. She is always harping on the "cracker mentality."

Daddy comes in with the first armful of roses of the spring. He agrees with her that the field trip was a stupid idea and that the school principal has not got the sense God gave a billy goat. He pulls me to his chest, forgetting that the roses pierce through my blouse, and kisses the top of my head. "You're my buddy," he says. For a space, they're the parents I want.

The thousand Étoile de Hollande rosebushes he had planted along the mill fence are coming into bloom. Blood red, his favorite. Out come the brownies in a whoosh of steam from the oven. The dark chocolate scent and the light, spicy perfume of the roses blend with the western sunlight slanting into the kitchen. Daddy lays the roses on the drain board and hands me the scissors. I start to snip off all the thorns.

Even now, the white heron can walk through swamp water across my dream. The pig can rise in the air with a fast jerk. I have baked a thousand pans of brownies in my life and planted hundreds of roses, none red. Out of the endless expanse of school days, from all the birthday parties, wiener roasts, movies, overnights, carnivals, tests, piano lessons, homework, what rises in memory? Swamp and abattoir. Thinking hard, writing about these specific days long gone, I think I'll get to the bottom. Why are they remembered? But what one finds in the enterprise of writing is that there is no bottom. Only a contraction into the rhythmic, blood-pumping heart of the past and sometimes an expansion out of it.

WHATEVER WAS HIDDEN

Something must be hidden. I pried up floorboards in the barn and found an old baby shoe and a bill for tires. I tossed all the navy caps and shirts from my uncle's war trunk. "Stop that plundering." My mother shoved the uniforms back inside and snapped down the lid. I riffled through the pages of *Art in Everyday Life,* a college textbook of my mother's. "Don't strew," she said when she came upon me with a drawer pulled out, old photos scattered on the floor. "You strew faster than I can pick up." "Plunder" and "strew," ancient words: spoils of war, recklessness, booty, scattering, mindless ransacking. I was voracious to solve a mystery. Whatever was hidden, I would find.

When I lift the dust ruffle of my parents' bed, I know at last I have found something. I pull out my father's calfskin suitcase with the Boca Raton Club sticker and slide back the locks with my thumbs. Inside, a tarnished silver flask and a box. I pour the last few drops into the cap, smell it (I know the smell of bourbon), then rub the drops into the blue rug. No one will see, since it's under the bed. The box is full to the brim with gold, but foil, like chocolate coins in my Christmas stocking toe. Pieces of eight, doubloons, as in peg-legged pirate stories. The edges unloosen easily, like pulling paper away from a cupcake.

The foil is silver on the inside and I almost know what the rolled balloon is for. There's a larger one in the box too, with a forked plastic stick shaped like branches that magic people way out in the country hold to find water. What is that? It has something to do with the rubber bag in the bathroom, with the box of powder that smells like peppermint. I've heard the word "douche." I stuff my pocket and go to the porch, where I blow up one of the balloons, but it doesn't feel like a balloon. More animal. The skin on the inside of my arm feels smoother than the skin of the balloon. I fit one over the front yard faucet and hold it tight while it fills, stretches to bursting. Mrs. Tuggle, the dentist's wife, walks by and stares without speaking to me. I ball up the gold and rubber, bury them under the house in the doodlebug mounds, and then hunch there, peering out through the foundation vent at nothing passing down Lemon Street, nothing happening in the yard except my dog Tish rolling merrily, probably in Daddy's bird dogs' do-do. Nothing else moves, not even the light, faint blossoms at the top of the crape myrtle. This is *something*, this box of pirate gold, *something*, but not it.

What are they hiding? Knowing them, they probably don't know themselves. Two blocks away, at The House, I pillage every room. Three times a week I practice on the piano there. Daddy Jack and Fanny don't care what I do as long as I stay out of the kitchen. She looms over the stove, madly coating everything she cooks with cayenne pepper and several shakes of Tabasco. Sometimes she cries because her husband tries to beat her. "I was running for my life last night," she says. "Bud gets mean as a snake when he gets into the bottle." I don't like his name being the same as my nickname. "Fanny, why don't you stay here? He's mean. You could sleep in Hazel's old room." She shakes her head. "Oh, honey." I stare at the cabinet lined with green and pink parfait dishes. I wish we could make ice cream right now. On the back burner, she keeps a pot of once green beans falling apart in salt pork.

I find Hazel's tattered sheets of music, still in the piano bench even though she's been gone from Daddy Jack's house for twenty years. They flake as I turn the pages. In my grandmother's desk, untouched since she died, a dozen cubbyholes must hold one secret. One paper shows Mother Mayes's maternal family tree. Her mother, Sarah America Gray, was born on January 30, 1848–before the War Between the States. *Her* father, George Alexander Gray, was born in 1802. I don't know what happened in history in 1802. Then the drawing branches: *His* parents, Ransom Gray and Narcissa Alexander, married in 1800. Narcissa Alexander Gray! Married to Ransom. At last, something worth knowing. I'm sure they had a great romance. Too bad this was before the days of photographs. I want to see Narcissa and Ransom. The last name, down in the taproot, says George Alexander, born in 1743, even before the Revolution. I copy the best names on the palm of my hand. Other than that: my uncles' Georgia Tech diplomas, dull letters from Hazel in Miami complaining about how much she missed home. I'd heard Daddy Jack's family in North Carolina had a French maid and a place in Nova Scotia for the summers. Some family war occurred and Daddy Jack spoke to no one in North Carolina anymore. No information at The House, only cabinets of painted china, scratchy afghans folded on the twin beds, dance cards in yearbooks, a buzzer to signal the kitchen under the dining room rug, and the key to the grandfather clock, whose Westminster chime every fifteen minutes reminded Daddy Jack of England, where he was born. Because of a song I learned in kindergarten, I believed firmly that it would stop short, never to go again, when the old man died.

At home, jars of swollen pickles glint in the back corners of cabinets where the shelf paper runs out. I look in every chest for secret compartments in the backs of drawers, places to hide amethysts, love letters, and hand-drawn maps with Xs on them. I press the floor, hoping for a panel to spring open, revealing a staircase going down, down to a dirt room full of trunks, or an entrance to the underground railroad where slaves had escaped, although I know our house is not that old and that the town of Fitzgerald did not even exist during the War.

Was I always alone? Where did they all find to go in the long afternoons? I rubbed against every splinter of the house. A cat, pouncing, examining, equally curious and indifferent. Outside, I lift the iron door at the base of the chimney and let the ashes fall out into the azalea bed. I climb closet shelves to push open the attic door with my head. Nothing there but trapped light and enormous whirring blades of the attic fan exhaling like a hot beast. In the hall, I lift the heavy lid of the cedar chest and breathe in the dark resinous smell that is death to moths. My hand knows what to push aside to feel the satin lining of my mother's lingerie holders. I know the touch of the cold mesh evening bag she carried in college, its fragile chain, and inside, the round little mirror she'd looked in so long ago, back in her belle-hood, when her father said she was born to break a thousand hearts. In the bottom left, my fingers find the velvet box, almost soft, like a just-dead mouse, that holds a cool locket and a blood ruby ring, surrounded by chip diamonds. Among the bolts of silk and cotton and flowered chintz, I feel for notes, secret wills and deeds, but find nothing: baby clothes, sheets too good to use, report cards, my birth certificate with the brown ink imprint of my foot before it ever touched the earth.

I spy also. Move silently from pecan tree to privet hedge to outdoor fireplace to behind the barn, listening to my parents, who sit in the yard in the early evenings. My ear, against a jelly jar, presses to the wall when my mother has the bridge club. But she only says, "Lilanne was a terrible bride. What could she have been thinking of, carrying those calla lilies? She is far too short—and wide—to carry calla lilies." Opening the door to a closet close to the dining room where they play bridge, I find mother's friend Martha there before me, crouched down trembling. The summer thunderstorms scare her and every time she's dummy she runs to the closet to hide. When the storms magnify and the ground shakes with thunder, she even bids three hearts from the closet floor. Adults are pitiful.

I taste all the sharp pink medicines and liver pills in the

bathroom and know the sour bush whiskey someone from out in the county brought my father. He calls it monkey rum and won't touch it because it could make you blind. I even sample the cloudy cordials Great-Aunt Bessy sends over from Vidalia, syrupy concoctions steeped from elderberries and scuppernongs.

I'm interested in steaming open letters over the coffeepot, but nothing arrives except bills from Rich's and the Nifty Shop. My red diary with a small key I keep in code. Since the letter "e" occurs 131.5 times in every 1,000 letters, I try to use as few *e*'s as possible. My own privacy must be maintained. I want to break wax seals. When I walk on the beach, I keep my eyes open for bottles with messages curled inside: *I have been on this island many years.*

I was reading under the covers late, late one night. Not that anyone cared how late I read, but I preferred the blue light my blanket made. This year, sixth grade, we studied the War Between the States. I kept a notebook of the battle plans of Gettysburg and Shiloh. Jeb Stuart was all action, my favorite man. I would love someone like that but no one else, except possibly Heathcliff. I was stirred by Jeb's cavalry troops singing "Kathleen Mavourneen, the gray dawn is breaking . . ." as they rode off to battle, how he saved the day for Lee. I could relive the time, envision it so strongly that I broke into time. I didn't see myself as a plantation belle burying the silver tea service in the back forty as the Yankees arrived. I loaded a gun and took slow aim, dressed wounds on gangrenous legs, stuck my hand in blown-open stomachs to probe for bullets. Since I often went bird hunting with my father, I knew how to shoot. He had given me a BB gun of my own. The war also held some secret—something happened that could not be undone, and I wanted to know. We were branded "Southern" because of the war, different—better, really—from every other part of the country. I had to find out everything. I knew Robert E. Lee's birthday was January 19, and the name of his horse Traveller. My mother was a Davis and I looked at the Confederate president's face for family resemblances. His wife, my mother said, was known to be notoriously unattractive.

Breaking into my reverie, the voices of my parents in the kitchen made a low rumble. I was reading about Judah Benjamin, brain of the Confederacy, much more interesting than their late-night snarls of accusations, denials, ups and downs. What would they talk about into the night if they were not angry? As though under the anger a deep silence waited.

"You're walking on thin ice," I heard my father say, "and you'd better be careful."

"If I were on thin ice," she answered, "I'd skate as fast and with as much style as I could. If you're slow," she said pointedly, "you will fall through." Her logic was maddening but I often agreed with it. I knew neither of them ever had seen any ice. But I could imagine her skimming fast across a frozen lake in a red skirt, the cracking ice always just behind her. I heard the bench of the kitchen table scrape back. "Besides, you *knew* that was the song and you didn't come to me." She flings supper dishes into the sink.

"What the hell are you talking about?"

"On the radio. They were playing 'When Day Is Done.'" She sings in an awful tremolo "When day is done and grass is wet . . . I think of you." She is close to tears.

But then the tone of my father's voice changes. Instead of rising and rising again, as usually it did in their long night sieges, it falls. "All you can think about is some idiotic song." He slams down his glass on the table. "I am dying, God damn it. Dying." There is silence then. I throw off the blanket and sit up. I shine the flashlight out the window into the backyard. A gold panel of light from the open back door falls across the lawn. Beyond that, only the spring night. Nothing moves.

The panther came into my dreams when I was twelve and never left. In my dream, I am sleeping. I wake up and find the panther along my body, its black back to me, my arms around it, my hand curled around a big paw. The claws are retracted but I feel their possibility. I lie totally still, thrilled, terrified, hardly breathing. The ropy, oily suppleness of the body of the sleeping animal, my face against the back of its head. When light starts to slant into the room, I slowly tie a blindfold around the panther's eyes and slip out of bed.

My father was a nuisance with his illness. All his operations were performed at a Catholic hospital in Atlanta. He'd linger for weeks, with my mother staying in the Henry Grady Hotel. I had to live with Daddy Jack, friends, or my aunt and uncle.

Finally he needed treatments for so long that my sister came home from college to take care of me. We thought they were going to cut off a leg in one operation. Whatever he had was spreading. When I visited him in the hospital right after that, he said it felt good to wake up and reach down and feel his leg. Nuns fluttered around him and he flattered them and flirted even then. I had never seen a nun, and found their wimples and starched white robes apparitional.

My sister was the sweetheart of Phi Delta Theta at Georgia, and taking care of me was not what she imagined. Even though she hadn't yet graduated and was only nineteen, she got a job teaching fifth grade ten miles away in Ocilla. Since I was in sixth, I was able to grade her papers for her. One of her pupils said Lax was the capital of Georgia and another said the Flint was the largest river in the world. Willie Bell took care of us. This suited me fine but finally Daddy came home and never worked again. I saw his stomach when my mother changed the bandages. He looked as though he'd been torn at by a wild animal. His big suppurating wound would not heal.

Daddy was a bleeder. My own blood goes scarlet and viscous, thickens even as I'm cut. *Nothing, I'm nothing like him.* "Blue blood," he always said when he nicked his face, the sink swirling with pale blood and water. "Blood like the English royalty, all of them hemophiliacs." His dull nails were almost square, beautiful really, with fine long fingers. Soft hands that never did a lick of work. When we went on a trip, Drew loaded the car. My father did not even lift a suitcase. My thumbs are square like his but the rest of my nails are oval with clear moons. I don't have his flat bottom, his flat feet, his eyes the color of crude oil. Is he really my father?

Whoever he was, I was not. A point of definition. But we all came out of the landscape. In the Carter years, the Yankee journalists were dumbfounded by Plains, just down the road from Fitzgerald. They tried every whichaway to condescend but the place, so completely itself, confounded them. One columnist finally said the stars were so bright they could drive a person mad. I knew he was on to something but he dropped it right there.

Up close, like the trees on the edge of the riverbank, our roots are too exposed to thrive. A vast shallow sea used to cover this land; it left us swaths of silky white sand, with chinks of ancient shells. Prehistoric looking garfish meditate on whatever fish meditate on in the brackish sloughs. Leaning oaks and pines trailing their moss in the water are romantic from a distance; up close the branches twist out like arms and legs. The far distance was in our eyes, all of us. A high school photograph of me shows a pure uninterrupted face, but my eyes look like the eyes of someone blind from birth. Cypresses grow in standing black water. We are like that, trees growing out of their own reflections.

He dies for three years while I rise, making my escape from childhood. He gets pains at the table, and I don't know whether to stop until the waves passing over his face subside or to keep chewing. Before he takes to his bed permanently, he rests in the afternoons. Sometimes he calls me but I play Elvis over and over in my room, ignoring him. He could call Willie Bell with the little button by his bed that buzzes the kitchen. I can hear her: the good sound of pots and pans clattering. Separated from him by a hall, I lie on my bed reading and eating peanut butter cookies. The afternoon perfectly quiet. One window open and the curtain lifts, falls, billows, ripples. "Frances . . . Bud, do you hear me?" he calls. Sunny light. I adjust my three pillows, hug my book to me: This is my secret and pleasure. I have a new stack from the library: Edna St. Vincent Millay and Frances Parkinson Keyes's *Joy Street,* Emily Brontë. I have a fine-tip pen with purple ink. There's a blot of it on the pink linen bedspread. In my black speckled notebook, I copy "What lips my lips have kissed, and where, and why / I have forgotten, and what arms have lain / Under my head till morning; but the rain / Is full of ghosts tonight." Willie Bell comes in with a stack of laundry. The hairs on her arms are little black curled wires. My skin, white as a lightbulb, my leg jutting out, faintly blue, my shoulder with light freckles like beach sand. She flashes her gold when she speaks. "Don't you hear your daddy calling you? Him lying in there and you won't answer. Shame."

Everyone but me seems to forget his terrorist past, holding a match under the kitchen curtain, saying the house would explode like fatwood; clicking his change in his pocket after you'd asked him to stop; ripping in half the new too-expensive blouse. I never could have friends stay over because of the unpredictable night escapades. His violence never turned toward me and I know he adored me, but I do not, will not, forgive

him. Somewhere Chekhov says that it would be strange not
to forgive. But was there no one in Russia like my father? He's
losing his life, losing us, leaving us. Visceral fear of his wasting
body assaults me when I go near his room. My love for him is
something I must hide, like notes from Calhoun Bruner, in an
outgrown coat pocket. If only a wild bolt of lightning would
strike him in the head. What if he lifts from the bed, a wafting
spirit who never leaves the house? This illness is endless. And
isn't it just like him?

How brave he is. How very young. Everyone says so, over
and over. My mother becomes a tireless Florence. For months,
streams of visitors faithfully bring his favorite coconut cakes,
lemon pies, and flowers. Soon he will be under the ground.
Maggots in the candy bar. Worms in the decayed possum. *The
worms crawl in, the worms crawl out, the worms play pinochle upon
your snout.* This can't be. I reject death. Death mocks every live
breath. The house is somber and sober and smells of cleansers,
rotted stems, sun-dried sheets, bandages. He will just wake up
one morning, well.

I stay in my room. I stand naked on the wicker dressing
table stool so I can stare at my body in the mirror. My hips
are smooth as an empty bowl, and I think my new breasts are
astonishing. Some girls got big brown nipples; I hope I never
will. I make sarong dresses from scarves my sisters left in the
chest of drawers, practice casual, indifferent poses so that when
I see Sonny Stone again, I can look sophisticated for an eighth
grader. My mother's sister Mary raises her right eyebrow when
she is skeptical. When I practice this, I look bewildered rather

than sexy. Sonny is a junior and lives two blocks down Lemon, above a grocery store. His father has one arm, a war injury. I watch Sonny on rainy days at school when all the students whose classes are at the same hour can just dance in socks on the basketball floor because there's no room inside for all the activities. He can really dance, and he wears only black T-shirts and fitted jeans. No one else dresses that way. I can see that the way he holds his partner makes it easy to dance with him, unlike the bobbing boys who'd been in my class since kindergarten. "Stranger in Paradise" and "Unchained Melody," my favorites, seemed written for him—his tight mouth, skinny, muscled torso, blond hair with a hint of red.

I'd had boyfriends since fifth grade. We all gathered on Saturday night and sat on steps talking endlessly. Still children, really, we chased each other through dark neighborhoods and peered in windows. We threw triangular folded notes in class, talked on the telephone about who liked whom. But on the arm of six-foot, 110-pound Clifton MacDuffie, box-stepping to "Ebb Tide" in the humid sock-smelling gym, my thick pink angora sweater feeling more like a live rabbit every minute, I lock eyes with Sonny Stone, as he rolls by with Pamela Puny Paleface Poor Posture Peterson in his arms. I look down, then slowly back at him. His sharp elbow jabs Clifton. He doesn't say "Excuse me" or anything, just throws his head back and winks. Then he starts talking to Pamela, who wears makeup because her mother owns a beauty shop and fixes her hair and face all the time. She has wavy hair and looks up at Sonny with a loose red smile that shows her sixth-year molars.

. . .

In my father's last year, thinned to a boy again, he is hard to imagine as the swaggering, powerful, big boss who could scare me so much that my teeth chattered. His eyes lose all jolt and spark; it's like looking into old campfires. I still run hot and cold on his sickness. At last, the house is peaceful. No waving of guns, no bottles thrown across the kitchen, no keys jerked from my mother's hand at three a.m. I had wished he'd just evaporate for as long as I could remember. Still, he reached for my hand with his old warmth. "Bud, we're sweethearts and buddies. That's why you're my bud." He'd always said that but now he sounds sad. I had to check to see if he always had a fresh glass of water. He listened for the noon whistle from the mill. "They're going to dinner," he said, and I knew he could see the mill workers walking out under the arch he built. A sign hung from it: THROUGH THESE GATES PASS THE BEST PEOPLE ON EARTH: OUR EMPLOYEES. When the five o'clock whistle blew, "They're going home."

Every morning Mother and Willie Bell freshened his bandages and dressed him in a clean pair of pressed pajamas. They changed the sheets the way tablecloths are changed in dining cars of trains, rolling him to one side and making up the other, then rolling him onto the clean side. Sometimes I was forced to sit with him when my mother had to go out. Francis Ward, our doctor, came by frequently to shoot him up with morphine, so mostly he just lay there in a haze. Now and then, he'd rally and talk with frightful clarity about how beautiful the river was

when he was a boy and how he picked up the tiny bird arrowheads, as I still did. Long-lost events seemed to be happening
again, even to me as he described them. I could see him as a
child, picking the shy Confederate violets for his mother. I saw
him with white doves resting on his arms the year he spent in a
wheelchair. The cages still rotted in back of Daddy Jack's house.
What caused his anger in high school when he pushed a teacher
and was expelled? And there was a photo of him in a uniform
at military school, looking oddly small.

He smelled awful, like a raccoon run over on the road, a
smell I still feel in my nose years later. I have a horror of illness.
When someone I love gets the flu, I say, "You'd feel better if
you'd just get up and *do* something." I say, "It's not good to just
lie there." I'm mute at the bedsides of dangerously sick friends,
can say no easy words, my heart racing at the hospital smells,
the efficiency of the nurses. His skin peeled. I flicked big dry
scales off the top of his hand when he was unconscious. Irresist-
ible, but I really didn't like to touch him, either, and would soap
my hands when I left the room.

In his illness he became sweet, not wanting to cause trouble.
He became the boy his mother had doted on, the "Boofa" of
the family, the courageous one who took the bullet for his father. And he was silent in pain, never moaning. *Backbone made
of iron,* the doctor said. *A saint,* the preacher said. When he
slept, I read *The Secret Garden,* imagining hunting speckled but-
terflies in a walled garden. I did not want him to die with me in
the room and listened for the sinewy rhythm of his breathing.
Would I be able to see his death, the transparent scarf, float out

of him and out the window? Would it flutter over me as it left his body?

What my mother does the nights of those long months, I have no idea. I stay with my best friend on Saturday nights. Her parents go out to the club for supper and as soon as they pull out of the driveway, all the boys in our group appear. We make popcorn, talk, talk, talk. Edna Lula and Virgil bang out four-handed "Heart and soul / I fell in love with you," and suddenly I like Sammy Dixon but as I lean back against the piano, laughing, my first kiss happens with Jeff Hardy. They switch to the first chords of "Blue moon / You saw me standing alone" and he quickly kisses me hard with his thirteen-year-old lips and I let him while everyone shouts and stomps. Sometimes we end up at Angela Moore's (her parents go to the same place as Edna Lula's for supper). There, playing spin-the-bottle, I kiss nine boys. These cold, slippery tight-lipped kisses are dry runs for the real thing—Sonny Stone, for instance. I am sure he wraps Pamela in his arms and kisses her deeply, her back bent as in movies. I imagine kissing someone so powerfully, we both pass out. But when? I practice on my ancient musical teddy bear and on the folded washrag in the bathtub.

Often at night, my friends and I walk through the Willcox's woods to a wide stream with beautiful springs. David Willcox, more handsome than Montgomery Clift, lives a block from me and later becomes my real love who loves me back. I played kick the can with him for years. He is a natural in the woods and loves all waters, as I do. In daylight you can see through clear water to the boils, which bubble so blue and pure far below that it seems a goddess could be born there. Such pleasure, diving through sunlight in water. Deeper and colder I swim down, my eyes open. I press my face into the icy surge, my fist into the opening in the earth. At night, it's different. We build a fire on the bank and step out of the circle of light to change into bathing suits among palmetto bushes. In the spooky light, which just reaches to the lower tips of swaying Spanish moss, one by one we push off with a running start, swing on a vine, up, out, up, then, at the highest point, drop into the spring, darker than black. When Lard goes, howling out the Tarzan cry, I hold my breath, afraid the vine will snap. We love the exhilaration of the fall into the night, our shouts scaring away every polecat and fox. Crocodiles, rattlesnakes, and snapping turtles lie concealed among the grasses—we know they won't bother you if you don't bother them.

David had green eyes and was shy. His father was a doctor with a balky heart. The family went to their cabin in the woods so no one could find him on weekends. When I am invited along, David and I take a rowboat on the river, throw out an anchor, and slip in the water. I shimmy out of my suit and tie it around my ankle, and we float and swim downstream with the current for a mile or so. In places the river becomes so shallow that my bottom surfaces. David swims ahead of me as I pole myself along, hoping no fishermen are casting nearby. In a deep spot,

I slide back into my suit, red with mud. Somewhere, we crawl out and walk back through the oaks. Once, as we are bumping the rowboat into the bank, a water moccasin the size of my leg thumps down into the boat. Even in the shadows the snakeskin looks greasy and I see the sliver of black fang slipping in and out of its mouth. Instinctively I jump into the water where all its relatives hide. The live panic that seizes me as I touch the water sends me straight up onto the bank. David stuns it with an oar, finally flinging it back into the river.

We accumulate a collection of arrowheads, as my father did as a boy. We search for Yamacraw burial grounds or middens, and I watch for unusual contours along the ground. We fish under bridges, climb up the sides of an abandoned granary, complete with waterwheel, and cross the swamp on a railroad trestle, hoping we won't have to jump into the water hyacinths and alligators below. We hunt in waders at dawn in cold duck blinds, taking warm birds out of the jaws of the dog. The cabin was my favorite place to be. Geneva, his mother, cans fruits. His father rests under the scuppernong arbor reading Robert Service's murderous poems of the Yukon out loud. We fill milk bottles with blackberries growing out of graves in a cemetery and his mother bakes cobblers.

One night, walking back to the cabin where Geneva is cooking ducks full of buckshot on the outdoor fireplace, we stop. The sand road, once on the bottom of the prehistoric sea, glows white as the surface of the moon. What stops us is the pure perfume of honeysuckle, rampant along the barbed wire fence. My father loves gardenias, roses, honeysuckle. When we drove to the mill, he'd always slow at a low dip in the road, where tangles of honeysuckle bloomed. He always said the same thing, "Smells better than a million dollars." When he came home with roses, he put them on the kitchen counter and said, "See there, we don't even have to go to heaven." The soft road at night and the fragrance seem like heaven. David never thought of kissing before, even as an experiment. We kiss twice, lips closed, chaste and amazed. He breaks off a sprig and sticks it behind my ear, then we kiss again, closer this time, our lips slightly open, just long enough that I feel his breath enter my mouth.

The last summer of my father's life, my sister Nancy married. I had a case of poison ivy that looked like leprosy and everyone was mad because I was supposed to wear pink tulle in the wedding, to be a lady, even though I'd only recently come down out of the trees. Heavy creamy invitations went out to a thousand people, and all Mother's friends went into a frenzy of luncheons, showers, teas for the bride. My father made his last trip out of his room to see her wedding presents on sheet-covered tiers in the dining room. He braced himself on the back of a chair and surveyed the rows of glittering silver flatware, pitchers, and trays. "God Almighty," he said, then turned back into the hall, slowly making his way back to bed, totally exhausted. For weeks, the wedding took over everything, and he had to lie there dying on the edge of the celebrations. We all got new dresses prettier than Princess Elizabeth's, who was going to become queen as my sister married. Flowered drifts of voile, peach linen with panels of pleated silk, aqua cotton, pale as the Gulf. My sister's wedding dress fanned out into an immense train. Her fiancé came with droves of people from Atlanta, probably amused to be down in the sticks for a country wedding. I was just learning to flirt, the art southern girls are destined to practice throughout their lives. That I already wanted all the boys to love me did not produce any sense in me that I could return the feeling. The object was romance, something like David felt about hunting. Jeb Stuart. Tristan. The Snow Prince. My friends and I knew our bodies were semidivine, never to be bestowed except in an Irish castle, on the moors, or at least in Atlanta, on the wedding night in a glamorous hotel, with the trousseau overflowing from a trunk, flowers filling the room with a secret sweetness, a white peignoir that floated as one walked toward the bed, like the robes of an angel lighting on earth. Yes, we were short on realism.

Meanwhile, kissing would do. I wasn't exactly sure why anyone would want to do those other contorted things, so awkward and comical.

The adorable blond groomsman, just out of college, flirts back, though I am in the eighth grade. He wants to play golf and I hear myself telling him I play often and will take him to the club. He ties a sweater with a crimson insignia around his shoulders and wears monogrammed shirts and baggy Bermudas. Possibly Sonny's tight black T-shirts aren't so great. Forest Ripley Harley III has been to Paris, France, and the real Vienna, not the Georgia one pronounced Vie-anna. He's never seen sand greens before; I don't know any other kind exist. I hardly know my way around the course, having played only twice with my mother. The last time, I'd swung back with a driving iron, my eye on the fairway rather than the ball, and thwunked my mother in the forehead, knocking her cuckoo. Forest must be already used to women acting incompetent at sports; he doesn't seem to notice how often my balls pop fly toward the rough, or disappear into the pond. On the seventh hole, by pure fluke, I hit a hole in one. Forgetting to be cool, I'm thrilled and jump up and down, waving the club.

"Too bad you're so young," he says driving home. "You're just so *sweet*." Sweet. I don't want to hear that. Dangerous, mysterious, fascinating. I pout my lips: sweet. "Looks are deceiving," I answer, trying to make my eyelashes brush my cheek as I lower my eyes. I've practiced how to look down, then very slowly up with wide eyes.

I hang my arm out the window for the air. My long sleeves in the hundred-degree days keep anyone from seeing the seeping crust of poison ivy, remnant of a day in the woods with David. Surges of an itch beyond itch flood my entire body, at times so intense I stop breathing. The poison ivy courses in my bloodstream. It's on my thighs, too, hard welts, horribly alive. My father's cancer—no one utters the forbidden word out loud—might feel like this, but worse. I look at my arm, thinking *How can this be my arm?* I want to unscrew it at the shoulder and replace it with a well one. If the surges were constant, I could see how you'd fall unconscious or fall into a fit. At night I run hot water over my skin and the sensation of pleasure, just at the crux of pain, is unbearable. The blood-stimulating heat and the water might spread the poison ivy like a gas fire over my body but I let it run anyway, smiling and biting my lip. How could he be so silent in his room? I easily could scream. Odd, my arm has a memory: Anytime I'm under major stress, I get a faint rash along the tender inside of my elbow, a slight itch I don't touch, lest it take hold of me.

A bee flies under my sister's veil at the wedding and she gasps and jerks, lifts the lace, fanning wildly until it buzzes off. A woman from Atlanta loses her half-slip in the church vestibule, daintily steps over the clump of satin, and walks on. My father lies at home, watched over for the evening by Drew and the sheriff, whose gun on the dining room table guards the hoard of sterling and crystal.

My sister and Cleve, her new husband, stop by the house to say good-bye to Daddy. She's stunning in her going-away suit, shining with happiness, and crying as she leaves because they are off to Nassau, then to French Morocco, same blistering latitude as Georgia but a world away. Cleve will be a navy lieutenant for two years and she knows they will be among foreigners when the telegram arrives with news that Daddy has died.

Forest kisses my forehead and says, "Look me up in five years." I smile and lift my shoulders; Daddy has said I have lovely shoulders. Someday maybe someone will drink champagne from the hollows my collarbones make when I pull my shoulders forward a little. I fold my inflamed arm around my bouquet so he can't see the oozing pus.

Mother cried all night. The next day we were left with packing up boxes and tiptoeing around the house again. Summer burned. I wished we were at Sea Island on the edge of the palmetto jungle. Daddy holds on, refusing all the ground has to offer. We hire nurses around the clock. There was little for them to do except tell me to be quiet. I walk by in the hot afternoon and see the nurse staring at the trickle of urine dripping into a jug on the floor, the only activity in the room except that sometimes a fly crawls over Daddy's face and the nurse leaps up to fan it away. I have a telephone in my room, with my own number. I talk, till my ear goes numb, to Monroe and Jeff, and to Richard, who sets up bowling pins at Bowens Mill. I've met him when I've been swimming at the pool there, ten miles outside town. Son of the fish hatchery manager, he's the one my parents would most violently oppose. His voice comes from another world; I can hear the miles between us. He's darling. Often my phone rings once. When I pick it up, no one answers me.

At home late on Friday nights, I look out the window from eleven on, waiting to see Sonny Stone walking home from Pamela's house, right behind mine. After flirting with Forest and knowing David, I can see that Sonny won't do, but the very thing I see that won't do is what attracts me to him. He rolls up his sleeve and pokes in a cigarette. When Mother and I pass him in the car, I say, "Look, that's Sonny Stone—he said he'd ask me for a date if I were older. He's the cutest boy in the eleventh grade!" She glances at him. "Generations of ignorance," she says, "and probably Vitamin D deficiency." Still, I crouch in the dark dining room that faces Lemon Street. At eleven fifteen, or eleven thirty, or sometimes midnight, he walks by, obscure as a shadow in his black T-shirt. Sometimes he glances at my house, where I peer out from the edge of the draperies.

Before I go to bed, I look in my father's room. His covers are not disturbed. In the middle of the canopied bed, he looks like marble. He already could be dead. The light from the bathroom shines like a white plank over his sleeping form. He won't die and won't die. Frozen like this, he's better than his former swaggering self. "No-fun bastard," I whisper at his door. "What did you ever do for anyone? On whose arm will I come out at the Sub-Deb Dance? You *would* do this."

His reign ends two days before Christmas. His forty-eighth birthday passed four days ago. Relatives are all over the house. I sit in my uncle's Cadillac all afternoon, listening to the radio, pushing the station bar over and over, unable to find anything except moronic gospels and chestnuts roasting on an open fire that I don't want to hear. We have a tree but no one decorated it. When my uncle comes to the porch and motions at me, I pretend not to see him. He raps on the window. I am bloody cold and no one I know has even ridden by. "Sugar, you better go in and say good-bye to your daddy. They don't think he's going to make it," my uncle said, as though this were news.

My mother leans onto the foot of the bed and squeezes the daylights out of my hand. Daddy Jack stands at the door mopping his bald head with his handkerchief: his son, the one he'd worked with every day, the one who'd proved with blood his astounding bravery. The nurse says, "Mr. Mayes, here's Frances, do you see her?" He's been in a deep coma for days, his breath light as a newborn's. The mill whistle blows. Suddenly he opens his eyes. Not jet-black now: faded like an old horse's. He stares. I press my knees hard against the bed. "Yes," he said clearly, "she's beautiful."

Last words. He seems to frown and look out the window and he is gone from this world. The doctor comes in and my mother starts to yelp like a hit dog and says, "Oh, no, not after all this." Who knows what she expected, but I understand what she meant.

Just because it is Christmas Eve and we are having the funeral, it rains. Hard. By the time the coffin is lowered, there are inches of water in the hole. I look down and the casket blanketed with red roses floats, a last refusal. Then he lurches and settles into the clay. I close my eyes and cross them hard beneath my lids to keep from thinking.

The next day my mother and I drive home with my sister Barbara to Florida. The round lakes in the town are where the limestone substrata collapsed. The earth can do that, just sink, and then fill with water. One day we see the movie *The Merry Widow* with Lana Turner and my mother cheers up, then cries. My sister has three small children who seem to cry a lot also.

I begin to feel the buoyant emptiness I was to feel for so many years. Even though Daddy wasted for three years, death surprises me, so insulting. It seems like such an unlikely thing to happen, especially that his great force could cool. I thought he was powerful, and to fall—or rise—from mean and adoring to pitiful and brave was too tangled.

When we came home ten days later, Willie Bell had moved his bed to the other side of the room and put on a different bedspread. If only he hadn't said that about me at the last moment. Beautiful. Me, with the pointed incisors that made Wivoni Harden say I looked like I should hiss instead of smile.

The house feels blank and clean, no mysteries hidden anywhere. I recalled a day a long time ago when my sister learned to drive. We were all at Fernandina, and Nancy and I took Daddy's new Oldsmobile into town. At a stoplight, she rammed into someone from behind. My fault—I had shouted "Look" at an antique hearse displayed in front of a mortuary. The entire front of the car caved in. Scared, fearing the brunt of his anger, we knocked on the hotel door, where my parents were taking an afternoon nap. Obviously annoyed, Daddy opened the door and we told him that his car was smashed. "Is anyone hurt?" he asked. We said no. "Well, why in hell did you wake me up?" He slammed the door. I really loved him then.

Since my father read no books, played no records, collected no stamps or clocks or coins, nothing tied down his memory. Willie Bell had given his clothes away, thrown out the tree, baked a pound cake. I'd missed Rosemary's party. I didn't want to go to school ever again. I didn't care about logarithms, *passé composé,* or the new Supreme Court announcement that segregation was over. Nothing could touch me. Once his clothes, hunting guns, and the white box containing an old watch, gold cuff links, and his tuxedo studs were hidden, he was entirely gone. How quick is oblivion. Over Christmas, all my friends learned how to fast dance. I could dance perfectly in my mind but with a real partner I couldn't follow a lead and stepped on his feet. I thought, *Now I'll never learn.*

FRANKYE

A White Tucked-Chiffon Crystal-Beaded Dress

My mother was forty-seven when her husband was laid beside his mother under marble slabs at Evergreen Cemetery. She thought she was still young. At fourteen, I did not think she was young, but I was about to notice that, although she was full of high spirits and wants, she was—to my astonishment—utterly helpless. Not that she didn't warn me. *You think I'm made of iron. I am not made of iron,* she repeated over and over. What was she made of?

Without either the high drama of her entanglement with my father in his swaggering days, or the day-and-night vigil over his decline into brave-and-sweet ghost of himself, she emerged like a spooky velvet-winged spectral moth that flaps toward porch lights.

As for him, she didn't know which to prefer—the hand pouring the Southern Comfort over ice, or the hand weak and bony on the bedspread, constantly reaching out to us as we walked by his bed. Arrogant (*You low-down pissant*) or pitiful (*I'll be dead and you'll be fastening those pearls* and he yanks off the pearls, sending them scurrying all over the kitchen floor). Raging big boss (*I want it yesterday*) or supplicant (*Please, darlin', some chipped ice*). Wild (roaring into the driveway at dawn) or snagged (pus-stained bandages over wounds).

In the first winter of our loss, Frankye found that we had no money. The mill check came, even while Daddy was sick, but when he died, nothing. Mayes Manufacturing had long since sold to New York owners and Daddy was their manager, while Daddy Jack sat on the money. There must have been health insurance then but we didn't have it. My parents had neglected to pay the installments on the life insurance policy; they simply forgot. The life insurance would have made all the difference in our lives. When I asked why, she replied, *You have no idea what I go through.* Months in the Atlanta hospital, operations, nurses, medicines, doctors—the costs never were mentioned but must have been staggering. When all the medical bills were paid, the First National Bank statement said one thousand dollars.

Because I am four years under eighteen, she can apply for government aid for minors. When the first check arrives, she looks at it incredulously. I can tell she's concentrating hard from the way she works her bottom lip back and forth, as when she focuses on spreading hot peanut brittle fast across the porcelain-topped kitchen table. "Don't do that with your lip," I complain.

"Do what?"

"That sticking out your bottom lip. It looks stupid."

"You don't know what you're talking about."

"I do too."

"You certainly do not. You think you know so much."

I drop it with *I know more than you* on the brink of my sassy lips.

She lets the check float to the floor. "You can have these. They're useless to me. Use them to buy clothes. Use them to light fires." The sum is around two hundred dollars a month. At today's value, a thousand dollars or more.

Out of instinct, I begin to call her Frankye instead of Mammy or Mother. I sense that the mother role is now in question. I open a checking account and buy anything I want. A nice pleated wool skirt costs fifteen dollars, a cashmere sweater about twenty-five. I collect Capezios, which, via an ad in *Mademoiselle*, I order all the way from New Rochelle, New York. Pink ballet flats, pointed-toe loafers in red alligator, blue sandals with ankle straps, suede pumps with kitten heels, fur-cuffed little boots—my closet floor is littered with shoes. Miss Leila, our neighbor, sews Capri pants in pink linen, a yellow dress with silver dollar–sized buttons down the front, a hydrangea-printed organdy formal dress, strapless and with a trailing purple ribbon at the waist.

Daddy Jack felt obliged to step in and pay the bills. Not only did he remember that bullet meant for him, he confessed that he had promised Garbert, and a promise is a promise. When I've heard someone say *He'd take a bullet for me,* I've known exactly what that means and, no, it's not likely that someone would. But one had.

A local florist asked my mother to help him out a few days a week, since she was a founder of the Magnolia Garden Club and known for flower arrangements. She went to his greenhouse a few times then decided that she didn't want to. The humidity made her hair sticky. Then there was something about the owner's bad taste—red anthuriums and screaming red ribbons—and not being able to stand looking at his mossy teeth. She bought a typewriter and enrolled in an English course at a college thirty miles away. To get there, she had to get up at seven, even before Willie Bell arrived. She lasted a few weeks, and then gave the typewriter to me and I used it all through high school and college. I brightly suggested that we move to Atlanta, where my sister and her husband lived. Surely there was a job she'd like in Atlanta. "What do you expect me to do, clerk in a store?"

They'd always tipped the bottle. Now Frankye sometimes drank a bit in the daytime. After school, I'd find her at the kitchen table with a gin and tonic, not even looking at a magazine. What was she to do? She always wanted to go somewhere, anywhere. She had the vibrancy, the looks, the determined helplessness that made you step forth to take over, even if you were eight or nine years old. She had nowhere to go. I watched her energy start to fizzle. Neither my sisters, who were nowhere near, nor I knew depression; we knew bad mood. We didn't know drinking as disease, but as character flaw. Weakness. We didn't know "dysfunctional," but we lived it. We knew that if you were miserable, you brought it on yourself. She taught us.

She gazes in the mirror of her dresser, with two side mirrors reflecting her three-quarter profile. She is multiplied, faceted, broken into aspects. I look at her with blame. When I mention a job, she stares at me as though I'd suggested she walk the streets. Work is not going to work out. She becomes interested in competitive bridge. Unlikely as it is, she's an excellent bridge player and begins to accumulate masters' points. When Daddy Jack says she can go on a duplicate bridge cruise in the Caribbean, she has several linen sundresses made, packs her bags, and leaves.

Bridge was the focus of the trip but I knew my mother hoped to meet someone exciting. She'd already surveyed Fitzgerald and found no one presentable. Or, instead, just found no one. During Daddy's illness, when he still had the wherewithal to drink bourbon, gin, and vodka, I overheard him say, "You'll be remarried before I'm cold in the grave." She did not dispute that.

· · ·

During the day while Frankye cruises, Willie Bell tends to the house and I get myself to school. I'd started driving when I was nine. By twelve, while they were away at the hospital in Atlanta, I'd back out of the driveway then speed back in, over and over. I still can back up as well as I can drive forward. By fifteen, I drive everywhere.

After school, my friends and I "ride around." Up Lee, down Pine, out the ten-mile stretch where I floor the blue Buick and see how fast it speeds up to 110 mph. At night, I read *The Foxes of Harrow* and other Frank Yerby novels one after another, although the librarian had called my mother to report that I was reading "unsuitable" books. (Yerby was a mulatto.) Reading omnivorously across the library, I by fluke choose Jane Austen, Hamilton Basso, Willa Cather, Flaubert, Hemingway, Thoreau, Fitzgerald, Dreiser, Steinbeck, and Turgenev. (I know this because I still have the blue Reading Log I kept for fifteen years.) Propped in my white spool bed, a tin of cheese straws within reach, a stack of library books on the table, the house quiet, protective. I am perfectly happy. Imagine, writing a book. What else could you do with your life that could compare with that? I began to keep lists of good words and quotes, to underline sentences I liked, and write notes in margins. Carson McCullers, from right over in Columbus, how did she do it? "In the town there were two mutes, and they were always together." You can begin a book like that, and, yes, the heart is a lonely hunter.

• • •

Every day Willie Bell leaves a pan of chicken and some dev-
iled eggs, or a pot roast and a plate of icebox cookies. I spend
some nights at friends' houses, sometimes one of them stays
with me, and once or twice I stay at Daddy Jack's, but usually
during the two weeks Frankye is gone, I am alone. No one
seems to think this odd, so I don't either. We never locked our
doors. I read late, listening to LPs that I ordered from a record
club. Often they sent the wrong choice so I ended up hearing
Rachmaninoff, Tchaikovsky, and *Concierto de Aranjuez* and
Boléro. My favorite is a dramatic reading of *John Brown's Body*
by Stephen Vincent Benét. The spinning rhythms and haunting repetitions of the story of the War Between the States ex-
pressed my sense of the land I lived on. I underlined "the
old wise dog with Autumn in his eyes," and descriptions that
named my feelings:

> *For, wherever the winds of Georgia run,*
> *It smells of peaches long in the sun,*
> *And the white wolf-winter, hungry and frore,*
> *Can prowl the North by a frozen door*
> *But here we have fed him on bacon-fat*
> *And he sleeps by the stove like a lazy cat.*
> *Here Christmas stops at everyone's house*
> *With a jug of molasses and green, young boughs,*
> *And the little New Year, the weakling one,*
> *Can lie outdoors in the noonday sun,*
> *Blowing the fluff from a turkey-wing*
> *At skies already haunted with Spring—*

Oh Georgia . . . Georgia . . . the careless yield!
The watermelons ripe in the field!
The mist in the bottoms that tastes of fever
And the yellow river rolling forever . . . !

With the lights out in my room, I listen as the lively voice reads to me, imprinting the Old South myth. What if you could write something that sings? I know the breeze does not smell of warm peaches, but it seems as though it does. And the Lost Cause, that's a subject still reverberating. It had occurred to me that there was another side to the whole story but at that time I was like the Mayas, who used the wheel in toys but never made the leap to chariots and carts.

A couple of postcards arrive. One day in Barbados, natives who shouted *Yankee, go home* pelted the cruise group with rotten fruit as they walked around the port buying straw bags. The card, a view of the harbor, said how insulting to be called a Yankee when she was with Southerners and Canadians and that her turquoise linen dress was ruined.

When Frankye returned, she confessed that she'd been quite taken with a man from Vancouver. His name, Cliff, caused me to imagine my mother in the arms of Montgomery Clift, leaning into his kiss on the top deck of a ship sailing farther and farther south, as south as you could go. Cliff, slick black hair I saw in the snapshot, was not Montgomery Clift by any stretch. Instead, the word "swarthy" came to mind, and I hoped I never had to move to Canada (the moon) because of him. He escorted her on the day trips, she said, had been a *grand* dance partner, and my daddy would never dance. A few days later, I asked if she'd heard from Cliff. Then she admitted that she found on checking out the last morning that the bar tabs he'd signed for all the lovely rum drinks they'd shared while the moon rose over the water, he'd signed in her name and room number. He was off the boat by then. Was it then that she realized that her flamboyant college romance days were not going to reappear? That all the men who flattered her when she was married (sending Daddy into apoplexy) somehow had fast-faded into the background? *John Brown's body lies a-mouldering in the grave. . . .*

Daddy Jack doles out money parsimoniously. We should be grateful, but we are not. I think *If Daddy had not saved your life, maybe he . . .* but I'm not sure how to end the speculation. Daddy Jack is rich and stingy, a bad combination, Frankye says. "Tight as Dick's hatband," she says with a laugh. "Who's Dick?" I always ask. No one questions my "allowance," as Mother calls it.

She rests in the afternoons, reading fashion magazines or condensed books, or she lowers the slant-top desk, pulls out her blue note cards, and writes to my sisters while I browse in her fabric cupboard. The convex mirror above the desk enlarges her forehead and magnifies her eyes when she looks up.

She collects bolts of cotton polka dots, stripes, flower prints, good linen in solid colors, folds of copper or herringbone wool—enough to make a skirt—sheer dimity, seersucker stripes, gossamer voile. A few remnants remained of prints—cowboys, sailboats, and big cherries—left over from my camp shirts. On the bottom shelf are yards of flowery blue and white chintz, raspberry toile, and a green and brown deco design she'd once chosen for my room. When I'd said I hated it, she explained, "Your sisters had the pink. You can't do the Degas dancers twice," so what were my choices?

Some of the fabrics came from the mill, where I'd seen the barefoot women at the looms that looked strung with light in the long room of oiled black machines and bins of cotton. Strong armed, they pulled the warp (weft?) beam across the harp strings of white threads, interweaving heavier threads for texture. I liked the muffled bump with each pull. All the thin women worked in faded cotton shifts they'd run up on their treadle machines. Their lank brown hair swung with each thrust, their eyes, paler blue than my mother's, smiled at me as I followed Daddy down the aisles.

Wedged among the white fabric for linings, Frankye keeps a box of buttons, which I loved from babyhood—gold blazer buttons with anchors, horn toggles, shirt buttons, mottled tortoiseshell, red and yellow Bakelite that seemed very old, jet-black sparklers, diamond-shaped faceted rhinestones, gold baubles, leather-covered knobs, square metal ones beginning to rust, teardrop pearls, and cloth ones to cover with whatever fabric you chose. "When you see nice buttons, buy them," she advises. "By themselves, they can inspire a dress."

If I had become a Coco Chanel or a Diane von Furstenberg, the origins could be traced to these afternoons in my mother's bedroom, with me spreading out the fabric at the foot of her big canopied bed where Daddy died, drawing a sundress or a bathing suit cover-up or a lavender wool coat with mother-of-pearl buttons. My mother is propped up on pillows in her slip, offering her opinion. "Not that. The coral linen would make a cuter shirtwaist dress," and "You can't wear that muddy green. It makes you look like a piece of rat cheese. Look at that *eau de Nil* instead." Water of the Nile. The name set me dreaming, though I looked like rat cheese in it, too.

"So," the biography would go, "she developed her heightened sense of texture and line from her mother, whose incisive taste forever influenced her designs." But I did not become a designer, nor did my sisters. They are better dressed than I, despite my rigorous indoctrination. But always, we are examining the seams, the hem, the quality of the fabric. But, Frankye, there, polishing her toenails with Fire and Ice. I imagine her with parents—experts, say, in the Etruscans—who'd told her as a child about the printed scrap of cloth around a mummy that provided a key to the lost language. Told her that the underthread in the weave is the "subtle." (Sub-tela, under the fabric.) They might have taken her to the Cairo museum to see the Coptic cloth or to the wing at the Pitti Palace where the lush brocade dresses of the Renaissance are displayed. They would have explained the relationship between text and textile. *Texere*, to weave, as I'm weaving this memory. Texture: bumpy dotted Swiss, papery watered silk, stiff khaki (from the Urdu/Hindustan word meaning dust colored).

For you, Frankye, a context and a place to go forward. *Yes, that's my mother's atelier. Just ring the bell and her assistant, Hortensia, will show you the collection.* But, she has her closet of bolts. Daughters to dress. The afternoon is sweltering and her silk slip clings to her breasts that look saggy when she's lying back on pillows.

Why were we fabric obsessed? Were we like Adam and Eve, running out of the garden, inventing fabric to cover ourselves? (Probably they grabbed some flax and started weaving.) Who's to say our designing and dreaming of beauty was not important? Was this how we entertained ourselves? Was it visionary, creative, with the underlying possibility of transformation? Where would we wear these creations? (Everywhere.) Not that she could piece together a pattern.

Our horizon widened. Soon after Nancy married, she and her husband settled into his first and only navy post in French Morocco. She began to write about shopping trips to Gibraltar, a duty-free port she could pop over to on a warship. (Surely this kind of thing is no longer allowed.) She began to send us tweed coats and cashmere twinsets in pearl pink, camel, and cobalt blue. How did she afford this? The question never has been on the lips of my family members. Money is to spend. The coats were English and made me think of hounds and foxes and crumpets. The sweaters were triple ply, lush and voluptuous. And so exotic. *Oh, thank you. I got it from the rock of Gibraltar.*

. . .

Frankye was burned with a powerful cultural lens. Her father doted on her; her mother constantly criticized her and every other living being within her walls.

My maternal grandmother, blind Big Mama, was referred to by my father as "that snake." Because she lived seventy-six miles away and my father's mother lived only two blocks down the road, my Vidalia grandmother was referred to as "your other

grandmother." I suppose I heard my mother call her "Mother," but I thought of her as "Other."

When Mother and I make an obligatory visit, Big Mama always rocks in the breezeway. As soon as the car doors slam, she begins her complaint, her dirge, indignation, grievance against the world. She rocks faster, keeping time with her faultfinding. My mother has heard this caterwaul too many times. She leans casually against the porch rail with her arms crossed, smoking and staring out at the corn fields. She's bright as a quetzal, impatient but silent. Still she frowns down at me, smiles, and shakes her head *no* as I cross my eyes, pull out my lips, and wag my tongue at my blind grandmother. Big Mama rails on against every ungrateful member of the family, then catalogs her ailments, which I count on my fingers until I run out. A little froth of spit gathers at the corners of her mouth. Jesus and the Lord are hauled out frequently to boost her charges.

She was always feeling my arms, as when Gretel held out sticks to the witch so she wouldn't be eaten. She asked what I had learned in Sunday school and I always said, "Jesus wept." I didn't want to go into my feelings about a God who put a father to a test to see if he'd kill his own son like a lamb to roast, and then sent his only child to be nailed onto a cross and fed vinegar. Like Big Mama, the Sunday school God was just mean.

While she only insinuated that I was misbehaving and that Jesus had his eye on me, she openly castigated my mother for her profligate ways, for driving my father to drink, for not obeying the commandments. My mother was shiny metal for her raspy voice to scrape. Garbert Mayes was blameless. Generous.

He sent her checks. My mother was lucky to have married *into money*. What had *she* done with that luck? If she had the sense God gave a polecat she'd get right with her Master.

Big Mama lived with my aunt Mary, who mostly escaped the holy wrath because Big Mama was canny enough not to bite the hand that fed her lavishly. Only Mary walked free. Mother referred to her as The Saint. As the youngest, she'd been stuck since she graduated from high school with the care of her mother. Frankye and the other two siblings (both died in their forties of heart trouble, magnified by drink) had already struck out from there, never looking back.

No one mentioned Big Daddy, dead for a decade. Big Mama had inherited a good hunk of south Georgia land from her mother, iron-face Catherine Phillips Williamson, but Big Daddy, a jolly drinking man, had gambled it away over the years. All that I had of him—no memory at all—was a pine chest he made for my mother's doll clothes when she was small. Big Mama, whose given name was Almeda, had her crosses to bear, for sure, and she bore them quite badly and with as many grudges as she could remember. She had hands so small I had the urge to squeeze hard and hear the fine bones crush. Her vitreous white skin revealed no wrinkle (no worries when you're always in the right). Her feet made me want to say "prim." She kept them together like a good girl at church. Her black hair, thinning, never turned gray, except for a few stray streaks. She kept it in a knot at the back of her neck, arranged over a horrid net doughnut she called a "rat." Biscuits were her redeeming talent.

Always when we arrive, she bakes a sheet pan full of delectable, light biscuits, soft inside, toasty outside. Mary sets out the ingredients and turns on the oven; Big Mama mixes them by feel. A crock of fresh butter, a jar of Mary's blackberry jam, and a plate of those steamy, airy, crunchy biscuits: worth the trip. I help myself to four.

Big Mama secretly can see, surely. Her staring green eyes look like marbles, and her lard-white forehead gleams. When I later saw the first photo of earth from space, I thought of her eyes.

"Take those things back, Frankye. I don't want them!" she grumbles, sliding off her lap the velvet robe and fuzzy shawl my mother brought in extravagantly wrapped gift boxes. She pronounces her name as though it's an accusation. Frankye: I wonder if my mother substituted the "ye" for the plain "ie." It seems unlikely that Big Mama would spell any name in a fanciful way.

Named for her father, Mack Franklin Davis, Frankye must have been a disappointment. The firstborn a girl, slapped with a feminized version of her father's name as small consolation. Her middle name was Catherine, mother of Big Mama. At least it wasn't Almeda.

"You could get me something useful," she barks. "My eyes are on fire." My mother brings a cold washrag with lemon juice squeezed on it and lays it over the bald eyes. *Let's go,* she motions to me, tilting her head toward the door. I pretend to look in the glass-doored bookcase—my aunt Mary is a reader, too—but really I watch their distorted reflections in the foxed mirror above. They seem to move in a haze, as though from another time. "Come out from back there," my mother snaps.

She's tense as wire hanging a picture frame. I wonder if she, too, thinks it impossible that Big Mama can't see.

After every exit from Mary's house, my mother drives fast, lighting one cigarette with the other, burning up rubber all the way back to Fitz. When we turn into the driveway at home, bugs streak the windshield and the hood ticks.

Apparently, she was just as poisonous before she went blind. On the other end of the seesaw, Mack Franklin Davis indulged Frankye endlessly while she was growing up. Frankye told me that when her mother said *no* to the pleated chiffon crystal-

beaded dress in the window of a shop, her father brought it home in a box that night. She dove into the tissue paper and held it up, twirling in front of her mother. Maybe that night Big Mama's eyes went stony for good.

When her mother said college was a waste for a girl, her father ordered the application. If even half the stories of my mother's conquests are true, she was a femme fatale, if for a very short period. She met my father at twenty. Not much time to break hearts. My father was considered quite a catch, and I don't know how long it was before she realized that she was the one caught.

My sister was born a year after they eloped. My other sister four years later, and I, "the baby of the family," was born a long eight years after her. Obviously a mistake.

My mother told me they were happy only for the first year. She said the Depression "destroyed our generation." By their midthirties, they'd lived through World War I, the influenza epidemic, the Great Depression, and World War II. Daddy sat out the war. Since he was engaged in making cotton cloth, his staying in Fitzgerald was considered essential to our nation's well-being. Perhaps if he had gone, his life would have been better. He would have been out of small-town patterns and cast against history instead. As in books, shouldn't he have a quest? Then I could have discovered, as a friend did, a stash of photographs of stick-and-bone people and learned that my father was one of the liberators of Dachau. A handsome young Italian would have knocked at our door, searching for his birth father. *I am from Anzio, where a Garbert Mayes met my mother,*

Costanza. . . . Or, he'd just been stationed, like his brother, in San Francisco on a gray battleship. He might have written to us: *Sell the house; this could be home.* If he'd come back from war to Georgia, he might have brought the luck to live.

If he'd gone, perhaps she'd have developed some resilience and pluck. She would have stepped in and managed the mill in his absence, have all the millhouses painted yellow, and the swept dirt yards planted with butterfly bushes and azaleas. She could have opened a café out behind the mill where the workers could sip iced tea, play dominos, and listen to blues.

But they were fated to the one-mile-square town, wearing out the streets with their heels and tires, wearing out their expectations, wearing out their love. When I read about an eighteenth-century table decoration in Naples—a live goldfinch in a cage of spun sugar—I thought of Frankye in her saffron silk slip, fluffing her hair and spritzing her pulses with Shalimar.

I can get no real satisfaction with first causes, the reasons they wrangled constantly. Clearly, they were bored and created drama to give some high resolution to their days. Beyond that, there's the mystery of other people's lives. How do the early years shape you? Raising children, you think you're forming their character. But one of them with a steely eye may be determined to be just what you are not. We're fated to wonder, *Of those so close beside me, which are you?*

FRANKYE AND GARBERT—A MATCH FOR 20 YEARS was printed in gold on the white matchbooks their friend Marteel gave them for the anniversary. I was seven and it might have been the first little double entendre I got. Ha! The matchbooks suggested many guests at a celebration, all smoking, dressed up, leaning to light one another's Camels, the flaring lights isolating happy faces, the yard decorated with lanterns and the table set with my mother's favorite Country Captain Chicken, tomato aspic, green beans with tarragon. My father in a white suit toasting his bride of twenty impeccable years. But I don't really remember a party.

I knew that you could strike one match and set the whole book on fire; my parents seemed, over and over, to do that, so I must have understood metaphor, or at least the limits of the literal. They were no match for each other. They smoked, so they always were looking for matches. "Light the candles," my mother said. "I want to bloody see what I'm eating," my father answered.

For months the white matchbooks sat in crystal ashtrays rimmed with silver, prizes my mother won for flower arranging. I had my own supply for my playhouse in the front room of the barn, which I'd divided with trunks and suitcases into individual rooms, the kitchen being near the door where there were shelves for my tea set and the toy stove heated by a lightbulb. My dolls ranged along the discarded sofa cushions and their clothes hung on miniature hangers on nails. "Don't you dare light any matches," I was warned. "That barn could go up like a tinderbox." But in a cigar box, I had many candle stubs and when my mother's car backed out of the driveway, leaving me with Willie Bell, I lined them up on a box and struck one of the matches for twenty years and by candlelight fed my dolls gruel made of sand. I liked the sudden burst of blue flame, the sulfuric smell, how quickly the matchstick bent and charred toward my fingers. *Frankye,* I thought. *Garbert.* I had no way of knowing that matches, made in heaven or not, continue to flare, lighting up the mind as they burn the heart.

Soon after Daddy died, I began dating juniors in high school. We were all football mad, then in the summers the bush league baseball teams came down from North Carolina and all my friends went to the field in the sweltering nights under the bug-hazed lights and the girls decided which players were cute. A few girls even went out with the gum-chewing boys but my mother said they probably were not from nice families and I was not to speak to them. She took a stand; usually, she didn't notice what I did or when I came home.

I loved high school and became part of every activity. I worked on the newspaper, acted in plays, decorated the Legion Hall for dances, joined the sub-debs and came down the ramp in the ethereal pink tulle I wore in my sister's wedding. The only deb without a father, I held the arm of my brother-in-law Cleve. David, a year older, who'd been like a twin, and I fell in love. I swam in his green eyes, like reflections of pines in the stream.

He was so handsome. I reveled in his jealousy when older boys paid attention to me. That was passion, I thought. We parked on the side of the house after movies and kissed until the windows steamed. Frankye came out on the porch and shouted, "You are making a mistake you will live to regret." David crouched down and we laughed, though it was mortifyingly not funny at all.

I ignore Frankye as much as I can. I am in high school; she is in free fall. I zealously pour out all her gin when I find bottles hidden in the clothes hamper or the hedge. "Why do you do this?" I ask her. "You are ruining everything."

"You always exaggerate. I don't drink more than anyone else. Look at . . . well, lots of people." My sisters, out of the chaos but sometimes home for weekends, plead and she quits for the length of their visits, pouring a big glug as they back out of the driveway.

One morning I skip school and go over to The House to ask Hazel for help. Not only was Frankye drinking like crazy, Daddy Jack was, too. He ate every meal at our house. Though he mocked, he never overtly criticized Frankye, but with the pot roast, I had a big helping of his criticism. "You don't know what you're doing, wasting time with David." He clatters his fork on the plate. "That two-by-four, the most common piece of wood in the stack."

Hazel listens carefully, I think, then says, "Sugar, you always were an imaginative child but, really, this is the limit. Why,

Daddy sits in the same pew every Sunday and is just tireless in good work, a pillar of the community." She adjusts the lace dickey around her neck and straightens her spine. "Now that Boofa is gone, he's the one who gets the nigras out of jail. He sits on the bank board." Her voice rises for her final pitch. "He's the one who named Fitzgerald 'the Colony City.'"

"Yes, but that's not what I mean. . . ."

"As for Frankye," she interrupts, "she's your mother, *the only mother you've got,* and you should have more respect, even if Frankye didn't come from here and I know nothing about her people." She flips me over like a little hotcake on the griddle.

At night, Frankye stumbles to the door of my room and berates me for causing the "ruination" of her life. She'd always ranted a bit against Daddy, especially focusing on his adoration of Mother Mayes and Hazel.

Now it is my turn. She improvises fast as a jazz musician on my faults for an hour or more. "If it were not for you I would not be stuck in this hellhole," she begins. Then she's off and running, performing her riffs—*you keep your head in a book when you could be doing something, you drive everything into the ground, you just live in the woods, go to the woods, see if I care*—and listing her missed chances, Daddy's licentiousness and transgressions. An apparition in a transparent nightgown, she seems to glow around the edges of her body. She's weaving and slurring. I'll end up sorry, sorry, sorry. I'll make a bed I'll have to lie in. I'm courting disaster, and will end up sorry, sorry.

I stay silent. I will myself into a long-stemmed rose, imagining the leaves sprouting off my shoulders, the thorns, my face a bloom where a bee might want to slumber. A rose cradled in green tissue paper, and I must keep still so there is no crackle. If I respond, the sizzling fuse of her face explodes. I am unappreciative of everything she sacrifices, a smart aleck, and will waste my life with a local yo-ho. My Little Richard records particularly incite her. When I play "Rip It Up" and "Long Tall Sally," my friends and I gyrate as we sing *whole lotta shakin'* and imitate what my mother calls his "jungle" cries.

"He's nasty! He picked cotton at your boyfriend's grandmother's farm. Even the other nigras wouldn't drink after him." I would like to turn up the volume of "Rip It Up" to maximum decibels to drown her out. I would like to stand on my bed and belt out "Keep a-knockin' but you can't come in." But she's rockin' it up, rippin' it up on Saturday nights and all other nights, when she does not feel at all fine.

On some nights as she wavers in the doorway, I imagine that I am a skeleton with thin bones lying under the linen sheet. No sensation in my skin, just the slow growth of my hair and fingernails. I think of turning a fire hose on her, washing her down the hall, her blue nylon gown skidding. I must have laughed because she shrieks that I am the worst of her three children. As though we are all bad, when usually my sisters are held up as paragons who married well. She suddenly burns out like a lightbulb, turns to the dark house, and wanders off, finished with her mad and fearful lamentation.

I have many normal friends. Normal lives exist. I spend as much time as possible with them. I am embarking on a quest

to live a normal life. By day the raids against me never happened. Frankye spent sunny mornings with Willie Bell, making lists and accomplishing them. They baked caramel cakes, rearranged closets, and waxed what didn't need waxing. Some days, though, she wouldn't get out of bed and would still have on her robe when I came home for dinner at noon. On the kitchen windowsill, the weather forecasting house she brought me from Macon sent out a witch or a beautiful girl from a shingled Alpine doorway. The girl, though, often swung out when it was cloudy; the witch appeared on bright days.

At school, I'm out from under. I'm elected "prettiest eyes," "best personality," "best dressed" (don't tell Daddy Jack), and "most original." I'm reading more than ever. I've started on the left wall of the Carnegie Library and plan to read my way around the room. Frankye returns from a shopping trip to Macon and brings me *Anna Karenina*. Neither of us has heard of Tolstoy but she picked it out because it was thick and would take me a while to read. She gave me the first book that lifted me off my chair. Anna also raised a disquiet that formerly belonged only to Frankye. That train, coming round the bend.

I could remember Daddy telling me that I was smart enough to do anything I wanted to do, although he impractically used as examples that I could scale Mount Everest or juggle three oranges. I'm selected to edit the yearbook because the French teacher thinks I might have some writing talent. I can't wait to meet my friends at night when we work at her house on the layout and photos. She's a widow, terse and controlled. I glimpse into the guest bedroom with plain white curtains and bedspread, and wish that I could move in. She says I can name the theme of the annual and I call it *Spirit of Place*.

Our plays reach state competition, and I win an essay contest. Some reluctance keeps me from cheerleading, though I go to all the games to watch David, number thirty-five. The football team elects me their sponsor. I adore every moment of Fitz-Hi. Frankye occasionally tosses me a line, too. She'll vary her accusations and shout, "Don't do what I do, do what I say do." "Don't follow my footsteps." "Fend for yourself. There's no one to fend for you." *Fend*, I thought. What a nice word. She bought a revolving bookcase from a law office and refinished the "garish" oak, so that it resembled walnut. My books, she said, deserved a good home. So finely spun, the threads to hang on.

. . .

Daddy's brother Mark let us use his house at Daytona Beach, a two-story gray shingle, where the tough St. Augustine grass lawn met the dunes. We've never owned a dishwasher, and put in the wrong soap. We come back to find the whole kitchen engulfed with suds. We scoot around the kitchen, laughing like crazy. At the auction near the beach, Frankye bids on and wins a diamond watch. Her friend Gladys and her daughter Nancy come down to visit. Nancy buys a monkey at the dime store. He's cute at first but turns nasty in Aunt Emmy's immaculate house and swings around the room, dropping smelly turds. We play constant canasta and take long walks on the deserted beach.

I try to flirt with the lifeguards, but they have their own bronzed-breasted acolytes. Gladys and Nancy leave, and we are

alone. I read in the sunroom, which smells like moldy puzzles, while my mother paces outside, ice rattling in her fifth or sixth drink. On the beach every afternoon, I run my hands under the warm sand, feeling the big pulse of the ocean. She's out in the water. I want her to wash in this primitive surf, turn clean as a scallop shell. The water clears around her ankles. She turns to me and says, "Cold."

When I look at photographs of my mother at forty-eight, fifty, I see what I did not see then. Even in black-and-white, the intense blue of her eyes is beginning to fade. I would like to step into the frame, take her hand, and lead her away. If someone had, surely she might still have thrived. Fallible, fragile, she was saved by no one. Least of all by herself.

At this time, I began the dream that was to reoccur for twenty years. I am in water up to my chin. The current rises and falls, and I am only barely able to breathe. That I am above water at all is because my feet balance on the submerged shoulders of my mother.

TEN THOUSAND RULES TO LIVE BY

I couldn't wait to go to college. Daddy Jack walked into the dining room where I sat at the table reading catalogs. I wanted to go to Sophie Newcomb but knew nothing about it other than that it was in New Orleans. For years late at night, I'd listened to a black-Cajun radio station that somehow made it across the airwaves all the way to south Georgia. The music! I was pulled toward that raucous sound. The disc jockey advertised White Rose Petroleum Jelly night after night. I knew about ruined plantation houses with oak alleys, and I kept a record album propped on my bedside table so I could see the cover photo of the golden crescent of the Mississippi at sunset. I was interested in Vanderbilt because I heard that's where poets went. I ordered catalogs from Pembroke (Brown) and Wellesley. Reading those two, I had visions of myself in a gored tweed skirt and starched white blouse editing the school news, a practical and serious person. The catalog from Randolph-Macon Woman's College came, too, sent by a very nice friend of mother who went there in the dark ages and told my mother it was the finest school for girls in the United States.

Daddy Jack thumbed through the Wellesley catalog and tossed it back on the table. I knew what he was going to say. "I went to the school of hard knocks myself," he rewarded me. "I didn't have any of this fancy education, and I've done pretty well if I do say so." *And you do say so,* I thought. "Well, you've got your head in the clouds but I tell you one thing, sister, you can go anywhere you want as long as it's not north of the Mason-Dixon Line. I'm not paying a dime for you to go off and marry some Yankee two-by-four much less mix with nigras not three generations removed from cannibalism." He puffed like a bullfrog. "What is wrong with the University of Georgia? It was good enough for your sisters." That they had gone there was the reason why I didn't want to. I wanted something different, not to follow in their footsteps.

My mother at the door, years past the middle of the twentieth century, said, "And you can forget New Orleans—that's the white slavery capital of the world."

"*What* is white slavery?" I asked.

"White girls are kidnapped and sold to Arabs and other foreign sheiks, and besides Tulane is only for Jews. It's known as Jew-U. You would not fit."

I couldn't wait to go to college.

Given my strictures, I finally opted for Randolph-Macon. Virginia was within striking distance of places I wanted to know, whereas Tennessee was just as "hick" in my mind as where I sat, poets or no.

I drive up north. From the passenger seat, Frankye com-
pulsively presses the floor when she thinks I should brake. We
pick up my sister Nancy in Atlanta so Mother won't have to
drive home alone. In my trunk, dance dresses—red taffeta, gold
strapless, the old, still good, pink tulle—are layered with blan-
kets, books, and sheets. The blue luggage my family gave me for
graduation is packed with sweaters, fall outfits, and a suit for
church. Frankye has planned my college wardrobe all summer,
something fun for her to do. Now she says every few miles,
"What will I do without you?" until I feel I should make a
U-turn and head home, get a job at the library, marry as she

always warned me against, and try to write. From the backseat, my sister says, "Just speed up."

When we turn in the redbrick entrance, I let the car creep while I savor the feeling of entering a new country.

Two men haul up my luggage to my assigned room on the fifth floor. Frankye insists on making up my bed. Then she starts to cry and my sister puts her arm around her as they head for the car. Before they drive off, Frankye rolls down her window. "Bud, take this." She folds into my hand the delicate diamond watch she splurged on at the auction in Daytona Beach. "I want you to have it." I wait in the bathroom stall until I think my face is not too red to meet my roommate.

We were not gearing up for hippie times; we were still clutched in the last grasp of Queen Victoria. Although Betty Friedan must have been putting the finishing touches on *The Feminine Mystique,* not one word of that news, as far as I know, had leaked inside the redbrick wall that surrounded the campus. This was the cusp of the sixties, the last of the fifties. Marriage still was the first order of business; any career ideas could be tucked in around the edges. Though we were walking up to the verge of change, the college still remained in the holding pattern.

Randolph-Macon girls arrived with a lot in common. Many of us had similar reasons for being there: Our parents had insisted. Randolph-Macon was thought to be better than the places we put first. We didn't know to ask: *Better for what?* Louise wanted Radcliffe badly but her parents told her it was R-M or nothing. Anne longed to go to Stanford; her parents knew

California was too strange. Determined to leave the state of Georgia, I simply chose the farthest point north I could.

Academically the school was good—too good. When Eudora Welty made her first foray out of Mississippi back in '27 she chose Randolph-Macon. After a short time, she had to leave. The administration decided that her credits from Mississippi State College for Women wouldn't transfer. Welty would have to repeat a year. She headed for Wisconsin, left "weeping across the James," and thereby escaped into literature. I had no goal other than to read, make friends, meet someone fantastic, and have fun. My purposes didn't fit the onerous requirements to master two languages, mathematics, economics, and a bag of other unintelligible subjects. I never saw the necessity to attend all those classes, so many days a week, or purchase unreadable texts when so much fiction and poetry waited in the bookstore. I was an ideal candidate for "alternative education," a concept unknown at the time. My grades tilted from A to F. Greek and Latin etymology fascinated me whereas whatever class happened at 8:10 a.m. sometimes escaped my notice. When I returned to graduate school as an adult, I could no longer remember why I'd had trouble in college courses. By then I'd caught on to cause and effect, the basic idea that one sometimes does one thing in order to be able to do another.

One rule at Randolph-Macon was the belt-to-breakfast rule. We could go downstairs in our robes when the bell rang, but we had to be belted—no sloppy free hanging robes allowed. A student inspector, earning her scholarship, stood at the dining room door. My robe had no belt. It was a copy Miss Leila, our seamstress, made of one my mother saw in a magazine, a bubble line with narrow hem. A belt had nothing to do with it. But every morning I had to tie around me a string belt in order to eat. The dining rooms for each dorm were identical: round tables for eight with white cloths and the special floral-edged R-M Wedgwood. At lunch and dinner the rule was skirts or dresses. No one could leave the table until everyone had finished. The few Yankee girls hated this and even the Southerners, who didn't know any other way of eating, hadn't counted on Harriet Bowles from Mississippi chewing every bite twenty-seven times while the housemother drawled on about her youth and about the good families of former students. Scholarship girls waited on tables. (Didn't they just *hate* that?) They went down early for their dinner, then donned whites and served.

I was picky. So was Rena, a friend I spotted right away as a wild card in the deck. Across the street was the Columns, a big house turned restaurant. By the end of freshman year we were regulars. Even though Daddy Jack had to pay for my meals at school, I headed across the street several times a week, always when the odor of "train wreck," a tomato stew, or "mystery meat" drifted up the stairwell. Rena was always ready. We charged, blithely signing tabs that ran up into horrendous amounts by the end of the month. During the week, crossing the street was our only venture outside the brick wall surrounding the campus. Sometimes we walked a couple of blocks to the ice cream shop on a spring evening. Leaving the campus became a distinct feeling. R-M felt like an enclosed world, such a microcosm, such a nunnery, that to leave began to feel odd. We became, some to a not mild degree, institutionalized. The only facts from the great world I remember from then are that Alaska became a state and that a handsome Latin in camouflage acting up in Cuba kicked out the sugar mills. Somewhere they were reading *On the Road* but behind the red brick, we weren't. We swooned over "The Lake Isle of Innisfree." Freshman year, we could not ride in a car during the day unless a senior accompanied us. We could have horses, not Jaguars or Jeeps. From this distance, our slowness seems impossible. I see myself trying to run underwater.

I told Daddy Jack the Columns was the name of the school store and I needed tights for modern dance, kneepads for hockey, a school blazer, a choir robe (choir robe!), endless pads and notebooks. He paid but was not amused. He wrote threatening letters. This person who went off to a woman's college (we are not a girl's school, we are a woman's college) and sounds as remote as Emily Dickinson, was, to Daddy Jack, a wild girl who must be broken.

The school agreed. What might we do if we didn't have the ten thousand rules to live by?

My time at Randolph-Macon was just before girls were able to grab a little wheel of pills, that gesture that changed us forever. A nice girl got pregnant the year before I arrived and her family was furious with R-M, so now a gym teacher lectured to us. She spoke in such vague abstractions that no one had any clue what she was talking about until she concluded by holding up a diaphragm between thumb and forefinger as though dangling a dead bird, and saying, "Now gulls, gulls, I have no idea what you'll do in your four years at Randolph-Macon Woman's College, no idea, but just remember if you're a good little actress on your wedding night, your husband never need know. There is no reason for him ev-ah to know."

Those old wise birds sniffed the winds of change and tightened the grip on freedom one last time. Dating R-M girls had a built-in obstacle course. Each dorm had date parlors. If you were dull enough to want your date to stick around the campus, you sat in there on flowered chintz or linen and kept the door open six regulation inches. The dorm mother paraded through, smiling and chatting about her courting days in Milledgeville (she had gone to the same school as my mother so always mentioned that). The boys rolled their eyes up, as if on an elevator. They'd just driven the Blue Ridge Parkway or back mountain roads sometimes jammed six to a car from the University of Virginia or Washington and Lee in Lexington. They wanted to party, not see Miss Montgomery's sensible shoe and nose poked in the door. When a boy arrived he approached a podium and filled out a date slip, stating his name, address, destination for the evening—everything but the occupation of his father. My luck was to have dates who listed their addresses as Mars or 10

Downing Street. This, the dorm mother said, implied disrespect toward me. Usually dates were blind dates, never seen before or after. Distance, the number of girls' schools, the rules, everything stacked against getting to know someone normally.

We did have a unique advantage among Washington and Lee students. Early in the fall, all of us had to line up at the gym for nude posture pictures. Why did we docilely line up? The gym teacher in wide khaki shorts planted her muscular legs and feet on the floor and explained that posture was important to health. We had to strip and walk naked and solo across the floor while they sized us up. We then were photographed in profile and straight on. We were later called in and a teacher would go over our body photos with us, giving us a grade and telling us to walk with our fannies tucked in, stomachs tight, shoulders back, chin up. I can walk for blocks with a book on my head. Those with big busts were told they'd always have backaches and should wear dark colors. Those with small breasts were given an isometric exercise we could do in chapel or anywhere: grasp each forearm with the opposite hand and push, repeating rhythmically, "I must, I must, I must develop a bust."

Our rush in popularity happened when a drunk W&L boy climbed in the gym window and stole the photos, neatly labeled with our names. His fraternity passed them all over W&L. Somehow we didn't find this out for a long time; we simply thought we were noticed for our cute haircuts and sharp clothes at the freshman mixer, when boys were bused in and dumped and tagged.

I loved the University of Virginia. Not the boys, especially, but the thrilling serene classicism of the architecture in the somewhat rough landscape. The columns under the sweep of fall-colored trees appealed deeply to my sense of ideal education in an ideal setting. Those Thomas Jefferson "ranges," little rooms with fireplaces, each one opening to the walkway, seemed the epitome of romantic, intelligent design for students. I imagined Edgar Allan Poe scribbling madly in the firelight. But the boys were hard drinkers by night. By day, dressed in suits and ties, they lounged about pretending, as Rena said, that they were at Oxford. Actually they were just hungover. When we went to Charlottesville for parties, we were placed with a lady with spare bedrooms, usually a widow who had attended R-M so very long ago. Three or four girls would be garrisoned with her. One of us was charged with the "yellow sheet" for signing everyone in and out over the weekend. It was an honor to be selected to monitor. All rules applied even though we were dreaming under Mrs. Blankenship's Martha Washington bedspread, miles away.

The most stringent was the Twenty Mile Rule. No drop of alcohol could be touched within that radius of the school. Even those who didn't drink began to plot ways to get 20.1 miles away every weekend.

I have my first drink in Washington—a Cuba libre, naturally. We elect Rena to go in the liquor store. She turns her ring around to look like a wedding ring and orders a bottle of rum. What kind? "The best," she answers.

"Young lady, are you twenty-one?"

Rena looks amazed. "I wish I'd see twenty-one again," she says, laughing. Anne and I are crazy with admiration for her. The three of us sharing a room at The Willard rush up and open the bottle. Anne's brother Paul is in town on leave from the navy. He's older, a pilot, gorgeous, and engaged. He's not interested in us at all. What a pity. For hours we play bridge with him and sip rum out of hotel glasses, feeling we've succeeded in something but not knowing quite what. In Washington, we don't have our usual restricted hours but we don't know anywhere to go after dark.

On weekends, I go farther and farther, though there's a limit to how far you can get on trains and buses and still get back by ten thirty Sunday night. R-M made it difficult to stray far afield: They scheduled Saturday classes. I've never heard of another school in modern times with Saturday classes. Girls appear at eight thirty, raincoats wrapped over their nightgowns or pajamas, hair unrolled, barely combed, deeply demoralized, vacant eyes staring at Dr. Voorhis as he consults his yellowed three-by-fives. He harps on the Hapsburgs. World history. Invasion from without, decay from within. All wars begin in spring.

I cut. Skip to Annapolis or Princeton or Chapel Hill. Annapolis was one school more mightily skewed than ours. Those constant salutes! And all the crew-cut officers always around. But one of the ladies who takes in dates has a basement room that is a true pit. In the few minutes the midshipmen have to deliver the dates at curfew, something could happen, though not much can take place on those cushions in the dark. For sure, everyone is stone sober after a dance with fruity fruit punch and crackers, the same snack served in Robert E. Lee kindergarten in Fitzgerald, Georgia. My friend Joan already is in love and knows she will marry Mike, whose friend I dated. He came from Des Moines, Iowa, but loved the sea. West of the Mississippi, my imagination flattens out into an endless corn prairie. I simply can't see that anyone irresistable could come from such a place. Even so, he is. But he kisses fast and I'm glad of the dark so I can wipe his saliva on my sleeve rather than swallow it. Joan and I feel stirred in chapel with all the midshipmen singing "Eternal Father" under the cold light from the highest windows. We love sailing in yawls on the Chesapeake Bay, holding hands under the table in crowded tearooms crammed with uniforms and lovely girls who streamed in from girls' schools every weekend they were allowed.

Princeton, oh, even better. The dreaming spires of Scott Fitzgerald, pink blooming trees along the lake, the big talk in the eating clubs, the town that looks like a model village for an HO scale train set. Rena's high school boyfriend Jamie fixes me up with his friend Ernie. The football coach's wife gives us the run of her house. The coach had died and one room is filled with his trophies and ribbons. Ernie calls me *cara mia* and we take long walks across campus, past the Princeton Inn, to the grad school where the students dine in robes. Late at night the living room is littered with couples making out in armchairs, on the floor, four to the sofa. Someone plays "Misty" on the piano. We kiss until we are dizzy and sweaty. Heaven. That was heaven. Sunday mornings at Ivy Club we sip milk punch and listen to a string quartet, and begin counting the minutes until the train south.

Rena and I make it back at the last instant. All quiet on the western front. We slide our bags down the hallways then bump them up the stairs, looking up for waiting friends who want to know how it was, what did he say, did you meet anyone else, looking up at each scrubbed, creamed face, hair in rollers, book in hand. *I probably should have stayed here and studied for the anatomy quiz tomorrow.*

The reason we follow the elaborate rule book is the honor system: a system devised not just to prevent cheating in classes but an inclusive, strict code of ratting on anyone who broke any rule. Anyone's broken rule was tied to your "honor." If you see someone 19.9 miles away from school pop a beer, you are on your honor to turn her in to the council. Any infraction is up to you. Your conscience should burn if you know someone sneaked out the window after hours at Mrs. Clark's in Charlottesville. You can't just turn over and go to sleep. For this girl's own good, you must turn her in. This is extolled as a system of mutual trust.

Once turned in, the culprit would be summoned in the middle of the night to march down to the dean's office to face a black-robed tribunal of faculty and peers. At this mini inquisition, you could be drummed out of school. Helen, who caused a ruckus at UVA involving two boys in a bed (reported from fraternity mother to date-house mother to R-M dorm mother) never saw Monday morning at R-M again. Calm-spoken, outraged faces greeted her at the door. Since the process was secret, I never learned the lesser forms of retribution.

Was my going against the prescribed academic grain a perverse way of rebelling against rigidity, a freedom stakeout that didn't haul me before the midnight court? Not sure. I do know that a rigid sense of truth took root in me. My mother always encouraged the "white lie." *Just tell him you are going out of town. Say you're sick. You have another invitation. Tell them someone backed into you.* After my R-M years, I can't even tell someone I don't particularly want to see that I'm busy, if I'm not. What is just? Fair? Right? I open my mouth and the truth spills out. As a result of R-M indoctrination, I've had countless tedious lunches and dinners. There, I never actually saw a rule broken and so was spared an acute moral dilemma of ratting on friends. Such good girls. We were kept in place by the appeal to a higher sense, morality; the rule was the thing, not the judgment of the act behind the rule.

Faced with a real crime, the system was useless. For a while a klepto was loose in the halls, picking up our wallets casually left on desks or beds. Emptied, they were discovered floating in the toilet tanks. Gradually a rumor surfaced that X, from one of the First Families of Virginia, was the thief. A girl who went to high school with her said she'd done the same there, too. We were not allowed to put little dime store locks on the door. Rena tried and was told she couldn't deface the door and besides that was contrary to the atmosphere of R-M. Apparently the school was reluctant to confront Miss First Family. We just learned to hide our ten-dollar bills and driver's licenses from her.

Virginity seems quaint in light of later days of genital warts, herpes, AIDS, and other fallout of the then-nascent sexual revolution. An old granite statue in front of a dorm was supposed to wink every time a virgin walked by. His eye must have been permanently fluttering, even though these were the last days of the virgin cult. Many of us didn't think for a minute sex was "wrong," but fear of pregnancy was a powerful deterrent, as were stories of coat-hanger abortions in a Boston apartment smelling of cabbage. Those, compounded with the big word "reputation," kept us relatively chaste. A high school friend got pregnant her first semester of college and was forced into marriage by the parents. She cried when we wished her well and tried to act excited about the baby. "I think babies are dirty," she kept saying. Frankye had brainwashed me into thinking that life would end if I slept with my boyfriend and turned up "pg."

Some did have developed senses of sin. Anne worried about the exact moment a kiss turned passionate and therefore sinful. She went to confession for such things. The priest defined passion as beginning after fifteen seconds, no tongues included, so, while kissing, Anne also had to count. Many girls had never kissed anyone; they'd been sentenced even in high school to other tidy girls' schools and never dated at all.

• • •

Fitzgerald is not the antebellum, heavy-duty South, with pa-triarchs reading Tacitus on the porch, but only the backwoods of Georgia, stratified as a midden, but not hidebound like the tidewater South. At home, like all my friends, I'd stayed out late, kissed dozens of boys, fallen in love. I'd had steamy nights at drive-ins and summer cabins and swum naked down the river with my real high school love. This corseting rubbed me wrong. I liked boys but never got to know any well while I was "up north." Given even the smallness of the pond, wasn't I popular in high school? Now I began to feel less attractive. My natural instincts to be expressive started to snuff out. I couldn't think of anything to say to the Scotch-drinking Virginia school dudes. Being "cool" never interested me. The endless loud party in a crummy fraternity house got old quickly, as did football games, especially since the University of Virginia team had endured a three-year streak of solid loss, and the tanked-up boys now cheered for whatever team theirs opposed. Everyone I met had some Civil War name, Moseley or Stuart or Meade. Besides having to jump through hoops to date us, boys faced the stigma that we were "smart." The Sweet Briar and Hollins students had better reputations as well-rounded, party girls, May queens, debutants. We were rule-ridden, and with a tight bit. Horses like that tend to spook easily. I began to spend more weekends at school reading or scrambling down through the brush to the edge of the James River, where I tried to write poems or just sat there thinking moody thoughts. I didn't even want to go home, not with Frankye circling the drain. At least with Daddy Jack, I always knew where things stood; he was utterly predictable. He blundered through the world, scattering effects from his disinterest about any life beyond the absolutely practical. David and I agreed that we wanted different lives. He planned to live in Fitzgerald. I wanted something else, not that I knew what that would be. Things at home were awful.

With a few others, I even remain at school over Thanksgiving. Those big echoing halls, the trees bare, our little places set for meals, and nothing going on. My big sister in the sorority insists on fixing me up with an "older man," twenty-four, who teaches at a prep school. He drives a sports car and likes to dance, she says. I'm not excited to date someone who has settled into teaching high school boys. He's handsome and attentive, and unlike the other boys, doesn't drink. After the movie, though, when we're driving back to campus (curfew rules still applied on holidays), he takes my hand and says, "You don't know how fond of you I've grown."

Fond. "Oh, thanks," I answer, trying to sound sincere. Rain sloshes over the tiny car. I want to cry myself because I'm missing David, eight hundred miles south, with his Hermes by Praxiteles mouth, more beautiful than anyone in Virginia, even if he has grown up only a block from me. The TR3 windshield wipers scrape back and forth; the windows steam, not from my hot breath. He squeezes my hand then lifts it. At first I think he's placed my hand over the gear knob, then I realize that the bony protuberance is sticking up in his dress pants. I jerk back my hand and look at it as though it were burned. This, and we've never even kissed. He apologizes all the way to the college gate and I never go to the telephone when he calls over and over.

. . .

The alma mater is in Latin. The composer, Miss Willie Weathers, was oblivious to the fact that in such a repressive atmosphere, the Latin words *quae ubi pinus exit* sung by a chapel of girls might have other reverberations than the context suggested. When we come to those lines we thunder out the word *pinus*. The deans all look down; some of the younger professors smirk. To mention it would be an acknowledgment that penises existed in the world, and that did not happen. I wonder if Miss Weathers ever noticed and if so whether she cringed or suppressed a smile.

The most telling activities we were urged toward were the custom of "stomps" and "odds and evens." I thought from the outset that both were beyond belief. Stomps were marches at night when several secret societies such as STAB (said to mean Stately Tall Attractive Brunettes) "brought out" a new member—girls selecting other girls with their own type looks for mutual glorification. The group, folded arms up, stomped through the dorm just before closing, chanting their special chant. At the room of the new member they all stomped their feet hard and shouted out her name. Everyone looked out of their doorways, clapping and calling congratulations. Underground, there was a group that thought this was all too corny for words; I was "brought out" SOB my sophomore year. We had no rituals like the rest, only a bond of contempt. No alternatives occurred to us. The rumor mill was always churning up names. So-and-so should be Pi or AmSam, whatever they were. My roommate spent hours each night in beauty rituals. Her hair was her glory, but was it enough to get her into Omega, the blond beauties? For an hour and a half each night she rolled her fine pale strawberry hair. Every morning she applied mascara and crimped her lashes before going down to breakfast. I was the only person ever to see her sweet, washed face. She was brought out, to many happy tears and congratulations.

Stranger was the odd-even hoopla. If your year of graduation was '64 you were the sister of the class of '62. Classes often serenaded the sister class at night, winding through the halls with candles. The downside was that the Evens had a set of "trophies" that were hidden around the campus, as did the Odds. In your spare time you were supposed to search under rocks and in storerooms and behind books in the library for the other classes' trophies. If you found one (the only one I remember is a horse's tail) you sounded an alarm and gathered at the Odd Tree or the Even Post for various songs extolling your class. Sort of a perpetual treasure hunt. Several well-adjusted friends actually loved scavenging for trophies and thought I would too if I "just would try."

This roaming tribal fervor is channeled, at the end of sophomore year, into a performance of Euripides's *The Bacchae*. We barefoot girls in fawn skins dance around the amphitheater in the moonlight in the service of Dionysus, god of wine and fertility. Whoever chose the play had a diabolical streak. We are perfect for whipping up into a froth of fleshy, religious ecstasy.

We can get into these parts as we cannot get into *The Glass Menagerie*. Racing around night after night whirling torches, wild with divinity, ludic maenads:

> *. . . crowned their hair with leaves*
> *ivy and oak and flowering bryony. One woman*
> *struck her thyrsus against a rock and a fountain*
> *of cool water came bubbling up. Another drove*
> *her fennel in the ground, and where it struck the*
> *earth*
> *at the touch of god, a spring of wine poured out.*
> *Those who wanted milk scratched at the soil*
> *with bare fingers and the white milk came welling*
> *up,*
> *Pure honey spurted, streaming, from their wands.*

Power, mythic power we feel in the blood. We sing in Greek. The words ringing out all across the dell:

> *When shall I dance once more*
> *with bare feet the all-night dances,*
> *tossing my head for joy*
> *in the damp air, in the dew,*
> *as a running fawn might frisk*
> *for the green joy of the wide fields*

The green joy feels cathartic. We wind back up the trail to the dorms, flashlights beaming the edges of the path, singing like maenads, in touch with all that fire the entire mechanism and history of the school seeks to suppress, suppress, suppress.

I do not regret going to R-M in the last throes of repression because of the friends I made there. I'm happy that I followed the president, Dr. Quillian, down Crush Path with my classmates singing "Gleam Little Lantern." We were supposed to be pure, coiffed, gracious, intelligent, unselfish, subtle, capable. We were. Semi-isolation from men at the very time many wanted that most turned us toward ourselves and one another. Life without the friendship of Rena and Anne—unthinkable.

We had the bond of loving books. We spent the summers traveling from Fitzgerald to Rena's in Birmingham and to Anne's in New Orleans. Frankye, who'd criticized all my friends in high school, loved Anne and Rena. To my surprise, they liked Fitzgerald. Frankye became her charming self again. She gave teas for them and took us to Jekyll Island and baked pound cakes and Toll House cookies, and served us frozen fruit salad and delicate chicken sandwiches with celery and nuts. She wanted them to stay, to fill the house with their grace and loveliness. Rena and Anne both thought I should think again about giving up on David. Rena was stirred to quote Yeats's line about *more beautiful than thy first love / But now lies under boards*. And couldn't I at least influence him to move as far from Fitz as Atlanta?

In Birmingham and New Orleans, there were more parties, their old friends to meet, new things to taste at restaurants, and always books to pass around and read from aloud, and blouses and belts to swap.

After holidays, we took the long train back to Lynchburg. Beginning in New Orleans, the Crescent swung through the South picking up hundreds of college students and depositing them at schools all the way to Washington. We adored the little compartments and read *The Magic Mountain* and *Light in August* aloud, sharing tins of cheese wafers brought from home. Rena came up with a copy of *Lady Chatterley's Lover.* I admired a natural dignity Anne was born with, admired Rena's passionate response to everything, as though she had one less layer of skin than the rest of us. Dozens of splendid young women, idealistic and nasty, intelligent and naive, adventurous and unsophisticated.

We began to forget we were supposed to please men. There weren't any. We were like the Spartan women during long wars. We were hell-raisers on sabbatical. At R-M again, we bought strawberries and sat in the rain on front campus whooshing them with Reddi-wip and screaming with laughter as our hair dripped and the whipped cream ran. We were unconsciously developing a strong core self. Confined as we were, we enjoyed one another thoroughly, and so acquired the talent for friendship, one of the two or three chief pleasures of my life.

Beyond my two closest friends were circles and circles of other friends, Kit, Gwynne, Lucy, Alice Neale, Joan, Linda, Nancy, Rebecca, Catherine, Marion, Mary Jo. I visited in Greenville, Atlanta, Lexington, Washington. The whole South was our playground. Each friend stays indelible and unique in memory. Rebecca, doubled over with cramps, wrapped in a blanket telling jokes while her roommate strummed endless verses of "The Eddystone Light." Lovely Joan dressed in red on the wisteria-draped Main Hall porch. The night watchman's flashlight passing briefly, late, under our doors. Sue, who slept in her panties (the same Sue who called out "Oh hell, I'm awake," when her alarm went off), often met him in the hall on her way back from the bathroom. She crossed her arms over her bare flat chest and stared straight ahead as he passed. Gwynne and I acting out the hare and tortoise tale for drama class, feeling humiliated to be hopping and slugging along the rug. Everyone swaying in a chorus song from a play about isolated life in the remote country of Andorra one of us wrote. The first story I wrote was about the imaginary death of Daddy Jack by tumbling down the stairs at his house, vivid in detail. I was thrilled to be published in the school magazine, *Potpourri*, but could not show it to anyone at home—my first brush with the edgy situation of the writer's life.

Ten thousand images, one for every rule.

Many are of the Virginia seasons, unparalleled. To see the fall trees on the campus blessed my days. A golden rain tree on front campus gave up all its fan-shaped leaves on the same day, a brilliant shower falling into a circle like the melted tigers in "Little Black Sambo." I loved kicking through the leaves of hundreds of scarlet and yellow maples, and that clear fall air touched with some stirring, unnamable scent. When snow fell in huge wet lovely flakes, we built an altar to Zeus on the lawn. In spring, a sharp green newness lasted weeks, then arrived the white and lavender lilacs, made to sing about, and the immense Japanese magnolia filling the library windows. First the buds seemed so tight they almost quivered, then they splayed open, offering streaked lavender petals to the eyes of girls reading, dozing, dreaming in armchairs at the windows, in a world of their own, though not of their own making.

The weeping cherry tree outside New Hall exists in my mind's eye as the paradigm ever after for all trees. This tree was twisted and large, the limbs trailing, effulgent with white blooms. I took pictures, wishing I had the Chinese landscape painter's delicate hand instead. To stand under those blossoms looking up at the intense spring sky was a pure pleasure that never diminishes. Rena and I typed Housman's "Loveliest of Trees" and tacked it to the trunk. Every spring since, after all these years, someone repeats the gesture, that instinct for tradition at its best.

When I dream the anxiety dream, that I have not started the work and the exam is upon me and they've switched the subject anyway, the setting is Randolph-Macon. At least once a year, I'm back there for senior year and must make up all the requirements I skipped. I wince at the memory of my professor Mr. St. Vincent's remarks in the margins of my creative writing notebook: "Maenad," and "What is to become of you?" *Vita abundantior,* the Latin motto on our blazers, meant "the life more abundant." But Anne's brother on a weekend visit said, "I've been in navy barracks all over the world and this is the most depressing place I've ever seen." Sandy tried to slit her wrists. Louise broke out as soon as she got the lay of the land, a woman before her time. I was balancing. I loved my friends and my sense of the place and the traveling. Often I returned to R-M's structure with relief, sheep to the fold. There was just enough abundance to keep me attached, not enough for me to commit. No loneliness of any year has been as bad as freshman year, staring out my fifth-floor dormer window at bare trees, the river hidden, and no clue where I'd been or was going.

As soon as The Pill hit, R-M as it reigned, was lost. The truly revolutionary consequences of women having control over their own bodies kicked those date parlor doors closed, ripped up those destination slips, put those ladies in Charlottesville with their white toast, teapots, and emery-board towels out of business forever. As preservers of The Way, how wise those women who ran the school proved; they invoked tradition, grace, protection, the concept of respect, culture, decorum: all those paternal gods of undamaged goods. We were imprinted with an intricate moral code of rules, from belted bathrobes to bedtime a hundred miles away. Soon, the little wheel of pills—we will cross a great divide. Didn't those deans and dorm mothers foresee exactly, unleashed, how complicated our lives would become?

Rena and I were foolish enough to think our families would allow us to pause for a year and go to Greece. We thought we'd figure out a way to work and pay for ourselves. We wrote away for pamphlets on freighters that took passengers. The *Hellenic Destiny* would sail in July. We tucked all the brochures in our luggage as we packed for the summer break.

THE WALKING RAIN

Below the southern fall line, that place where the hard, as I imagine it, soil of the North meets the silty coastal plain I lived on, stream beds are pure white sand, so beautiful when dry—the meandering course patterned with the shimmers of flowing water. In droughts, I walk these sandy watercourses, looking for flint arrowheads and quartz crystals, which once I found in handfuls. I walk, too, for the pleasure of the fine sand under my feet, powdery soft in places, grainy as ground glass in others, and for the occasional clear pool; I am following the idea of water.

The summer after I turn twenty is the longest in the history of the world. No sign of rain. No dream of the dead, no peacock screaming, no sweat on a glass of cold water. Just chiggers and ticks. The heat has to break.

"Suffocating," people say. But really, I feel more like the turtle must in its carapace, the whole atmosphere weighing on my body, and I carry the heavy air step by step.

"It's going to be a scorcher," Daddy Jack says at breakfast every day.

"Sweltering," Fanny Brown agrees, as she breaks a raw egg into his shot of bourbon. My grandfather believes in high-octane breakfasts. He takes it in a gulp.

Willie Bell used to fix cinnamon toast and hot chocolate for me, but she's gone to the North and her kitchen's been over-taken by Fanny, a big knobby woman with skin the color of a room when the lights suddenly go out. Willie Bell's gingerbread-colored face has moved to Chicago, or is it Detroit? No one can seem to remember which, both being equidistant to the moon. "Up and left six days before the bridesmaids' luncheon Marga-ret and I were having for Dottie Richards," my mother had writ-ten to me at school. At our house, her exodus has raised what Daddy Jack calls "the Nigra Question." Frankye and I aren't in-terested. Mother thinks anybody with half sense who can walk out of Fitzgerald should. I just miss Willie Bell. She found a job cooking in a pool hall; Willie Bell, who'd specialized in the freshest lady peas, just shelled butter beans, fried tomatoes with tomato gravy, watermelon rind pickles, brown sugar muffins, pressed chicken, tarragon beans, and airy biscuits.

"She won't last up there in Yankeeland. She'll be back beg-ging for her job before Christmas," Daddy Jack predicts. "Nigras don't know when they're well off." He unfolds the *Atlanta Journal* and blessedly covers his face. We dread the news. My grandfather recently had cast the first Republican vote of his life. My mother had not. She thought John Kennedy was very attractive and Nixon's nose looked as though it were carved from a baking potato. Daddy Jack, therefore, held Mother personally responsible every time Kennedy or his "upstart fool" brother Bobby made a move. "Where do you think the nigras are getting these big ideas of theirs?" he shouted at her frequently. The words "march," "demonstration," and "freedom riders" were beginning to be heard. When he reads that Bobby *asked* the freedom riders to cool off for a while, he rails, "Why don't they have the fortitude to call out the tanks? What are tanks for?"

The head of the freedom riders, James Farmer, countered, "We have been cooling off for one hundred years. If we got any cooler, we'd be in a deep freeze."

At that, Daddy Jack rips the *Journal* in half, staring at Mother, Fanny, and me as though we'd caused the whole thing. "Fanny, you know sure as you're born, anybody who works for me, colored or white or speckled, gets a fair deal."

"Yassuh, Cap'n," she replies. They don't see her mouth twist down when she turns back to the sink.

I cross my eyes at Mother and she rolls hers. My mother looks at her arms. "My skin is on fire," she says every day. She gets hives by August and wonders what she's allergic to. Citrus. Sugar. Heat. Fanny tells her the only cure is to find a man who's never seen his own father and to have him blow in her face. Soon Mother excuses herself and heads toward the bathroom, where she has a bottle of gin hidden at the bottom of the wicker clothes basket.

. . .

Willie Bell called a few times. "You've got to come back," I'd say. "The recipe for fudge cake isn't even written down anywhere." She'd laugh. She was elusive on the subject of returning. Once she said to me, "I just had to take a chance, Miss Frances. You know nuthin' was ever going to happen down there." Within months, she'd disappeared from us forever, swallowed by the North.

I put up with Fanny's cooking. Her idea of summer vegetables is boil them to pieces with a hunk of salt pork. The barbecue practically catches fire, with sauce so hot you have to go sit in a creek. Her pound cakes always had gooey sad streaks in the middle. Bud, her husband, beat her so badly that Daddy Jack had him put in jail. I have to drive her home in the afternoons and she cries and asks me to go by the jeweler's so she can pay a dollar on a layaway Bible for her son, also in the penitentiary. Alarming to have two family members locked up. She lives in a square house, the boards gone shiny with age, near Willie Bell's old place. What had her son done? She won't say. What she does say as we pull up is, "I hear tell Willie Bell's doin' fine up there. You can bet your bottom dollar Willie Bell won't be back." She doesn't quite slam the back door.

"Hey, Fanny, you think I'm thrilled to be here in the garden spot of the South?" I tease her, and I don't say I worry about when Bud gets out of jail. When I let her out she always stops to water her scraggly purple petunias growing in rusty cans on the front porch.

It was bad enough to be imprisoned in Fitzgerald; my

college friends found jobs as waitresses in exotic places such as Ogunquit, Maine, or Yellowstone National Park. Daddy Jack would not allow me to work at something "ridiculous" like that. "A waste of time. You study Greek, of all things, and you want to wait on tables for people who have no manners at all?" He was similarly enlightened about scholarships: They were fine for people who did not object to welfare, which he did. No one in our family was going on the dole. I just leaned on my fist and stared at him when he went on and on. From excerpts I'd read in Philosophy 101 at Randolph-Macon, Marx was dead on, I thought, about the idiocy of rural life. I knew better than to quote Marx. I tuned out everyone on the home front.

But I did come home. I knew he would not send me to college except on his terms and I didn't want to end up as a clerk in the dime store selling nasty pond slider turtles all my life. I was supposed to do what, languish at home polishing my toenails and going to bridal showers? Read one thousand books? He didn't seem to approve of anything, especially any boyfriend.

My last two years of college were coming up. What did I plan to do? All I desired was to go to Greece. I frequently consulted the tonnage, Libyan crew, and the other information on the freighter *Elysian Fields* until Daddy Jack saw the pamphlet on the table and tore it up. "You'll find out, young lady, that the world is under your nose."

Under his nose was Drew, our yardman, who had to cut Daddy Jack's toenails when they got long enough to curve down and click on the floor. Fanny came over with the broom to sweep up the curls of horny yellow clippings that looked like curls of old wax or buzzard talons.

My only goal was to memorize poems. I cauterized the memory of my recent lost romance with John Donne's Holy Sonnets. I copied them on index cards and stuck them around my dressing table mirror. While I daubed Sortilege perfume on my pulse points, rubbed my gleaming just-shaven legs with baby oil, plucked three tiny hairs from between my eyebrows, outlined my lips with the sable lip brush, I repeated over and over, "I am a little world made cunningly. . . ." and:

> *At the round earth's imagined corners, blow*
> *Your trumpets, Angels, and arise, arise*
> *From death, you numberless infinities*
> *Of souls, and to your scattered bodies go*

It was the time of Donne and Dostoyevsky, Lawrence, Keats, and Yeats. All the books I'd charged at the Randolph-Macon bookstore, and Daddy Jack had sputtered over, now stood in the heavy revolving bookcase in my bedroom, my name on each flyleaf and black ink underlining the significant parts. I read for six or seven hours a day. "Would you get off that bed so I can make it up?" Fanny huffed. "*Do* something!" my mother shouted. I looked at them from Russia or New York or Spain.

Early in the summer, I'd fallen in love. Paul was Anne's older brother. I'd met him twice before I visited her in New Orleans, but he'd never noticed me among the throng of friends we traveled in. Brilliant like Anne, he finished college at twenty and now, at twenty-three, was just out of the navy, where he'd been a jet pilot. Also, he was engaged. His fiancée sailed for Europe in June. When school ended, Anne visited me in Fitzgerald, then we took the Southern Crescent to New Orleans.

We love the train, the long hours of confidences. Someday we'll take a train from Moscow to Novosibirsk, reading Chekhov aloud and eating cold potatoes with chugs of vodka. For now, shuttling through Alabama, we discuss what we want on our tombstones. Anne decides on lines from Swinburne's "The Garden of Proserpine":

> *From too much love of living,*
> *From hope and fear set free,*
> *We thank with brief thanksgiving*
> *Whatever gods may be*
> *That no life lives forever;*
> *That dead men rise up never;*
> *That even the weariest river*
> *Winds somewhere safe to sea.*

A bit dreary, I thought, but Anne was Roman Catholic; that explained it. I liked Lawrence's "Moonrise":

> *. . . beauty is a thing beyond the grave,*
> *That perfect, bright experience never falls*
> *To nothingness, and time will dim the moon*
> *Sooner than our full consummation here*
> *In this odd life will tarnish or pass away.*

The Magic Mountain gets us across Mississippi.

Anne told me she had a summer job in her father's office, but that she really had to go to work while I was visiting stunned me. At first I lounged around in her room, reading all day and copying Rilke and Larkin quotes in a notebook. After a few days, Paul asked me to go to the French Quarter to his favorite bar, Café Lafitte in Exile. It rained just after noon, when the heat hit the unbearable point, rained just enough to steam the streets. We talked books. We ran from bar to bar and sat in doorways getting wet. He looked like the photos of the young Hemingway, and I'd heard he got smashed with a friend at the officers' club and took a navy plane up without permission. They landed it with the wheels half up, laughing and oblivious to the rage that greeted them. So Lawrentian, his black curls and terse humor. We began to go out every afternoon. Some of the bars opened into rainy green courtyards. Strangers began to make remarks, "Ain't love the damnedest thing?" and "Enjoy it while it lasts." One bartender translated a sign in Italian: Love makes time pass; time makes love pass.

Now when Anne came home at five, it was plain that I had not been bored and waiting for her. No one said anything because the family was wild about the fiancée. Lovely girl. Sweet and innocent. Sweethearts since she was twelve or something. I thought I should go home.

My mother called and asked if I'd worn out my welcome. Paul inched behind me in the hall and whispered, lips against my ear, "Don't go. I want you to stay."

Anne arranges a blind date for me for her friend Ginger's party. A chartered bus drops us at her house across the lake where we walk up the oak alley behind a band playing "Saints." Soft-shelled crab gives me the creeps to eat and the lake bottom feels mushy and dark to my feet. My date looks down on dancing, probably because he can't, and just wants to talk all night about Dorothy Sayers's sense of religion. Somehow we are home early. Anne has a late date with Jimmie and they ask Paul and me to go listen to jazz. We bar hop, laughing all night. Just at dawn we drive to the river and Paul and I walk along the levee. Mythic river, the ruined plantations with oak alleys, the lilt and roll of Mark Twain, the brown swirling color of an old meandering looping wide river. A big gold sun hoisting out of the dark spreads munificent light over the Mississippi. He picks wild blue morning glories and strings them in my hair then slowly leans to me, so slowly that time seems to wind down and suspend. We kiss, then again. After all the kissing I'd done, this was the first time I felt passion like knockout drops. Like in books. Ecstasy, the word "ecstasy." So it's true. Kisses that I feel along the backs of my legs, in the hairs on my arms. "This is not the last time, hear?" Down the levee, I sense Anne's shocked face. What will happen?

As we turn in the driveway at six thirty, Anne and Paul's father in his bathrobe, a workday coming up, walks outside to pick up the newspaper. He looks at us with eyes hard as nickels and does not speak, just slaps the *Picayune* against his thigh and walks inside.

I sleep until two. Anne staggers out to work early, practically whimpering with fatigue. When I wake up, Anne's mother is out. I wash my hair and put on a straight black skirt, striped blouse, and a red belt that shows how small my waist is. I try not to remember overhearing Paul ask Anne when I first arrived, "Is your friend old enough to drive yet?" In front of the full-length mirror, I dance the way we danced last night. So sexy, his tight turns. *I* think I look twenty-one. He can really dance; they don't know anything in Fitzgerald. Paul is reading in the living room. He tells me he's looked in the bedroom four times to see me sleep. He says he can't break his engagement. I am too interesting, unspoiled. He loves her. Could he read *The Hound of Heaven* to me? He can't understand how he's become attracted to his little sister's friend. He wants to show Lisbon to me and a small village somewhere in Spain. His fiancée is the sweetest person imaginable. Shall we go to the Quarter now?

That live current in the air, no one escapes. Even dogs and cats feel it. Looking at him is more satisfactory than talking to most people. Holding hands, I'm conscious in my tendons, hair, shoulders, of exquisite happiness. His *hand*! Even looking at the rain together feels like an event. The house is zinging, this Catholic-to-the-core house, where the Latin words for "guilt" and "responsibility" should be emblazoned on the family crest in the foyer. When Anne comes home, I hear whispering in the kitchen. Will she defend us? She, the soul of justice, feels confused and righteous at the same time. The fiancée is her friend, too, poor thing off in Vienna with a busload of Newcomb girls. How *could* Paul?

I wear to the country club dance a white eyelet dress with a ribbon sash woven of three deepening shades of red velvet: rose, scarlet, burgundy. Paul is not a boy, I realize. He has an edge I like; he's complex *enough*, and gorgeous, in a dark way, a movie star from my mother's era. We dance under the enormous chandelier until no one else is dancing. As I look up at him, brilliant shards of light whirl behind his head. The night blooms, deep tropical night I've always loved, as fragrant as the word "frangipani," with a breeze the same temperature as flushed skin. Even Paris, I think, couldn't be better. We drive to three a.m. fishermen's mass in the cathedral then order beignets and chicory coffee at dawn. The gray air and lambent light of the French Quarter gives the iron balconies and faded pastel walls, and even the people, a tawny sepia tone.

Anne is torn. Her boyfriend tells her not to worry; everyone has a last fling. We all decide to go to Lake Pontchartrain because I'd never been on carnival rides. In Fitzgerald, they were always breaking, leaving someone stranded for hours on top of a rickety Ferris wheel. Anne looks annoyed when I scream on the swings that throw us out with such strong centrifugal force that I fear we'll be flung into the lake. Paul, a pilot, after all, laughs.

We ride the streetcar named Desire, walk in Audubon Park. We order turtle soup and play gin on rainy afternoons at the country club. We try mile-high ice cream pie in an old hotel, dine at Antoine's with the Maxwells, Paul's knee pressing mine while his father inquires what the news is from our little world traveler.

After driving the Maxwells home, we find a bar near Tulane. Paul alone, dance floor dark and cool, the smell of beer and— what?—something sweet, damp gardenias, heartbreaker, that song, wherever you're going, I'm going your way, two drifters, that's what we wanted, just drift off, read Russian novels aloud to each other forever. Then kissing in the car, sliding down, rubbing our faces hard together. Good animals, *soul*, though. I want to say *I want*, so this is giving, giving. I never have. "I don't know about you all." Anne opens the car door. "But tonight I have to get to bed. These hours are getting ridiculous."

Everyone's asleep at the house and she tiptoes down the hall while we stand in the living room doorway. All quiet, except for the cool whir of the air conditioner. I almost can feel Mr. and Mrs. Maxwell's breathing in their room just a wall away. "Wait here," Paul whispers. He comes back with a bottle of wine. "I bought this in Portugal. I was planning to have it on my wedding night." He opens the bottle and pours. Our eyes hold. Imagine such brown eyes; I've always liked green or blue. I take a sip and he kisses me, pressing his tongue into my mouth, and I give him the wine in mine. He drinks and I take his wine. We're falling into the down sofa. Grace of dissolving time, boundaries, the bloodstream a brush fire started by children. I want to pull him so close that our bodies absorb each other. He lies on top of me and through our summer clothes I feel the entire velocity of his body on mine, feel our bright holy skin, a swarming fierce right. "Love," I say. "Love." We begin to laugh; he licks my face, throat. His hands, my blouse, over. "I always knew it," he whispers. "I can love this way. I'm going to be the one to teach you everything there is to know about passion. I'm going to make love to you for the rest of my life."

The next day, three letters with big foreign stamps arrive from Italy, Austria. Anne, with particularly aulic posture, I think from my pillow, leaves for work without waking me to make a plan for later. Mrs. Maxwell is cordial but looks troubled. I call the Southern Crescent for the schedule to Georgia.

En route home, I stop in Atlanta. I have a sudden wild idea that I will not go home. I will not go to college. If he was going to marry what's-her-name, I'll just take off for . . . where? My sister Nancy picks me up at the Peachtree station. At her house, I look in the want ads and see that TWA is hiring stewardesses. I should fly like Paul. The next morning I go downtown to a hotel suite where a lot of girls wait in the hall. We're all weighed and measured and some are dismissed. At five foot four, 108 pounds, I'm afraid I am fat but I pass. I think of Rome and the little house where Keats died, the Pyramids, Ireland, the blue waters of Greece; the interviewer talks about evacuation procedures, safety chutes, loss of cabin pressure—a training program somewhere in the Midwest, then six months of routes starting in Des Moines or Kansas. I see myself in slow motion, emptying trays in people's laps. "Why do you want to fly?" "To see the world," I answer, thinking of Paul in the navy. How soon can I start? The interviewer looks raw somehow, and his Adam's apple dips and rises. Planes taking off make me sick, especially if the pilot banks so steeply that I look sideways down at the receding red clay earth. I want to read Chaucer in Middle English. I don't want to be a stewardess, even if I eventually can go to Europe that way. I want to go to Paris in black, with sandals, and big sunglasses, and write on a tiny iron table in the Tuileries while little boys with French maids sail toy boats. I flee.

In August, no one is reasonable, if anyone ever was. If it rains, it's over too fast to cool anything down. The only thing that comes down is heat; heat descends in sheets. Always the rain begins as a trapezoid of gray lines slanting against the horizon. I watch it "walk" across the field, pushing cool air toward me, until surprisingly warm, it hits, a hard pelting. I lie in the grass and let it soak through me. In August, my skin feels permeable. The sky cracks, lightning darts down so close I instinctively draw back. Then more rain. Just as quickly, it stops and the sun makes an angry comeback, pulling clouds off the hot streets, wilting the dresses of ladies who have risen from their naps, blistering the glaring white sides of houses. The rain, for all I know, walks somewhere else, walks all over the South.

To get away, I drive out to Crystal Lake. Local legend says it's the devil's winter home.

As I lower myself into the water, I forget if I am hot or cold. My feet feel the sandy bottom until I find the cold springs, spurting pure as Easter water. I am so cold I was never hot before; I was always ice.

To swim, as a child again. Like one of the brown and violet fish, the deepwater gars that look as if they oozed up from prehistory. I let myself be the fish. The soul is a swimming animal. Let it scrape the bottom; let it grow gills. The soul, flagrant and fishy. Let the cool mud settle. For there is no great dog in the heavens, only an abstract constellation, and who will connect the fiery dots? Let the soul somersault in clean water. Let me be still, a long amphora under water since the seventh century BC; let me be buoyant. Let me swim a psalm.

I climb out in my cleanest skin, burning with cold, and taste the sun all over.

The summer I was ten, I asked Willie Bell what "dog days" meant. "It means dogs go mad from the heat and run us up and down the street, foaming at the mouth." But that was in childhood on the sweltering back porch where the lattice cut the sun to bits. "This time of year, you better watch out." I was keeping Willie Bell company while she shelled butterbeans into a brown bag, keeping quiet while Mother and her friends played bridge in the dining room. We could hear the shuffling of cards and the click of ice in their tea glasses. Mother's friend Marion was back home from Asheville where she went for shock treatments almost every August when the year got to be just too much. "Bulldogs are the worst. They sink their teeth in your leg and they won't let go till it thunders. Just like snappin' turtles."

Marion never forgot a card, could bid baby slams and make them all the time; Mother said her forgetting had nothing to do

with diamonds and hearts. The treatments just erased life's un-
pleasant moments. Unless they singed you with too many volts,
then everything went haywire; you could lose the whole Spanish language, if you ever knew it. When Willie Bell and I took
in the chilled plates of frozen fruit salad, I saw Marion looking
at little rolls of paper she took out of her purse. Willie Bell told
me she saw *Amy, Harper,* the names of Marion's children, and
4469, her own telephone number, her address, and where she
was born. Mother said that was all there was to it. She said the
treatments were like reshuffling the cards after the hand. Our
dog Tish lay near the cool brick foundation all day, tongue dripping. Dog days; Willie Bell said if one bites you, you'll foam at
the mouth, too.

Cicadas, the deep end of summer, this is how night sounds
when it breathes. Looked at one way, there is much madness.
The chthonic spirits have it in for my family. Or do they, like
the Greek gods, create mischief to entertain themselves? I want
this part of my life to be over. Enough.

Out of the absolute fullness of nothing to do, on Wednesday
nights I go to the country club with Frankye and Daddy Jack.
Michael Wright, the only boy my age whose parents are members, always turns up there, too. "Well, Mayes, you're gracing
us with your presence. How about giving me a little sugar?"
He pushes out his cheek, and I give him a big pink-pursed-lips
kiss, which he wipes off with a handkerchief. Michael is polite
to all the adults, each of whom he hits with a mocking remark

as soon as he or she walks away. "Notice how Ellen had her sweater turned over her arm so we could see the J. P. Allen label?" I'd noticed. She tells us how beautiful, how handsome we are, asks about college, how we are enjoying the summer, and Michael says we are both going insane and she says how nice and drifts on.

He and I have known each other since we were born. At thirteen, his parents sent him away to a boys' school in north Georgia, the only person in memory to escape so early. This made his old friends uneasy. He must be a sissy; something must be wrong. David was his best friend, and Michael's high school girlfriend was my best friend. Our old loves probably are at the drive-in with dates right now, struggling around on sweaty vinyl seats. Over the years of our parents' friendship and our double dating, we have a habit of saying absolutely anything to each other.

We load our plates with ham, corn, potato salad, and hard rolls at the buffet and take our plates and iced tea out by the pool. No one else leaves the air-conditioned dining room. I hike up my dress and sit with my feet on the first step under water. Hot piney air and a great moon, which must radiate heat, too. Only the wet calls of the pond frogs cool the air. Both of us still half-think we'll marry our old loves. We've been to college in other states but, even so, the idea that we can actually leave Fitzgerald forever, simply invent a new life, doesn't have a firm hold. We're rooted down to the tap here, both of us. He has the powerful pull of his grandfather's, father's building supply business. I have Daddy Jack constantly telling me these are the best days of my life and I'm in for a rude awakening. I have Frankye, too. She's a fox gnawing through her own limbs but won't get free. She keeps to her own vatic litany, "This is the end of the earth. There's one road in and one road out. We are at the end of the earth." I'm sure Michael will stay; I'm sure I won't.

"Heard you had a little fling in New Orleans," he begins. "Is there a deflowering scene?"

"Oh, sure. Would that there were. Just some inspired groping." I keep chewing the salty, undercured ham and lower my eyelashes mysteriously. Like a creek spilling its banks, a memory surge flashes. Paul breathing on my face, my arms wrapped around him, the word "love" brimming over me.

"Is he rich? I'm sure Daddy Jack's first question was what his old man does, right?"

I tell him I haven't heard from Paul since I came home, except for one note I memorized: "When I think how I'd like to spend my life, it is with you. Great sunset clouds at evening, rose, pink, and for Frances blue. A sky clean with light over the river. Thoughts of you, always beautiful. My love, Paul."

"Pretty juicy, Mayes."

"Michael, how do you see yourself in five years?"

"In cords from Abercrombie's, hitting the links," he says in falsetto voice. "You're serious? Christ-ola, I don't know, not in this godforsaken place. Oh, I don't know, what if you'd . . . Hey, they're shaking up the corn for bingo. Big night at the Fitz CC." There, he hasn't quite said it again. We each wish, in a fleeting way, that we'd fall in love. Wouldn't our parents be thrilled? We've sat in his mama's black Cadillac a few times and kissed arduously, but neither of us ever felt inspired.

Through the glass wall we see our families and their friends laughing and settling down with their cards. Harmon Griffin calls out, "Under the O, seventy-five." Everyone pays; the winner takes the proceeds. That's not the only kind of gambling. In the bar, which has no windows, illegal slot machines line the walls. Daddy Jack buys a stack of silver dollars. No one minds that Michael and I sit in the bar. Mother wanders in from bingo after a while; she can take only so much. Late, the bar gets smoky and loud. I'm long past ready to go. Michael's sensible parents leave early and I'm left to wait for Daddy Jack and Mother to exhaust whatever it is that drives them. By the time we go, almost everyone has long since abandoned the place. Mother and I stop at the ladies', then follow Daddy Jack through the pines to his green Oldsmobile. He sways like an Easter Island stone on wheels. Too many stingers. We see him take out the keys then open the back door and get in. "Look at the old fool," my mother says. Tipsy herself, she grabs my arm. We watch him groping, then poking the back of the seat, searching for the ignition. "Where does he think the steering wheel is?" I shout. We start laughing and can't stop. We're shrieking, doubled over. We knock on his window. "You're in the backseat! The backseat!"

"God damn it, why don't they put some lights out here?" He harrumphs to the front and careens out the drive onto 129. Three miles of utterly straight road home. This time he keeps it between the ditches.

At home, all silent, I take my lotion out of the refrigerator and soothe my whole body with the chilly jasmine fragrance. Where will I be? The icy voice of a night bird spumes out of the pecan trees. I play Ravel, galloping an Andalusian pony through the music, my cape flying, across dusky heath toward Barcelona. Do they have heaths in Spain? Why do the cicadas sing together? I am twelve but I am twenty. Writing in my blank book, I am but I am not. I copy:

Thou my sacred solitude
thou art as rich and clean and wide
as an awakening garden.
My sacred solitude thou—
hold shut the golden doors
before which wishes wait.

RILKE

I write letters, placing a lined sheet beneath the thin blue paper to keep my writing from slanting upward like a nine-year-old's. I am waiting for the fiancée to return so Paul will tell her. I am waiting to hear that Paul will marry at Christmas. I write a sonnet entitled "Preface" about rain in the Quarter, drumming the iambs on my knee. I read about eternal return in a philosophy book. Everything, philosophers have thought since the Greeks, will come back again, exactly as it is. And what is happening has already happened hundreds of times. A fated plot. My time, the Holocaust raging as I was born, the Fitzgerald Purple Hurricane football team's number thirty-five standing out on the field under the misty lights, gigantic bombs on the Japs, my mother's camellias in winter, our street islands a dogwood fairyland in spring. Each blossom and blast coming around again in ten thousand years? My mother, a star losing

her heat. How slowly the dead subside. My father, igneous still—
Such a rainy night in Georgia . . .

What, in all this, is *will*? I know I have that, I feel the force
of it in my chest humming like an electrical tower in a cotton
field. *Will*, yes, but *to power*? *Yes. It's raining all over the world.*

Time for the back-to-school dream. I have not bought the
book, the exam is today, the teacher is speaking another language, where is my blue book, my number two pencil, what
is the subject everyone else is so intent on? I am in the wrong
class, perhaps the wrong cosmos.

TO FLORIDA

We're sprung. Rena and I haul boxes to the second floor. From the porch, we overlook a row of seven mighty magnolias. Ours is the apartment on the end—living room, bedroom, bath, and kitchen. "Can you believe this?" we ask each other over and over. Frankye finds blue and lavender carpet remnants and brings chairs. Rena arrives with lamps, pillows, and pans. We paint the bedroom lavender, with dangling bunches of grapes at each corner of the ceiling. We hang posters by Picasso, a castle in Austria, and bright paintings by Rena's mother. The small closet and chest of drawers from a thrift shop bulge with our clothes. As soon as we plug in the stereo, we turn up "The Great Pretender," "Only the Lonely," and the theme from *A Summer Place.*

Half the class transferred from the lovely woman's college at the end of sophomore year. In spite of the contemplation, intellectual challenge, friendships, the glorious Virginia seasons . . .

enough was enough. For many, the sense that an active world zoomed by the gates of the redbrick wall became too strong. We went off to big universities, Texas, LSU, North Carolina, and Florida. Some married. I didn't have much choice. Daddy Jack said, "You have your head in the clouds, young lady, and I'm not paying a cent for you to waste any more of your time. You can go to Georgia or nowhere." Two years "up north," and no husband in sight. And I'd brought up the idea of the freighter to Greece. He was explosively mad. He mopped his bald head with a Kleenex, leaving damp white balls in the remaining hairs. "And put a smile in your voice when you speak to me," he added.

But I had taken none of the requirements for Georgia and the admissions office remained unimpressed with my Roman drama, creative writing, dramatic interpretation, and Greek etymology courses. The University of Florida was more lenient and allowed me to transfer if I doubled back for intro classes such as Florida history, phys ed, logic, and a couple of Western civilization courses. Daddy Jack agreed. Gainesville was only three hours from home. "Rena, you've got to go with me!" I called her in Birmingham. She hadn't decided what to do about fall. Her family, too, nixed the Greece plan. At the last minute, miraculously, we were admitted to the University of Florida.

After Frankye hangs café curtains for us, she drives on to visit my oldest sister and her family farther south in central Florida. I'd been there many times since my sister Barbara married when

I was eleven. I love the hazy division between water and land, where the big-horned white Brahman bulls flicked their tails and cooled off, like visions from India, and stalky white birds looked perpetually startled while balancing on one pink leg. In the sandy soil, you can sometimes kick up a shark's tooth from when the land was under the sea. Frankye likes Florida, too, and forgets to drink excessively when she's there. If she permanently escaped, would she evade that scorpion roaming through her head? Couldn't she find a job there—flower arranger at the yacht club, housemother at the college—and a cottage covered in bougainvillea? She stays several weeks this time, playing bridge, shopping, and helping my sister with her three children. When she passes back through Gainesville, she throws out one plan after another. Bring Rena home for Thanksgiving. Let's go to Atlanta. This summer, the beach. She's in love with Florida colors and thinks she'll paint our house in Fitzgerald Bermuda-sand pink. She scratches off, waving out the window, beeping the horn till she turns the corner.

We have long ID numbers and make-up core classes with hundreds. We meet dozens of foreign students. The Caribbean boys teach us how Latins dance without moving the tops of their bodies; with the fraternity boys we learn to twist and to sip Scotch although we don't really like it. We cook spaghetti and Rena brings home Mustapha from Libya and Tyge, a thin Dane with a great laugh. I meet sophisticated Gary from Palm Beach and mysterious Joseph from Miami and Buzz, who takes me

shell hunting on Sanibel Island, where Ponce de León supposedly breathed his last after failing to find the fountain of youth.

Cruel, we occasionally call friends who stayed at Randolph-
Macon and let them know we've had five dates that week. We no
longer have strict rules to hamper us but we also no longer have
their protection. No handy excuse of curfew for boring dates or
difficult situations. At our place, the rousing Russian army chorus and the Academic Festival overture we keep turned up loud.
We put glasses to the wall and listen to the newlyweds next door
squealing and bouncing. We roast a turkey and don't know to
take the package of neck and gizzard out of the cavity. We thaw
frozen vegetables, mix frozen orange juice, fry hamburgers. At
R-M, we'd pledged sororities, but here we ignore groups of girls
and, instead, easily meet boys in classes. They seemed exotic,
coming from such evocative places as Lauderdale, Coral Gables,
Sarasota, Clearwater, Tarpon Springs, Tampa, Ocala. We are in
paradise. We are living the life of exiles welcomed home to the
large banquet of freedom. I can *go* from here. For the first time
ever, nothing is clamping me down. Like exiles, we are charged
and challenged. As we walk out of our apartment every morning, we feel as if live sparks fly away from our bodies.

I always have loved Florida. A million trees shade Gainesville. Moss-draped oaks feel right to me, the way trees ought
to be. Giant azaleas ("a ghastly pink," Frankye says) banking
the houses, palms, dogwoods, scraggly grass in sandy soil—the
atmosphere immediately feels like home. The wind through

pines, yes, but I love more the sweet breeze rattling the palms, and the habit they have of thrusting upward, unfurling green as fronds die below. I walk the few blocks to campus, taking different routes just to feel the comfort of trees and the houses built low, as if to stay close to cool ground. Cracker cottages, small brick ranches with jalousied breezeways, miniature Tudors, and gracious white-painted houses with screened porches and long windows—I imagine the lives inside, almost can slip in and take up residence. Someone told me that a lady left her back door open while she was hanging out the wash, and came back in to find an alligator in her kitchen. Nature, I read in Tennyson, "red in tooth and claw"—that's the far South, the scrubby, steaming, flat far South.

Rena starts dating an older graduate student in herpetology. "That's snakes," I say. "He's a snake handler?" But no, he's interested in some unsung salamander. There are plenty of impressive reptiles of every stripe and venom around here. She brings home the boyfriend and he's different, a grown-up who has been in the army and knows what he wants. Rena clearly is part of the plan. I sense that he thinks I'm a bad influence, since he would like to see Rena become more practical. When they go on collecting trips to swamps, she seems fascinated. I drive with them outside town to Paynes Prairie, what William Bartram called "the great Alachua Savannah" in 1774. Once a lake, the vast expanse suddenly drained in the late 1800s, leaving a steamboat stranded high and dry, and a marshy home for creatures, even for wild horses left by Hernando de Soto. (Why were the Spanish conquistadors always abandoning horses?) A fact of the southern landscape: Limestone foundations can collapse suddenly, leaving circular *bottomless* lakes. Or, a plug can open and a lake can disappear just as mysteriously, leaving prairie and a great expanse for sky. Sun, rain, evening, dawn—the aurous light ripples over the subtly changing grasses. If I were a landscape painter I would sit on a hummock with my brushes and hope the nuanced russet, sage, dun, and gold might seep into the canvas.

A raised narrow road, bullet-straight, crosses the flat, wide-sky prairie. In the heat the asphalt shimmers as though it wants to turn into water. After a storm, hundreds of snakes seeking higher ground slither up onto the road. As we drive across, we can't help but run over dozens. We pause and roll down the windows. Among arm-thick, five-foot writhers, we see the brilliant slender coral snakes. Scarlet, yolk-yellow, black—the pattern of color tells if it can kill you. Red and black, the rhyme goes, friend of Jack. Red and yellow, kill a fellow. But who's stopping long enough to see whether black abuts red?

Daddy Jack up and dies. As soon as Frankye hangs up the phone, my first thought is *Now she will be all right*. Frankye had prefaced her explanation of his death by, "Now, I don't want you to think I had anything to do with it." Why would she begin that way if she hadn't?

Daddy Jack's house, The House, burned. A neighbor found

him in shock, clinging to the monumental magnolia tree in his front yard. Daddy Jack died in two days, just stopped, with no apparent physical cause. Shock, all the newspaper articles lauding his life would repeat. Several stiff drinks probably caused him to fall into a little nap in his chair, where supposedly, his cigarette fell and started the blaze. No doubt he woke with a shock, found himself outside, watching flames rise in the windows of the house his father-in-law built for him and Mother Mayes, his Fanny, in 1906.

Another story quickly forms in my mind. *Red and yellow, kill a fellow.*

Earlier in the evening Daddy Jack and Frankye had supper at the Fitzgerald Country Club, and then stopped at our house for a few nightcaps. I know the bitter water mixed into each drink they shared. My mother was sick of his sour tyranny. "He has a mean streak," she repeated, and I pictured a broad yellow swath down his hairy back. Because my father never was truly well after his heroic act, and because he was the favorite boy, even though he often was a bad boy, and because my parents used all their money for my father's long illness, and because my father neglected to renew his insurance policy when he knew he was dying, Daddy Jack had by now "taken care" of us for six years. With a constant reference to the lack of appreciation he received (a drone that echoed my father's "You all think I am *made* out of money"), he doled out the cash that paid the bills at our house. Frankye, like a child reminding the parent of an allowance, had to ask for everything each week. I wanted a warm grandfather who genuinely cared about us. Instead, D.J. the D.J., as I called him (to his nonamusement), only criticized. He didn't like it that I wanted to go out with boys all the time ("Party, party, that's all you think of"). But he didn't like it that I liked to read six or eight books a week, either ("Lift your eyes off that book and you'll see life is not a bed of roses"). I was not allowed to work because it was "beneath" me, or to apply for a scholarship because "we don't take handouts," but at the same time I liked clothes too much. I was vain, frivolous, too serious, impractical, smart-mouthed. (Probably all true.) My mother's flimsy attempts to get a job were ridiculed. While Daddy Jack infantilized her, at the same time he resented her dependence. For the few months she commuted to South Georgia State College in Douglas, taking English 1A and trying to think of something she could do to get out of her financial situation, Daddy Jack denied she had a problem, and constantly made fun of "the college girl." The dark undercurrent was his sexual attraction to my mother, his favorite son's lovely wife. My mother used his attraction for her own purposes and hated him for it.

Is it my impotence that provokes the imaginary action now? Did I want her to burn his house?

In this fantasy, it's late and Frankye sends him home. Reeling a little, she changes to her red flats and walks the two blocks from our house to his. With no moon, the house looms large and solitary against the dark. She sees his profile in the window as he nods in his armchair. She lets herself in the always-unlocked back door and silently passes through the kitchen and dining room. As she leans into the living room, she hears him snorting in sleep. The yellowing chintz draperies, not changed since Mother Mayes died, hang stiffly with old dust. She glances out the window. No one. She strikes a match and touches it to the printed coral and pink roses. Immediately, a blaze erupts. She slips out the back door, down the alley to Roanoke Drive, and then turns back toward Lemon Street, throwing the match in the Arnolds's yard. By the time the sirens start, she is at home in her nightgown, sipping a bit of Southern Comfort, or so I imagine.

My sister from Lakeland drives by Gainesville and we head toward Fitz to Daddy Jack's funeral. "Do you think Mother set Daddy Jack's house on fire?"

My sister keeps her eyes on the road north. "Don't be ridiculous."

"Didn't Big Mama's house burn, too, that weird house in Vidalia?"

"I don't remember and I don't want to remember." She turns up the radio and I slump down, pretending to fall asleep. Perhaps the fire did spread from his fallen cigarette, and my mother remains innocent. Big Mama's weird house on Franklin Street did burn mysteriously long before I was born. And Big Mama's mother's house—I recall that sepia photograph taken on the porch where the big family squints into the light, with Big Mama in glasses holding a baby.

Frankye in white sits on the bottom step, a little flame. Later the house will burn. The matriarch, Big Mama's mother, Catherine, looks stony. I've wondered if she, too, was capable of a rant or two. Why all the fire? My aunt Mary said the burning house in Vidalia was the last thing Big Mama saw clearly before her eyesight dimmed. Did she start the fire, too?

Do we have an inheritance of fire, the same way we all got her waxy skin? In winter our too-white legs turn the pale green of cut turnips. Frankye's identity is housebound. Never able to convince Daddy to buy the big house she wanted, she coveted The House. Not, as for me, hills, pines, streams, rivers, but for

her wax, silk, canopies, silver, paint. She likes a gardenia, as I do, beside her bed. (*Baked from the same flour.*) For every drapery a cornice; for every plate a mat. A paper napkin never touches our lips. *Not as long as I'm in the mill business.* She draws patterns for needlepoint chair bottoms, serves quail with grits soufflé. When I was little she monogrammed my dimity doll dresses with the tiny cursive initials of the dolls' names, Amanda Anne Mayes, Baby Girl Mayes. She has a sofa that looks as though Napoléon should perch on it, covered and re-covered. She collects hand-painted *Gone with the Wind* lamps, even though we all tell her they're corny. Turn the doll upside down and the other pops out. It stands to reason that she'd want to destroy The House.

We cross into Georgia. The leaning oaks and pines trailing their moss in swamp water are romantic from a distance. Up close the exposed branches twist out like arms and legs. Frankye, a floating island, roots dangling. Bald cypress stumps look like burned people standing in black water, with sun-polished knees sticking up. Trees rising on their own reflections. They are wrong and beautiful at once.

As soon as we're home, I ask Frankye if she set the house on fire. She laughs but will not answer. My grandfather always said he would leave us my father's fourth of his estate. So, my sisters also believe, Mother can begin her life again. She'll go to Charleston for bridge tournaments, move to Atlanta and meet someone fascinating. I will go to Paris and write poetry. We feel the enormous lift of this Dickensian presence from our lives, a feeling that will prove to be temporary when his lawyer reveals the will to the whole assembled family.

Daddy Jack's will was read in the lawyer's office. As promised, my father's share came to Frankye, but with a hitch. My mother will have only the small income on her portion of the estate during her lifetime; my sisters and I will inherit the bundle of money upon her death. Diabolically, or shrewdly, he put my mother in the same position he had been in: *We*, he thought, would be waiting for her to die so we could collect.

There was a good-bye to me, too. A list of subtractions from our inheritance was read out in detail—expenditures Daddy Jack made that he did not approve of. Among them, my telephone calls to boys at several fraternity houses at Emory, Tulane, and Florida State. "$2.37, call to Jimbo Taylor, $3.11 to Carter

Thibodaux, $6.80 to David Willcox." He'd listed the minutes and time of day. My casual use of the telephone always drove Daddy Jack mad. I squeezed my hands together to keep from laughing. No one among the gathered relatives in black smiled, not even my aunt Mary Helen, who had Daddy Jack's number.

No math whiz, Frankye knew right away that interest on one-fourth of the estate was not going to support us, much less send her on bridge cruises to the Caribbean. He had far less money than anyone thought, and everything was invested in the most conservative stocks. No provision was made for my "worthless" college expenses. Hey, Daddy, so much for taking a bullet for him! Larkin has a poem in which someone realizes he is ugly, unappealing, and no one ever will love him. "Useful to get that learned," he concludes. Daddy Jack's retort from the grave remains: You never know what someone silently stores up against you. Useful to get that learned.

D.J. the D.J., with that annoying habit of the dead, took a long time to cool off.

My father's sister and one brother both have endless money but no one offers any help. My other uncle, always financed by Daddy Jack, recently has cleaned up his life and become a teetotaler, although he maintains that he "hasn't had a lick of fun since."

Clearly Mother could do the same, according to Hazel.

"Moral failure," she murmurs. "Really, she's an embarrassment and should get control of herself." Yes, that's rational. Rational doesn't count with Frankye, but no one sees that. I've been smoldering mad at her for years. But I am whacked by her helpless bad luck. "Your parents owe you nothing," my rich uncle says. Yes, not even love. Family. Those who hang you out to dry.

My mother has been the chief hostess of the family. What galls her most is all the times these aunts and uncles, who now look at us as though we exist at a great distance, over-ate at our laden table. The whole family had made fun of Hazel, who inquired at dinner what's for supper that night. My uncle buys an immense chandelier for the Presbyterian church. He sometimes invites us to use his houses at Highlands and Daytona Beach. Hazel keeps her kitchen as a storeroom and eats out at every meal, though that has become difficult for her since integration started to hit Miami. She keeps a warehouse for her clothes. Charity begins somewhere else, not at home. My mother and I are two flies in amber. Hazel buys The House, what's left of it, for almost nothing, and that little windfall from our one quarter sustains Frankye and me for the moment.

No one seemed to want it, so I drove back to Gainesville in Daddy Jack's green Oldsmobile '98. I collected forty-seven parking tickets.

. . .

Money or not, Daddy Jack's removal blesses the air. I can breathe. Gertrude Stein said, "As everybody knows, fathers are depressing but our family had one." Mine had two and both in their mildest forms were depressing. My father was maddening and unpredictable and violent but he was hospitable, wry (*Fitzgerald should be named "I heard"*), and generous with love and money. Daddy Jack was stingy and rigid. As a nine-year-old boy he sailed alone from England. His mother had died, his father gone ahead to America to manage a cotton mill. His aunt waved him off. A small boy with a satchel and a bag of apples. In the only early photo of him, his mother, Elizabeth Repton Mayes, gazes fondly down at him as he glares at the camera, mouth turned down, his tiny fists already clenched.

The story always touches me. Now and then he recalled being met by a redheaded stepmother who disliked him before he disembarked and proceeded to make his life miserable by criticizing every breath he took. Point of definition: one foot on the boat from England, other foot on the wharf in America. And, ah! How we learn.

"What's on the agenda today?" he asked every morning. His route for the day did not vary. Derail him and he'd have to start over, beginning with his liquid egg and bourbon breakfast.

With both Daddy and Daddy Jack gone to the same plot of dirt at Evergreen Cemetery, my mother was at last free. She was fifty-one—attractive and vivacious, until the point each night when every little bottle said Drink Me. Down the rabbit hole, she's Alice and she's the Red Queen.

All junior year I take five courses a semester to atone for my sins. Dr. Folger is the first man I've ever met who is "a queer." A small man in a large brown suit and gold glasses, he minces and gestures, rising to his tiptoes when he makes a salient point. His lectures are brilliant and I'm deep in love with his modern poetry course. At a conference on my Wallace Stevens paper, he asks, "Where are you from, Miss Mayes?" When I tell him Fitzgerald, Georgia, he says, "My God, isn't that a bit much?"

In French class, we translate *Les Misérables* and *Lettres de Mon Moulin*. The instructor, whose accent is not that great, smirks that I speak French with a southern accent. After that I hide in the back row. I devour all the texts for world religion and a double door swings open: Other religions are on a par with Christianity! Buddhism makes sense. Astronomy, which serves as a math requirement, collides with world religion. On nights of insomnia when I half-expect Frankye to materialize in the doorway and perform her sorcery, the unimagined vastness of the universe swirls through my brain. Every page in the astronomy text proves that I am merely a speck on a speck, so how to reconcile the importance of every sparrow that falls? Christianity, I fear, just isn't up to a satisfactory explanation of little planet Earth spinning in a minor galaxy. Does Jesus on the cross for our redemption reach all the way out to where space bends and black mass, black holes, and endless other galaxies begin? In the planetarium, the moving pointer across the sky map works like a Ouija board, searching for an answer. The big question, it seems to me, is the one posed by Leibniz: *Why is there something rather than nothing?* And here the Buddhists beg off by offering only a belief in the motion of birth and death cycles, a kind of thermodynamic principle: What's put in motion stays in motion; or, as I envision, the universe as a giant hoop snake. Aristotle seems to believe in the state of motion, too, except a force sets the motion in action. I like the idea of that unmoved mover. For first cause, the Bible offers a charming literal story that frankly begins to look quaint. But then, it is not that far from the unmoved mover. *Head in the clouds. Come down from the clouds.*

Religion becomes my minor. Except for architecture, which I don't dare go near, English is the only major I can imagine. Look how James Joyce illuminates a defining moment, and what an exact word for it: epiphany. Leap over to Virginia Woolf's *moment of being*: the private distilled instant caught, a cup scooping running water. T. S. Eliot's *Four Quartets*: My notebook fills with quotes about time past, time present. I'm whirling with the pleasure of so much to learn. My black-speckled composition books fill with quotes, questions, thoughts, ideas, fragments of poems.

The breakthrough class is the required logic. *Ad hominem, ad bellum, ad ignorantiam, post hoc ergo propter hoc*—ways to name what I know! Inductive, deductive. Up the ladder, down the ladder. How to think suddenly makes sense when you have precise language. How to analyze. In my family, we leap from A to D to F. We are walking fallacies. Ah! *Reductio ad absurdum*.

After a week at home for the summer, I start traveling. My sister in Atlanta likes for me to visit because I adore my nephew, which frees her and her husband to go out. We spend long weekends at their log house at Lakemont. Frankye behaves there, as she always does when she leaves the city limits of Fitz. Always we seem to arrive before anyone else and always we have the wrong key. The kitchen window pushes in. I've climbed in before. Here's the loft, here's the bed made of limbs where the water moccasin coiled on the pillow. Frankye goes into a cleaning frenzy. Mice have been in the flour bin, wasps, dirt daubers. Here's where I lay, eyes freezing on *Marjorie Morningstar* while I listened with my whole body to my aunt in the swayback bed, what is he doing to her, whimpering like a run-too-hard hound.

Then quiet. The lake lapping. Shadow of antlers on the window, spiders in the shower. Damp quilts.

Slowly everything works. The hoist lowers the boat back down in the water, Frankye's blackberry cobbler slides into the oven, waxy laurel blossoms float through my fingers. I can hear my hair growing. I suddenly realize: The cape jasmine sends up its fragrance whether I am here or not. Can it be made of words, the faint scent hovering along the edge of the lake? I imagine there is someone I can tell this to. My voice recrosses the lake three times. Hello. Hello. Hello.

We're in the water all day, swimming, floating, waterskiing, and at night Cleve, my brother-in-law, and I take the old restored Chris-Craft out in the dark and idle around docks, shining a flashlight into shallow water until we stun a frog with light and stab it with the gig. Late, we all line up along the porch facing the water and talk. Frankye and I sleep in the lower floor bedrooms in the log beds with red quilts. One morning, she steps out onto a gigantic furry tarantula, like squishing a banana. David comes for a visit, then Gwynne, my R-M roommate, and we go to the square dances in Clayton. The lake is pure joy, green as a Coca-Cola bottle, and furred around the shore with layers of other greens.

Back in Fitz, Frankye starts her night walks, and now I'm old enough to get away.

I take a bus to Gainesville, catch a ride, and visit Gary in Palm Beach. We're lying on a blanket on the beach at night, listening to music on a portable radio. The program is interrupted to announce that Ernest Hemingway has committed suicide. A policeman walks up and asks for Gary's license. He checks the address to see if he's local. Can't have just anyone making out on exclusive Palm Beach. I'm wild about the Addison Mizner houses. We walk in the ultrafancy neighborhoods, the bushes groomed within a millimeter, and fantasize about the princesses and princes who live in such mighty splendor.

After a few days, I visit my other sister, who now lives in a spacious house with a curved lanai surrounded by birds of paradise and banana plants. So much about Florida speaks my native language.

A week there and I make a call and catch the next bus, then train, to visit Oliver in Birmingham. I wish I were going to visit Rena but she's married the herpetologist. Oliver, a Princeton boy I'd met on another visit to Rena, picks me up at the station and we drive down to Montevallo, where Rena and her husband have set up house on a shady street near the college where he will begin to teach in the fall. Lizards, snakes, and toads. Looking around at Rena's tasteful lamps and cups and candlesticks and her mother's paintings, I feel sad that we never sailed to Piraeus. No more May baskets filled with poems and flowers. No more Beethoven turned up to the max as we painted our nails or sat cross-legged on our beds reading Yeats aloud. As she made coffee in the kitchen, I whispered a little about Paul.

Oliver and I are both quiet as we drive back to Birmingham to his family pillared home, firmly anchored in a century of southern charm and conservative history. In the pristine guest room that night, I hear handsome Oliver cough across the hall in his room decorated with lacrosse gear and model airplanes. He always seems to be congested. His mother has a library of leather books and reigns as the perfect mother and the consummate hostess. Willowy and slim, she stares at me with a slight bird-of-prey look. The father seems like most fathers—a remote figure, gracious but quick to hide behind the newspaper. This was my preferred trajectory according to Frankye: Houdini escape from Fitzgerald with a *city* boy from a *good* family. Junior League, a beach house, country club lunches and dinners ad infinitum, some "nice" church, not Baptist.

In a fetal curl, I relive my early and certain love for David, now lost, and my passionate connection with Paul, who is presumably proceeding down the primrose path with the New Orleans girlfriend. Then there's smart, funny, liberal Gary, and Joseph from Miami, a big crush who resists me because I'm not Jewish, and several others whose romantic overtures keep me bound to the quest for the jolt that arrives with love. I want ardent notes, wildflower bouquets left wedged inside the doorknob, poetry books wrapped in tissue, first kisses, the lips at my ear, the soft words, the *moment of being,* dance cards with tassels, midnight walks through old neighborhoods, laughter reaching up to the moon in the palms. Oliver and I, earlier, were lying in the grass kissing, kissing. For a moment I pretended that he was Paul but then I felt with my tongue his front teeth, one slightly crossing over the other. I turned away and nuzzled my face into his neck. A thread snapped. There, it's happened again. Even in the short run, he's not going to work for me.

I kick off the bedspread and bicycle in the air, my legs white scissors cutting the dark. I have been gone all summer. Time to go home.

THE LAST WEDDING

With Rena married, I moved into the Chi Omega house on Panhellenic Drive, all graceful old brick with wrought iron porches framed by long skeins of moss. Romantic, but a poor second to the *Hellenic Destiny* sailing for Greece. After Frankye asked them, my older sister and her husband offered to pay my fees (not easy for them with three small children). The Trust Company of Georgia, Daddy Jack's executor, refuses to allow her any money, despite the wording in the will that funds can be withdrawn from the corpus for "comfort, maintenance, and support." Every time I hear the word "corpus," I imagine Daddy Jack's rotund body in his casket, wormy and oozing. "Three years of college is more than sufficient for a young woman," the prim executor told her. Now Frankye becomes determined that I will finish college. When I revisit my impulse to work for TWA and travel, she throws a fit and starts one of her filibusters: "You are not going to end up in some dead-end or be like the dead-end Mayes family or live in death-in-life Fitzgerald or marry some dead-ignorant pilot or crash dead into the ocean— over my dead body."

Frankye spirals ever downward. What ever will lift her up? Red veins shoot through her blue-blue eyes. Her own sister Mary is so angry she barely speaks to her. *She was always spoiled rotten.* My sisters take her to their houses but all the encouragement goes nowhere. How to hold onto a falling star? Until now, Frankye could rally for visits from Mary or my sisters—camellias floating in a glass bowl, oyster stew, pound cake, new magazines on the coffee table, as if she cared what anyone in *Harper's Bazaar* wore to a benefit ball a thousand miles away from our little house in the pine barrens. Daddy long gone, Willie Bell gone, Daddy Jack gone, me gone to college: the shaky scaffolding has collapsed upon itself. Rising after ten, she skips coffee and goes straight to her tumbler. If I peek into her room, she's lying on her side looking out the window, frozen and silent. "Hey, Frankye, let's ride over and see Grace. She said to come pick some zinnias. Or Gladys. She's always fun." I stand in the doorway, half-hoping for her to jump up and say, "Let's go!" No answer. I would like to grab her ankles and pull her out of bed. I would like to shout *Get up this minute.* "Wonder if Mr. Bernhardt got in some corn today?" Finally, I back out and go to my books.

At times she waxes the kitchen floor at three in the morning or polishes all the silver. I try talking sense for the thousandth time. "There's AA in Macon. We could stay overnight. You could live with your cousin and go to meetings."

She sneers. "That's for bums and derelicts and hobos."

"*Hobos?* There are no *hobos* anymore. You are just *alien*. Do it for *us*! Your life is a blur." I'm shouting.

"Do what for you? I do everything for you. If it were not for you, I would not be in this two-bit place, and besides I don't *have* to drink anything; I can stop anytime I please." She's always slyly shifting the blame for her drinking onto me but I know in some sure place that I am not the cause, and neither is the two-bit place. Other people live vivid and valid lives here. I could stay if David and I had not canceled our love.

When she says, "I'm the best friend you'll ever have," I think *I'd hate to see the worst.* When she says, "I'm the only one who loves you," I talk back.

"That's what *you* think. Lots of people love me." My ephemeral romances slide across my mind and out. Am I *worthy* of anyone's love? "If you loved anybody, you wouldn't drink—what do you even mean by 'love'? Love! Damn, Frankye, you're committing slow suicide." My throat feels like a swarm of bees. I won't, won't cry.

"You have no idea what you're talking about. Don't cry for me; cry for yourself. You think you're so smart, but you're going nowhere fast."

"I'm going somewhere fast and that's out of here." I slam my door and crawl under the covers. Adrenaline feels like liquid hate coursing through my body. I am so angry that I think I could black out or go into a seizure. I'm appalled that I said "slow suicide." I've named it. The aftershock of that keeps shaking me.

An hour later, she pushes open the door and brings in a tray with Coca-Cola and warm brownies. "I thought you might be hungry. A slice of lemon in your Coke, just the way you like it. Brownies, your favorite." I bite into one. She has forgotten to add the sugar.

Fall, my senior year, and I must move back into communal living. My new roommate, Saralyn, and I share a corner room in the sorority house, perfect for stepping out onto the balcony for fraternity serenades when one of our sisters gets pinned. I'm on foot again. Frankye capriciously gave Daddy Jack's Oldsmobile to the yardman. A double blow—loss of the sunny apartment and of my wheels. I return to school with new determination to step closer to maturity. What will I *be*? Well, what else in the world is as riveting and important as writing? Since I first turned the pages of *Dick and Jane*, I wanted to write books. I will prepare myself to by analyzing the structures of books—outline enough plots and surely I will know how to do it—and I will keep my ideas in notebooks. What will I write about? Ezra Pound became famous with a single image: petals on a wet black bough. This was supposed to be equivalent to faces at the metro, but I just liked the fragile flowers and the contrast to the slick, stark branch. Since I love imagery, I will practice writing as though I were painting, as if my words could re-create a single glimpse of a panel of sunlight on the grass, the flash of a fish, antique gold in the murky pond, the first scent of wet lilacs, and then the underscent of ashes and rain. The blank leather book Rena gave me is where I will begin. I fill my pen with lavender ink.

. . .

Joseph, my big crush from last year, finally asks me out for the Florida State weekend. We stop in front of the sorority house a few minutes before curfew and sit in his car talking. The next day a committee of three takes me aside and informs me that Chi Os don't date the Jewish boys. Of course, they are very nice boys, but just *different.* I hate to get off on the wrong foot, but I smile and say firmly, "You all, I'm going to date anyone I want to. Wouldn't you, seriously, go out with him if he ever asked *you*?" I am not sure they get my little dig, but they never mention it again. During rush week, we cross off girls for the tackiness of their earrings, their hick accents (there's a sliding scale of southern accents), or simply their not-like-us qualities— too serious, too fat, too loud. *A figure like a deflated beach ball.* A Fernandina girl I champion is *not Chi Omega material.* I suspect that if I were going through rush, I would be cut after the first tea: *bad attitude.*

Once the pledging ends, a houseful of thirty girls, all Chi Omega material, settle in for the semester: shaving cream fights, three a.m. laughing shrieks in the hall, pajama study groups, chapter meetings with secret rituals, dinner served by fraternity boys, hall phone constantly ringing, communal bathroom steaming with scents of lime shampoo, Chanel No. 5, hair spray, and menstrual blood.

With no privacy available, I soon discover the library's music carrels, essentially closets with stereos, that I can sign out by the hour. I love to close the door and write in my notebook while listening to Wagner's *Tristan and Isolde* and Bach's cello suites, which sound like music the heart would write if it could.

I'm taking aesthetics, Renaissance lit, Shakespeare tragedies, French, individual work in religion, history of art—an intense schedule I devised to keep myself swamped with work. I will graduate and somehow work in Europe, where I will write novels. I'll play. I'll party. But I will not fall for anyone, not even the divine Joseph, whose wit keeps me laughing and whose walk seems smooth and oddly motionless, an animated Egyptian statue. The grader in my Shakespeare class asks me out, saying he'd like to talk about my Lear paper. After two dates, I don't want to see him again and my A papers are suddenly B papers. I drop Buzz, who has gained fifteen pounds. Even Gary moves on to another girlfriend.

In late October, I walk into the student union with Saralyn, and she stops to talk to a group of boys playing cards. One of them fans out his royal flush on the table and leans back in his chair. We look at each other and he stands up. "Hey, I'm Frank." His eyes are Atlantic green with flecks like mica. He's wearing a white dress shirt with jeans. Cool. I've never seen him before but I recognize him immediately.

I run into him the next night at Gatorland and we dance. He can dance! The way he holds his head back and tilted as he looks down at me reminds me of my father. His eyes are like David's. He's tensile and lithe. He seems like the boy I would want to be if I were a boy. Does this explain the familiarity I feel as we dance to "Unchained Melody"? The melody builds slowly, inevitably, rising like warm bread dough in a bowl. *I-I-I neeeed your love* . . . At the high trembling, heart-cracking *neeeed,* Frank tightens his arms, pulling me closer. *I'll be coming home, wait for me.* Next, the jukebox plays Ray Charles singing "Georgia on My Mind." He whispers in my ear, "Hey, Georgia." *The road leads back to you.* Right then I thought, I'd dance with him for the rest of my life.

Letter to Rena:

Rena, Rena—
My favorite kind of moon is tonight and Frank is tonight. Cool is tonight and I am content for the moment with two hours of my own, then a big red sweater, beer in front of a fireplace, and Mike in the background playing the piano.

It is different from the U. of F. of last year—like transferring again. Frank and I continue. Yesterday marked a month gone by. We have a riotous time together, we are enormously attracted to each other, we are alike in ways which will probably prove fatal (independent), and we still pretend to be playing the cool game although it has outgrown its purpose.

I miss you so much but I am glad you are not here. You were through with all this. I wasn't but I will be when I leave. I am glad for this year.

Oh, next day. I am sitting under the dryer. Frank and I are going to the ΣAE house for lunch, then to a circus with a group. Tonight is a party at Bob's apartment, The Bad Pad.

Tra la la la la.

Normal girl. Later in the year, I write to Rena:

Rena dearie,

Astronomy and Folklore finals today. Both were arduous struggles. But: *fini!* As are French, forever amen, and Romantic Poetry. Two left: Great Books Friday and History Saturday.

Mother came by today on her way home. I was completely surprised. She had a little trouble finding me, went in the AΔΠ house, missed the turn twice. She was with another lady who was sort of dizzy too. Hope they found their way to Fitz. She still hasn't met my true love. He had a test today. I haven't told my family yet, but Frank and I have decided, or rather Frank has asked me to marry him. It will be at midnight sometime in late, late summer. He has told his parents. They are agreeable. We have made no further plans. We are in love and it is new every day. We are the same and different. I can't imagine being without him and I am sure that if I were I would die of the Hopkins malady quietly without another word.

There was a full rainbow in the sky this afternoon with another one above it. . . .

From one who is writing exams in water . . .

Rena and I often had laughed over Gerard Manley Hopkins's description of nuns as dying of ingrown virginity.

Frank and I meet each other's family over spring break, spending Easter at his house in Pensacola, where we walk the sublime Gulf beaches, so undeveloped and serene, and buy a bucket of shrimp from the dock. I love the history of the town and the exotic street names: Zaragoza, Miramar, Salamanca, Palafox. I don't warm to his parents. His grumpy father props in his armchair smoking. Because of my rigorous training, I know a tyrant when I meet one. His mother waits on him like a servant. She's gracious and welcoming to me and I know Frank spent his high school years helping her peel and chop on Saturdays, while they listened to opera together in the kitchen. Sometimes one image can stand for a whole relationship and I take that as who they are together. Frankye always has advised, "Marry an orphan," but that is not going to happen.

Whatever they are, the visit is fun. We picnic at the Civil War fort among the wildflowers and I read Yeats aloud and Frank shows me his old schools and friends' houses. Voltage runs between us, the exhilarating feeling I always have when I fall in love, but this time there is a calm, certain center. With others, I always snagged on "but." But he has a girlfriend, but he's going to live a stodgy life, but he's not that smart . . . Now, we walk into a clearing, two would-be adventurers. A future to invent.

As it has to be, traveling to Fitz is fraught. I forewarn, but nothing prepares Frank for the moment when he asks Frankye for my hand in marriage. He sits down with her in the living room. "Frances and I, as you know, want to marry. I surely would like your blessing."

Without a pause, she replies, "That is the most ridiculous thing I've ever heard of."

"Boy," he says later, "how did you survive all this?" I introduce him to some of my friends, then we visit the church where the ceremony will take place. Late in the afternoon, we walk over to see The House. Hazel has restored it on the outside. Inside it's still burned. Peering in we see her charred piano, blistered walls, and the staircase sagging along the wall. Flowers line the front walkway. The brass door knocker gleams as though polished this morning. I'm relieved that he still loves me after we return to school.

I finish the year with a hideous case of poison ivy. Frank and I usually meet in class gaps and walk down to a sinkhole pond to talk and watch a granddaddy gator on the other side snapping at insects. We sit in lush weeds. The poison ivy starts on my inside arm, just where I had it when I was in my sister Nancy's wedding at age thirteen. Then, Daddy was busy dying, my sister about to move to French Morocco, my mother dancing on the head of a pin. I lather myself in chamomile lotion. The poison turns systemic. Soon it spreads to my face, which looks like the surface of the moon, then to my legs and arms—an advanced stage of jungle rot. I am allergic to chamomile. The doctors become alarmed at my listlessness and start me on steroid shots. Gary gives me a bell to ring, like a medieval leper. I stay in my room, reading *Candide* and swabbing myself with baking soda and water. In some odd way I cannot understand, the poison ivy eruption seems as though it comes from my fear of school ending and of making an enormous decision. My life has sped up, hurling me along toward the unknown. Should I stop it? Go home and try to force Frankye . . . I take long showers. The hot water on my live skin produces exquisite pleasure/pain. You do have to cast your bread upon the waters, yes? I'm not going home.

Frank sends flowers, via Saralyn, and she looks out for me. While the rash subsides, I have euphoric surges, a reaction to the steroids. With the energy of a ten-year-old, I return to class and write what I consider brilliant papers. They come back marked "I don't follow you here," and "This paragraph shows you know something more than the rest of the paper indicates." My make-up phys ed class is bait casting. We toss slow and elegant casts across a field, with Mr. Philpot shouting encouragement. *It's all in the wrist.* On one long and elegant maneuver, my line soars, then as it sinks, the fishhook embeds in Mr. Philpot's shiny bald head. A friend drives him to emergency, where the silver barb is—painfully—extracted. Graciously, he awards me a B for the class.

For a six-week session in the summer, I move to a dorm for my last gasp of requirements. Frank has gone home to work by day as a roofer and on weekends as a draftsman in a real estate office. He's saving for a car. What thrills me most about him is not his handsome face. He's not just smart, he's brilliant, though he maintains that he never does more than what's necessary to make an A. And he's open to living in Europe, not at all headed for the accepted idea of the future. We talk about living in England. He will be an Oxford don and I will write novels. He's sailing through a five-year engineering program. Since we must be in Gainesville another year, I line up my first job ever at a clothing shop. I'd applied for a social worker position but my whole family disapproved and, on second thought, I didn't want to be around more down-and-out problems when my home front was bad enough without further misery.

I adore Gainesville in the calm summer—the soaring temperature and the warm rain, wet streets with steam rising, the night scents of dripping leaves. There's something dreamy about summer school, more relaxed without the party frenzy. I'm memorizing the opening to the *Canterbury Tales*. Soon I'm walking home from the library with the studly, as my roommate calls him, Rich Herrin, who sits by me in Chaucer. Our talks grow more intimate. He throws his arm around me as we stop to look at the university mascot, Albert, a penned alligator. Rich starts a conversation, letting the gator say what it's really like to put up with football maniacs. Rich has thick blond eyelashes. He's funny. He leans to kiss me but I turn away. I suddenly realize that I could fall in love with him. He'll be a lawyer in Coral Gables. I will open a bookstore and write books. A phone call, and my life will go in a different direction. Wait. Could this cycle continue forever? Rich likes Middle English and is a total Florida boy, tan, muscular, ready to party. Ready to be ready. I slip out from under his arm. Time to close the fire door. Grow up.

The small wedding could not take place at midnight. The Methodist minister said midnight was a "furtive" hour and he would go no later than nine. He probably thought I was pregnant, since the wedding was hastily organized, and so unlike the Mayes girls. My sisters each had a wedding for a thousand, dinners of guinea hen and quail, honeymoons in the Caribbean. Now Frankye pivots. "Why can't you elope if you plan to go through with this? Well, sister, believe you me this is the last wedding I plan to attend. You should have married David and stayed home."

Summer school ends and I arrive home with my hard-earned BA degree. Frank drives up in his new car, a twelve-year-old Chevy named Old Blue. I'm ebullient. He has come for me. What luck we have between us. We are dying to escape into real life. We escape Frankye by spending as much time as possible in the party-room barn behind our house, wrapped around each other in the same chair. Miraculously, I am a virgin, barely so but still officially. Our local doctor refuses to prescribe the birth control pill—too dangerous—but has given me some foam to try on the wedding night.

On the afternoon of the wedding, as I lay out my hose and satin shoes, the phone rings—*Hey, babes. That you?* Rich Herrin calling from Coral Gables. *Please don't go through with this. Marry me. I'll take you to Paris. You're the only girl I want.* For a moment I think of bolting.

I wash my own hair and polish my nails. Lipstick, a brush of mascara, the hundred tiny pearls all buttoned. I'm ready.

Instead of flowers, I carry a leather book of Keats's poems. My little niece, Jane, seems to be the only family member who is excited. As I walk down the aisle Frankye leans out and grabs my dress. I turn to hear what she has to say; does she have some final redeeming words of wisdom? "It won't last six months," she says. I stumble slightly, suppress a laugh, and walk forward.

She has managed to arrange a supper afterward at the Elks Club, the only pretty venue in town. She looks faded in the silky limp dress she bought for my sister's wedding ten years ago. I'm just thankful that she doesn't bring down the house somehow and reveal to Frank's family that she has been shot out of a cannon.

In our furnished duplex cottage I tape poems around the sink so I can memorize as I wash dishes. Already, I can cook. Raised around women making great food, I've absorbed more than I realized. Our favorite is called Chicken Florence. Cut-up breasts dipped in egg, covered with bread crumbs and Parmesan from a little green container, quickly sautéed then baked in the oven with a half stick of melted butter. After work, I make spaghetti, meat loaf, or Willie Bell's fried chicken with a dash of red pepper. I love my kitchen and, as if all the future kitchens I will have flash before me, know that I'm at home cradling a bowl and beating something with a wooden spoon.

I'm the sole supporter—wouldn't Daddy Jack be surprised? Frank's father said if he was old enough to marry, he was old enough to support himself. Although the pay is low, I'm immensely happy at my sales job. Bill Donigan, owner of the shop, hires people he likes. The four of us fool around all day, but manage to sell fantastically and keep the shop pristine and straight. Bill is unusually handsome. Too bad he's so old, Saralyn says. He's thirty.

Frank studies while I work, and our nights are free. We are on the edge of Florida party world now. Bob, the Bad Pad host, has married my friend Patty and they're expecting a baby. We start the milder life of having people over to our kitchen table for supper, going to movies, or walking over to browse in the library. I'm studying my modern poetry tome, learning to scan for meters other than iambic, and dreaming over T. S. Eliot's *Four Quartets*. One night in our white iron bed, I've turned out the light after reading late. I hear a noise, a screen unlatching, and I look at the window just as a stick raises the white curtain. I see a shadowy figure outside. I motion "Shhh," to Frank as he sort of wakes up, and slip out on my side of the bed. Crouching low, I make my way to the phone in the hall. The curtain drops and we hear running steps. Soon the police siren splits the night. "How dumb can they get?" Frank wonders, but then they're at the door, having caught the peeping Tom. They just stopped by to reassure us that all is well. I look out to the street and in the backseat of the police car I see Rich Herrin looking straight ahead. That was the last time I ever saw him.

Into our idle comes the Cuban Missile Crisis. We store jars

of water and fill the bathtub. On the point of no return, we sit on pillows in the hall, an inside space, for hours, listening to the radio. The tip of Florida is only ninety miles from Cuba. We're holding hands, our backs pressed to the wall, imagining the unimaginable, that we will be vaporized and not all the love in the world can stop it. I think of Frankye, 150 miles north, probably unaware that her two daughters in Florida are in mortal danger, as is she, as are we all. Other drastic events have happened in my lifetime but with the home fires so incendiary, I have scarcely taken them in. If a door like this can open, what else might walk in? As I quickly wash the plates, the end of W. H. Auden's poem "Leap Before You Look," taped over the sink, gives me sudden shivers:

> *Although I love you, you will have to leap,*
> *Our dream of safety has to disappear.*

These unappealing men, Castro and Khrushchev, toy with us. Our president prevaricates. We hide in the hallway sipping hot chocolate. *Look if you like but you will have to leap.* Yes, I've always known that; I just didn't know that I knew.

The call came early one evening as I sliced onions for soup. Frankye has fallen. She hit her head on the heater and lay there; no one is sure how long. Matrel, a kind next-door neighbor, discovered her when Frankye didn't answer the door when Matrel went over to check. She's in the hospital and our doctor reports that she is incoherent and totally wacky. He says that she needs a "massive shock," she needs to "wake up," "come to her senses," and that he has experience. He recommends hospitalizing her for a brief period. Once there, she will be horrified and realize that she must change her life. "You mean he wants to send her to the loony bin?" I ask. In fact, she has agreed and already has gone, driven over by the sheriff, who used to work for my father at the mill and drive us when we took long trips. Frankye, sent off with a small suitcase, and apparently in confusion. Is Dr. Ward right? "You have to touch rock bottom before you can reform," he says. I picture Frankye touching bottom in a clear ocean, pushing off and breaking the surface with a smiling face.

It did not happen his way. What no one understood then was withdrawal. What transpired that first week remains unknown. The next call informed me that Frankye had fallen into a coma. Either the head injury or cold-turkey withdrawal was the cause, and she will not live more than a few days. If you want to say good-bye, the nurse says, come now.

My sister picks me up and we tunnel north in the dark, passing through Jasper, Florida, where Frankye and Garbert married late one night, having crossed over the state line where no waiting was required. Jasper, a mystery spot on my globe. Also the birthplace of a writer I admire, Lillian Smith, so ahead of her time. We cross the black rivers and speed through sleeping towns, reaching the hospital late at night.

We are allowed to see her. Lying on a stainless steel table under gray fluorescent light, she looks ashen and curiously withdrawn. Her head is shaved and a dime-sized hole has been drilled into her skull to drain blood. The metal bowl on the floor under her head is empty. A stroke, they explain. I want to stomp my feet, throw a tantrum, beat the walls. *A solitude ten thousand fathoms deep.* "Wouldn't she hate the hospital gown?" I say helplessly.

She does not die. For six weeks, she lies motionless. We try to talk to her. *Frankye, let's check out of this terrible hotel.* There is no flicker of eye movement, no responding squeeze of the hand. None of us is there when she wakes up as a large baby with low, low mental function that never will improve. She's gone. Throughout the extended family reigns the *she brought it on herself* sentiment and yes, she did, but for my sisters and me, what does that have to do with it?

She never will lean toward the light, moisten the thread between her lips, and thread the needle. She'll never throw the sheet on the floor and pile on the dirty laundry. Brush her hair a hundred strokes. Floorboard the Buick en route to Fernandina, singing "Oh my darling Clementine." No more—placing blue hydrangeas in a glass bowl, scraping her rings on the inside of the black mailbox, boiling jars for peach pickles, dabbing bath powder puff over her arms, refusing catfish because they're bottom-feeders, bidding grand slams, pulling meat off the bone for chicken divan, hand washing a peach silk slip, surrounding the birthday cake with pink camellias, tucking a seashell into the bosom of her bathing suit, shouting out the window *Go to the woods, live in the woods,* draining bacon grease into a jar, dipping kumquats and lemons in wax for a Della Robbia wreath, beeping the horn for help unloading groceries, stepping on a furry tarantula, insisting I buy the red taffeta dress with a balloon skirt—*just dynamite on you*—pounding a nail into the eye of a coconut, kicking a shoe up in the air, unmolding the loaf pan of tomato aspic, flocking the Christmas tree with white and hanging gold-sprayed wishbones on the branches, extracting a splinter from my heel, zipping her skirt and catching tender skin, cutting a cantaloupe into crescent moons, polishing the lion-face door knocker, feting a June bride with Pineapple Parfait, ripping up Daddy's birthday check because checks are not romantic, opening her handbag and showing fabric swatches of aqua like the waters of Barbados, saying *You don't know what it was like when every little piece of rubber broke,* hiding the bill from Rich's in the sideboard, skipping church missionary circle meeting (*Can't they see the poor three blocks from here?*), stretching the organdy canopy back over the tester, shelling pecans for Martha Washington Jetties: all her lost days, rolling away.

She is the lining of my coat I will have to shed.

I'm twenty-two; she's fifty-four. Her blue shot-silk eyes express an almost verbal intelligence, like a gorilla looking out from behind bars at the zoo. We move her to a family friend's nursing home in Fitzgerald. She recognizes everyone and knows our names but has lost the context for our lives. I want to unzip her and pull out the real Frankye. To her, I will be forever twenty-two, even when I am fifty and sixty, still visiting her in the small room, where she takes her long mystery ride to age ninety-two.

"Constitution of iron," the doctor says. "Good genes, Frances." Is he serious? Each time I approach the building, the mysterious rash blazes down my arm. On her door hangs her photograph from a prettier time. A woman on her hall has elephant man disease. When I walk by her room, she opens the door and sticks out her wild face, her eyes almost hidden by grotesque purple growths all over her. But her eyes—she's in there somewhere. I need everything I have to smile and say good morning.

Frankye has many friends and knows quite a few patients, who also have visitors. She's not alone now and nothing is expected of her. We move some of her furniture into her room and hang photos of the family. She has forgotten that she'd really like a drink. As I leave, I peek back in to see if she is crying. She is not. She lights a cigarette and reaches for the remote. A man with snuff-packed cheeks pulls my arm. "Gimme a nickel," he says. "Gimme a nickel." Others are strapped to wheelchairs, staring into the middle distance. A wizened woman jerks awake as I pass and says loudly, "It shouldn't happen to a dog."

I turn up the car radio louder than I can scream.

By spring, we see graduation looming. Gainesville floats on a vast sea of azaleas. We're in the wedding when Saralyn marries Bing from St. Pete. We take day trips to St. Augustine and to Cedar Key for Apalachicola oysters, and down to Lakeland to visit my sister and lounge at the Yacht Club and feast on People's Bar-B-Que. Outside Gainesville, we picnic at a lake with water hyacinths so large I'm tempted to step out of the rowboat and balance on one. *The Yearling,* a childhood favorite, propels me to visit Cross Creek, the citrus grove where Marjorie Kinnan Rawlings lived. "I do not know how anyone can live without some small place of enchantment to turn to," she wrote. And, "Cross Creek belongs to the wind and the rain, to the sun and the seasons, to the cosmic secrecy of seed, and beyond all, to time." The house charms me, though it is a simple cracker farmhouse. What would it be like to have a native place for my own? I love that: *the cosmic secrecy of seed.* Could I have written some of her words myself, if she hadn't written them for me? "I have walked it [the road] in despair, and the red of the sunset is my own blood dissolving into the night's darkness."

I have all of Frankye's recipes, her Black Bottom Pie, Grapefruit Aspic, Chocolate Icebox Cake, and the Custard Cups she made when I was small. In her few cookbooks, she has scrawled recipes all over any white space. Date Loaf, Date Bars, Date Roll, Date Bread with Cream Cheese, Macaroon Date Pie—why so many dates? I can't ask her now.

We've written letters to graduate schools for Frank, not for me; I'm not there yet. All the letters flew to places far from the South. Daddy Jack once said that God tipped America at the Rockies and everything loose rolled west. That sounds good to me. Frank's reward for his brains and perseverance: a full stipend to Stanford for graduate school. He will study physics and math. I will . . . I don't know what I will do. *Something.* We sell unreliable Old Blue, and make a down payment on a new VW bug, bright red, with seat belts. At night we plot a long journey through New Orleans, the Painted Desert, Big Sur. Because of the heat, we will drive from three a.m. until ten, find a motel, and see all there is to see. We set off with $500 and no place rented on the other side of the country.

Before falling asleep at night, I am on a road across the country, a meandering vine of road wending across Florida, the Panhandle, across the Old South, Natchez Trace, Mobile, into Texas, beyond, Grand Canyon, beyond, all the way across deserts the VW rolls along. No other cars are on this journey, and, oddly, I am alone. I have the landscape to myself until I top a hill and see the Pacific Ocean fanning out and out forever, and the red car comes to a stop on the last edge of the country.

I've cast my line far back. Now I'm flinging it forward. In California, I will create a life with my own two hands.

The End/Beginning

CODA: LIFE ALONG THE ENO

The solstice. Winter in the South: a blissful week of seventy-degree weather. *Skies already haunted with spring.* The garden is all put to bed, trimmed, tidied, and mulched. We've just planted four hundred daffodils, hyacinths, and tulips, which may slightly outnumber the amount munched away by voles and moles since last year. The native hollies and the ugly nandinas show off clusters of red berries, and the sasanquas' delicate white and pink blooms look out of place this time of year. What can they be thinking, tossing out spring-hearted pastels into the drear? Other than those spots of color, the landscape fades to grays, a vintage engraving of itself. But the air is enlivened—three cardinals cavort on the grass, chasing and flitting among bare branches. A redheaded woodpecker bangs its brains out on a walnut trunk.

I carry my small chainsaw; Ed takes his weed wench as we walk to the Eno River, which flows along the bottom of our meadow. When I was growing up, I haunted the rivers near Fitzgerald, the Altamaha and the Oconee. Writing my novel *Swan,* I let my character (somewhat modeled on David) J.J.'s first action be a swim in the river he loved. Opening line: *He loved the smell of rivers.* I couldn't wait to get him in the water. The Eno lured me to buy Chatwood because I also love the smell of rivers, the shots of warm current, the reflections of trees, the thought that rivers twist and join and reach the sea. There, Heraclitus, I *can* step into the same river twice. The water may have moved on, as you say, but surely it comes around again.

We are clearing the tangled, vine-choked woods for a view of the water. The river runs black at this time of year, at other times, a more tannic, sherry brown. Clearing is fun; hauling limbs and weeds is not. But we're spurred by the idea of a bonfire. As we prune, I look down, hoping to find a blue bead or a tiny flint arrowhead. But only milky quartz rocks glint in patches of light. Records mention the house's big stable in the nineteenth century. If I could locate it, I could dig up enough horseshoes to have good luck forever.

A property feels ideal to me if it includes a bit of a ruin. Just in the woods remains the foundation of a springhouse, built from local slabs of stone, where pure water bubbles from the ground. I think of the original gristmill owner's wife, Mrs. Faucette, who stored her milk and butter, cheese, and hunks of fresh meat on planks in the cool room. She must have sited the house, after the 1770 one burned. She might have watched the British general Cornwallis pass by, then gone inside to check on the bread rising in the south window, just where I set my focaccia dough. A faintly visible track to the river traces an Indian trading path. Maybe they exchanged berries for cornmeal. The old basement door has a three-lock barricade from inside, so who knows how peaceful the exchange was.

Inside the house, the mellow heart-pine rooms glow in firelight, and we're inside a thrumming hive, alive in amber light. The magnolia and pine boughs, berries, and mistletoe that I've arranged on all the mantels must have been placed there by many a hand in the last two hundred years.

Upstairs, one of the old doors pops open when I pass by. "Good morning, Mr. Faucette," I say, he who stood in that hallway in rough tweeds, needing a shave, heading out to help mule drivers through the mud. In a closet, Ed found tacked on the inner wall a list titled "The Stamps I Have on Hand." The yellowed paper dates only from 1958 but for fifty-four years no owner took it down. Now I know that someone who shared my writing supply closet once owned four Lincoln-Douglas Debate stamps, three Minnesota Statehood, four Overland Mail. A scrap. Like memory, how arbitrary what endures. Where are those stamps now?

Hillsborough lies two miles east. We have landed in a town of 6,500 souls, many of whom are writers, photographers, painters, book designers, historians, professors, singers, and other dreamers. As in Oxford, Mississippi, I'm reminded of Cortona: hospitality, raucous humor, the conviction that the table centers the universe. In Italy, one breathes art. The arts seem paramount in these parts, too. Books are handed around. Talked about. Recommendations fly via email. The riverine walk around Ayr Mount, a pre–Civil War house, is called Poet's Walk. Pencils and paper are provided at the outset, should you become inspired. This is light-years from the South I knew as a child.

Usually, dinner launches other fun: a spiritual sung by a guest, or a Puccini aria or two. Ed might want us to listen to the four best "Blue Moon" recordings, or to see which tenor holds the longest note in "Nessun Dorma." As in Italy, the hosts are lauded, then toasts outdo each other. Guests may read a play as they pass the olives and prosecco. We orchestrate black-tie potlucks with an array of oysters, slow-simmered quail in cognac and juniper berries, crown roast pork, and delectable lavender-scented panna cotta. Or, we spread quilts on the ground and serve retro food—bing cherry Jell-O, ham biscuits, fried chicken, and churned peach ice cream. I love it when someone throws a low-country boil in fresh-corn season, or just serves Brunswick Stew by the fire. To commence, there may be a blessing or, once, a reading of Yeats's "A Prayer for My Daughter." Light the candles. Turn up Eva Cassidy singing "At Last." Bring on the laughter and the goose confit.

These are the ties that bind. Daily life in Hillsborough draws me close to my earliest, best connections to the South. My father invited his office workers and other friends on Friday to our backyard, where everyone ate smothered doves and grits soufflé, Willie Bell's crunchy biscuits, potato salad, peach pickles she and my mother put up, and platters of pound cake, Pecan Icebox Cookies, and Frankye's Chocolate Icebox Cake made with ladyfingers and cloudlike mousse.

On certain Sundays, our church offered dinner on the grounds and my mother would bake a stupendous Lane Cake or, what still makes me feel deep lust, her famous three-layer Caramel Cake. Daddy preferred her Lemon Cheesecake—not a cheesecake at all but cloud-soft layers of butter cake, with thick curd filling that must have reminded someone of cheese. Maybe it's the food of the South that makes its children long so for home.

Now, how the traditions multiply and cube. Many of the obsolete North Carolina tobacco farms are given over to the production of organic kale, baby turnips, radishes, golden-yolked eggs, goat cheeses, and heritage livestock. What luck to come home in the midst of a food revolution, and one that circles back to the farmers who beeped at our back door, rattling a hand scale as Willie Bell picked out plums, collards, and butter beans at the back of the truck.

What a surprise to see that the fine old country manners endure, even a formality, so that our very handyman who can fix anything remains Mr. Farley to my Mrs. Mayes. Blessedly the good ol' boys have retreated, though they're not totally gone. At least no one any more offers to *buy the little lady a drink.*

I returned to a South where racism, while not erased, is no longer publically virulent, and this makes it an entirely different South from the one I knew. You still can see the Stars and

Bars flying over a trailer in the woods on Martin Luther King Day, still hear an occasional slur from someone who doesn't have the sense to see that you don't agree. But mostly the good inheritance of southern manners in both races prevails. Even in the worst of times, there existed a layer of deep familiarity, a shared bond of coming out of a place once ripped and ravaged by one of the worst wars in history. Because the land once soaked in blood remembers, we do, too. And there's a shared bond, too, of coming out of a place of unpredictable weather and terrain, a sun strong enough to melt your bones, a place where the second coming is still expected, where the night creatures sing the most soulful music that can be imagined. Back in the South, the tribal pulse of the place beats, the primitive gift that I sensed as a child riding to sea on the back of a turtle.

The day-to-day warmth that transpires in ordinary interactions simply thrills me. "Don't be a stranger," I heard when I was growing up. People talk to you everywhere. Waiting at the dentist, filling the tank, checking out at the grocery store. Each gesture may mean little but cumulatively there's a message: *You are not alone.*

My daughter remarried a Southerner. We live close to Ashley and Peter, which means we are also close to my grandson, Willie, or as only I call him, Wills. I can attend his first saxophone recital, help him with Spanish homework, serve Frankye's pot roast on a Wednesday night. After so long in Italy, where three generations of a family often share a house, the idea of living a long distance from one's family seems terribly wrong and the breaking up of a family even more drastic. I want to take over to them a baked pasta, pick up the sore throat medicine, keep the dog when they're away—everyday closeness, as well as state occasions and big celebrations.

The brilliant boy I married when I was very young was a long part of my life, but not my life. Divorce, which feels like being cleaved, sometimes can be one of those X spots. So it was for me, when at last I lived alone and worked. So this is what it's like, I thought. My inner compass began to align. I had the great luck of meeting Ed. Always fearful that what I love will be snatched away, I hesitate even to write that we are every day joyful. *Per ora*, the Italians say, for now, as a charm against the gods' envy of happiness.

I like the town's dignified white houses with black shutters. I like the cottages with friendly front porches, the fixed-up mill houses where someone's alone with his fiddle, the square brick houses of the fifties, the bottle trees to trap haints, the courthouse that anchors the square, and the street names that recall a town history I don't even know.

The interiors of friends' houses are wonderfully quirky—taxidermy that makes me squirm, walls of sagging books, screened porches on stilts so one can sleep as if in the trees, church windows inset above a desk, peculiar collections of skulls, plaster busts, Elvis memorabilia, retablos, folk art, model houses, Virginia Woolf's circles paintings, woven early American coverlets. Okay, I admit some of these are my collections. One writer keeps all the clothes he's ever owned, plus some of his father's and grandfather's, in the attic, and thus appears often in a big bear coat, a World War II uniform, or formal morning coat with spats. Another friend bought the contents of a costume shop that was closing, so that many of us have a vast selection to choose from for any occasion. The South always has enjoyed its eccentric people. I'm glad because I intend to become more and more that way myself. I'm done with my life quest to appear normal.

In Fitzgerald, the woman who kept a coffin in her living room was tolerated; the town klepto was tolerated—her husband was billed quietly for her picked-up trinkets. When she visited a bride's display of gifts, she was watched. Ella Mae drove with the windows down so her wild red hair flew out behind her. Her husband had his thing, too: He memorized the numbers of everyone's annual license tag and on New Year's, my daddy always said, "Poor Jim, he has to start all over." Ella Mae passed our house frequently and yelled out the window, "Are you having 'cue? I smell 'cue!"

As in Italy, old houses in town have names. Pilgrim's Rest. What a wonderful abode, with its suggestion of travel and return. Heartsease, yes, shouldn't home be that? Burnside, a Scot-built home beside the flowing burn. Montrose: Life is stately; life is upright. It Had Wings, named for a short story by neighbor Allan Gurganus. The owners collect antique model houses; hundreds of them line the rooms. Sunnyside, Mouse House, Seven Hearths, Teardrops, Woodthrush Cottage, Twin Chimneys—all have souls. Most houses' names recall the owner: Nash, Ruffin, Snipes, Forrest, Judge Gattis, many of whom lie still in the cemetery, along with CSA soldiers, a signer of the Declaration of Independence, and one woman whose epitaph reads SHE DID WHAT SHE COULD. I am sure there are many women's graves that could support that thought, maybe even my own someday.

One of my favorite pastimes is to "ride around," in the country, as I did as a child. So many simple pleasures come back, but without the complications. My parents, who touched not a drop on Sundays, took an afternoon ride in the country. I could hop out of the car and pick plums and violets or wade in creeks while they watched from the car. Here, I like to let the windows down and drive the lost roads, photographing abandoned farmhouses, wacky mailboxes, barns, and churches. The roads are named for churches, country stores long gone, or creeks. I pull over and explore tiny cemeteries, and lean over fences to pet the noses of horses. This is what I do in Italy, too, though it's a different world.

Frankye still is not behaving at Chatwood. In her frame on my chest of drawers, she slides down in the night, *thwunk*, waking me. The tacks fall out of the wood and she's often catawampus, although other family members stay in place, even Big Mama on the back row of her family group, cradling baby Annie Ruth, who later would raise quite a bit of hell.

As I lit out for California with Frank, I thought I'd had my share and more of trouble, that in the rest of life one adventure would cede only to the next. But just starting were decades of visiting Frankye. In the early years, when we had little money and lived three thousand miles away, that lonesome trip to Fitzgerald became my yearly vacation. My sisters and I met in Atlanta and drove the 180 miles south—green pines, green air, buzzards circling, heat wave rising off asphalt, possum smeared pink in the road, indelibly home—for an excruciating stay in Fitz's finest, a motel fast going from tired to grungy.

Half-paralyzed, Frankye still insisted on staying with us.

We'd check her out of the nursing home. Two queen beds; I bunk with her.

Who can sleep? Willful and bossy, she is terribly incapacitated physically, as well as mentally. We barely can haul her out of the backseat. She wants a bath, not her everyday shower. She has to be hoisted in and out of the tub, a terrifying ordeal always about to end with three of us in the water. Wrapped in a blue robe on the bed she looks like one of those beached seals we take excursions to see on the California shore. As in former days when she was beautiful, she is still concerned with her perfume, her nails, her rouge, which she rubs in clownish dark circles. Her skin stays luminous, without a sag or wrinkle, her hair silvery and wavy. Years down the line, she won't wear false teeth and keeps her lips pursed so we won't fuss at her about it again. She barely can walk but insists on lumbering into the drugstore, with my sister and me holding her up, to select new lipstick. We take her back to the car and she claws our arms as she cranks down, a lunging fall we control, rolling our eyes at each other behind her back. I go in again to get the rest of the things on her list. Lotion. Cigarettes. Eyedrops. There is a certain kind of compact she likes. Rose Ivoire. The one I selected will not do.

Often my sisters and I wanted to shoot ourselves but we lived on gallows humor instead. At least the trust company allowed the nursing home costs to come out of our inheritance from Daddy Jack, which lasted for the first thirty years of her care. A sincere thank-you, D.J. the D.J. What would we have done without his bequest? Then the last nickel was gone. One day, she forgot that she smoked. She acquired diabetes, then slimmed down and it disappeared. She was rushed to emergency with a ruptured appendix. My sisters and I arrived quickly, but she had recovered. We walked in just as she demanded omelets and French fries at the hospital.

Cataracts to cancer, she endured. We grew old ourselves, visiting her in the nursing home.

Frankye needs a new frame, something silver and gleaming. Propped beside her mother, will she, at last, just, please, sit still?

. . .

The day is mild, 21 December, and dark falls early. The shortest day. I'll start my own swing toward the light with a belated thank-you to Daddy Jack, the boy on the boat with the sack of apples and the gumption to succeed that he must have owned as a child. Already that kernel of determination and drive was sprouting as he balled his fist in the baby photo, and later as he boarded the boat to America. He could add a three-digit column of numbers in his head. He was kind to the people who worked for him. Sometimes you have to travel back in time, skirting the obstacles, in order to love someone.

Holding Daddy's photograph to the light at the window, I sense something frail in the handsome, wary face. Because he died at forty-eight, my memories of him are both sharp and vague. If I had died so fatally young, I would not have had the chance to write my books. All his possibilities remain unfurled. He willed to me the fatalism that is the lot of those who lose a parent when young. I'm phobically frightened that I will lose someone I love, that I will be left at the rest stop, and that the man next to me on the plane is the terrorist. When Rena's son drowned, I found out the worst that can happen to a parent. Other losses have been literally unbearable, but one bears them. You become sessile and keep small visitation rooms in your mind where those you lost still live. In one of those Daddy opens his coat and shows it lined with doves he's brought home for dinner. In another, he leaps in his white suit into the mill sewer to save me. His curse words still turn the air blue. I've recently seen where he was born in Mayesworth, North Carolina (now Cramerton), on a hill called Maymont. I've found his grandfather's big shingle house, he who exiled Daddy Jack to Fitzgerald, still standing in Charlotte. These threads, tendrils, let me travel way back to where he, Mother Mayes, and Daddy Jack launched, and to those people he came from, layers I never knew about.

From a recently found distant relative, I even have a poem written by Mother Mayes's father in Gastonia, North Carolina. John Laban Smith, a writer in this family! The house he built still stands. My sisters and I found it from an address on an old photo. Above the door, a stained glass panel was similar to the one in the house he built for his daughter, Frances, my Mother Mayes, in Fitzgerald. We have lists of cousins, grave sites, obituaries of relatives. The state of North Carolina is all over my DNA and somehow I was pulled here without knowing anything of that.

Tracing Daddy's family mysteriously realigned him in my mind. He has a context that has nothing to do with me. Recently, my sister came across several letters Garbert wrote to Frankye, full of passion and signed *I love you with worship*. For that, he has from me a red ribbon and gold medal around his neck.

Sometimes a dream offers a gift. I am near The House. The oak tree stands no taller than the porch. A stranger looks over the lattice fence and tells me, "You know it is 1922." In the garden, I see Daddy Jack. Young! Smiling. His hair parted, not the bald man I knew. "Where are the others?" I ask the stranger. "They are playing inside." I hear a faint few bars of a saxophone and I want them to come running out the back door, clattering down the steps, Daddy at sixteen, my uncles and aunt. I almost see them and although the dream stops short, I'm thrilled to have taken this dip behind time, when I was still out in oblivion and they were who they were, all possibility.

Forty-eight—a cruel age to die. My nephew hunts birds with Garbert's guns. Surely he would have tamed eventually. From him, I take my love of beaches. He liked to joke. In any grand situation—in a fancy car or restaurant—he'd lean over to me and say, "Wonder what the po' folks are doing, Bud?" He had sweetness, too, which I remember more as a feeling than an instance. Still, I was right to turn on him the hard spurt.

For Frankye, oddly enough, the word "munificence" comes to mind. Not that I ever forget her halo of negative ions. In the years since she's been gone, I've not had the wild rash on my arm. I've learned to relax when I shampoo my hair. Forever, when I poured on the shampoo, I'd feel my shoulders seize and my eyes squeeze tightly shut. One day I suddenly thought *relax* and I physically recalled Frankye's red nails scratching and digging into my scalp when she washed my hair over the sink. How much longer than memory the body reenacts what happened to it.

But from her, a shower of gifts. When I was at camp or in college, she constantly mailed boxes of cheese straws and peanut butter cookies. From her I inherited my gusto for food and the table it's set on—who's there, what's talked about, what's for dessert, the old linens and silver, the flowers, the ritual. The premise that you go all out for a guest. And from her, the impetus to *go*. Even if it were only to Fernandina, or St. Simons, or Atlanta, she was quick to yank her bag from under the bed. I'm on a quest to see everything I want to see, which is everything she never saw. Before her long fall, she had about her every day an air of possibility, as though she were riding in on the crest of a wave, there, balancing just where the wave starts to curl, always expecting something fantastic, ready to be delivered to shore.

From her fate, I know that friends and loves can take over if the abyss of family drops off. Her attitude toward money sank in. Nothing convinces me that it's not to spend and give away. And, *grazie mille*, for her force of life that propelled her to age ninety-two, against all odds. Her lit fuse. From her I have fierce currents of energy, a river in full tilt that I have reveled in all my life. She—and not only by negative examples—gave my sisters and me the fervor to thrive.

I've kept with me the feel of Willie Bell's strong fingers clutching my arm as we crossed a street. Her hand holding mine tight as she rubbed cut walnuts on the ringworm between my fingers. She had a big, toothy smile and I watched for the glints on her gold fillings. "You got wings back here," she said, tapping my shoulder blades. "You gon' fly, little girl." We never saw Willie Bell again. My sisters and I still miss her. "Swallowed by the North," Frankye maintained. "Swallowed whole."

· · ·

In the future, I plan to be braiding the garlic, reaching up to cut leaves from the tall holly that is right now waist high, harvesting bushels of heritage apples, gathering the last roses of the year. The garden will be burgeoning, and my dream realized of a pond below the parterre garden, just large enough for a blue canoe. We'll long since have remodeled the barn into— what? Exhibition space, guest quarters, or a library, adding a long screen porch for summer dining.

At that table, may Frankye be invisible to everyone but me, though the blue of her eyes looks straight at all of us from my daughter's and grandson Wills's sunnier glances.

From her, I understand in the marrow Yeats's line *A pity beyond all telling / Is hid in the heart of love.*

Frankye, who didn't raise me in that direction, would be shocked that work—starting with the high school yearbook—directs my days. Books, house restoration, vast gardening schemes, language, food, literacy projects, and a complex life in two countries. What would she say? And, where would she have gone, if she'd been lucky enough to make a midcourse correction?

Often in Tuscany, when I'm rolling out pizza dough, setting the table for twenty, poking an armful of hydrangeas in a pitcher, I think, *She would have loved this.*

Then, I know—her life blossomed into mine.

Too bad I don't believe she's beaming down from heaven, flapping feathery wings and sighing *At least she did it.* Ever since my faraway courses in astronomy and world religion, when I learned that even the solar system amounts to no more than a fleck in space, I cannot, unlike the majority of my fellow Southerners, take consolation from on high. All I've ever been able to figure out as my religion is to love the world and the people in it. Help those you can and relish the moment as it flies. I find strength in making grand plans for the future, and at the same time, in memory. In writing a life, you search for the white pebbles you didn't know you dropped to define your way. When they disappear, you instinctively follow the glimmer of swamp fire to the deep woods where time and event collapse, to the original source where love flourishes still.

As to the creation of the universe and our purpose on this blue spinning mote in space: Bow down before the mystery because you are not going to know. In that, I have faith.

ACKNOWLEDGMENTS

My good fortune is to have Vanessa Mobley as the editor of this book. She gave me thoughtful and useful responses and has understood from the start the vicissitudes and volatility of the memoir in my hands. My great thanks to her, to Miriam Chotiner-Gardner and Claire Potter, who steered so well, and to my excellent publicist, Rachel Rokicki. Elizabeth Rendfleisch was the book designer; I appreciate her fine work. Many thanks to: Julie Cepler, Jay Sones, Danielle Crabtree, Tricia Wygal, Rachel Meier, Luisa Francavilla, and to the whole team at Crown Publishing Group. Special gratitude to president Maya Mavjee and to publisher Molly Stern.

Peter Ginsberg of Curtis Brown Ltd. has lavished his attention on me ever since I showed up at his office with my memoir of Tuscany in a box and said, "Will you represent me?" I count on his perspective, astute ideas, and his humor. Also, my friends at Curtis Brown Ltd., *mille grazie* Jonathan Lyons, Holly Fredericks, Kerry D'Agostino, and Sarah Perillo.

Charlie Conrad was my editor for eight books, and although

he has moved on to new work, he continues to send encouragement my way. We've raised many toasts in Italy, and long may that continue.

At HarperCollins Australia, my gratitude to Katie Stackhouse and Shona Martyn, my editors, and to Fiona Inglis of Curtis Brown Ltd., Australia.

It's a pleasure to work with the Steven Barclay Agency for speaking engagements. Everyone there is a friend, and they are tops. *Amici per sempre!*

I'm grateful to the editors of the following magazines where parts (in early versions) of this book originally were published: *The Southern Review, Virginia Quarterly Review, Ironwood, The Gettysburg Review, Frontiers, Ploughshares, The American Poetry Review,* and *The American Scholar.*

Closer to home, I hope the book itself acknowledges my indebtedness to my family. Edward Mayes, my husband, shares the joys of writing and the celebration of living, as well as provides the correction of tenses (I tend toward the continuous present). He must have memorized these chapters by now. My daughter, Ashley King, insisted that this book be written. If not for that, probably the flowered folders still would be in a storage box in the attic. She and her husband, Peter Leousis, sustained me with cheer good times, and constant firing up of the grill. Many thanks to my dear tribes: the Davis, Jackson, and Willcoxon families. And to my grandson, Wills, who, at ten, dove into the manuscript with enthusiasm.

I am lucky to live among generous friends who read and write, live large, love to talk and to celebrate. A coffee, a walk, a dinner, these everyday and communal pleasures remind me that a rising tide lifts all boats. *Grazie,* Lori Carlson, Hal Crowther, Anne and Walter Dellinger, Nancy and Steven Demorest, Nancy and Craufurd Goodwin, Allan Gurganus, Eric Hallman, Michael Malone, Elizabeth Matheson, Jill McCorkle, Ippy and Neil Patterson, Maureen Quilligan, Tom Rankin, Randall Roden, Lee Smith, Ann Stewart, Sharon Wheeler, Elizabeth Woodman, Susan Wyler, and all the Revelers Club. Oscar Hijuelos is mourned and missed.

Not nearby, but always close, and in touch with the evolution of this book: Todd Alden, Alberto Alfonso, Robert Draper, Shotsy Faust, Steve Harrison, Toni Mirosevich, Daniel Orozco, Steven Rothfeld, Kim Sunée, Audrey Wells, and Rena Williams. *Cari,* you know who you are to me!

NOTES

xxiv No future I imagined took place: Running from Columbus to Augusta in Georgia, the southern fall line is the Mesozoic shore of the Atlantic Ocean. The line divides the sandy soil and sedimentary rock from the crystalline rock and clay of the Piedmont north of the shoreline. "Fall" refers to the waterfalls that burst out along the boundary at the first exposures of crystalline rock.

xxix When the Bartrams, early horticulturists and adventurers: Philadelphia-born William Bartram (1739–1823) as a boy accompanied his father, John Bartram, on botanical expeditions to the South. A naturalist and artist, he continued to travel the South, gathering information about the natural world and also the native populations. *Travels Through North and South Carolina, Georgia, East and West Florida* is a classic.

xxxiii Flipping through my notebook: The fragment quoted is from Ezra Pound's *The Pisan Cantos,* LXXXI.

9 *What was it really like:* For another Fitzgerald, Georgia, memoir, see *Born Colored: Life Before Bloody Sunday* by Erin Goseer Mitchell. We were contemporaries, but I never knew her. Now I see that we should have been friends.

22 *It was a cloying, marvelous, mysterious:* The fragment "happy as the grass was green" is from Dylan Thomas's poem "Fern Hill."

29 *A thriving Jewish community owned:* Encyclopedia of Southern Jewish Communities: www.isjl.org/history/archive/ga/fitzgerald.html.

41 *And as W. H. Auden's refrain goes:* The line "Time will say nothing but I told you so" is from the poem "If I Could Tell You."

77 *When I went to Nicaragua:* I've written more on this era in "Quetzal," published in *Better Than Fiction,* Lonely Planet, 2012.

85 *Jekyll Island was deserted:* Jekyll Island, Georgia, is fascinating to visit. To me, it seems an unlikely place to have been chosen as a playground for the extremely rich—so wild, so many mosquitoes, so remote. See www .nps.gov/nr/travel/geo-flor/15.htm and other sites for an introduction to the history of the island. The old Jekyll Island Club is now an historic hotel, and several of the "cottages" have been restored. With much of the island protected by the state, Jekyll has escaped rife develop-

ment. Strangely, the untouched neighborhoods of low-sixties ranch houses are beginning to look historic.

127 I was stirred by Jeb's cavalry troops singing: "Kathleen Mavourneen," a song popular during the Civil War, was written by Frederick Crouch in 1837.

154 Propped in my white spool bed: The idea that the house should protect the dreamer comes from Gaston Bachelard's *Poetics of Space.*

167 We're fated to wonder: The line "Of those so close beside me, which are you?" is from Theodore Roethke's poem "The Waking."

251 From one who is writing exams: "Writing exams in water" glances off Keats's epitaph: *Here lies one whose name was writ in water.*

260 Also the birthplace of a writer I admire: Lillian Smith took on the subject of race long before other southern writers. *How Am I to Be Heard?* is a collection of her letters. She's best known for *Strange Fruit* and *Killers of the Dream.*

262 . . . shelling pecans for Martha Washington Jetties: Martha Washington Jetties are the ultimate Christmas candy. Balls of pecan-studded fondant are dipped in warm chocolate. The recipe is on my blog: www.francesmayes books.com.

264 The Yearling, *a childhood favorite:* The Marjorie Kinnan Rawlings quotes are from her memoir, *Cross Creek.* Cross

Creek, where she settled in a cottage in an orange grove, is now a Florida state park.

267 *The water may have moved on:* Fragments of Heraclitus, number 21: One cannot step twice into the same river, for the water into which you first stepped has flown on. Guy Davenport translation.

277–78 *I've found his grandfather's big shingle house:* I first saw my great-grandfather's house when I moved to North Carolina. Now a law firm, it's the only petunia in the onion patch, an excellent architectural example of shingle style completely surrounded by freeway interchanges and high-rises. Some history is at www.cmhpf.org/S&Rs%20 Alphabetical%20Order/surveys&rmayes.htm.

278 *From a recently found distant relative:* Walt Whitman he was not, but I am thrilled to have "My Lucky Number" written by my great-grandfather John Laban Smith in 1926. At one place in the poem, he's seventy-eight, and in another, eighty. At another, his wife is seventy-eight, but a few lines down, she's dead. He must have later revised.

My Lucky Number

My lucky number is 8.
What is your lucky number?
I challenge the world to beat me on my lucky number 8.
The flood was in the year 2448 B.C.

My forefather, Noah, was 599 year and 48 days old when he entered the ark.

I had 8 ancestors saved by water.

The 28 American soldiers who were killed in the battle of King's Mountain were buried on October 8th, 1780.

My liberty was celebrated in 1880, the year of the great centennial at which time the old monument was unveiled.

The old monument is 18 feet square at the base and 28 feet high.

The distance from our home to King's Mountain Battle Ground is 18 miles.

My liberty was renewed in 1818, the World War, 8 years ago.

I am 78 years old.

My wife was born in the year 1848. She is 78 years old.

My father left the farm in the year 1858, moved in a wagon, and I rode 8 miles.

My great grandfather, Jacob Rhyne, was the father of 8 sons.

I was the 8th child in the family.

I was married in 1878. I have been married 58 years.

The first money I earned was 5 cents when I was 8 years old.

I married my wife out of a family of 8 children.

I went 8 miles to get married.

I celebrated my fiftieth anniversary in 1918, 8 years ago.

My wife and I lived together 58 years when death separated us.

The first cook stove I owned was Number 8. It cost $18 and was given to me in 1880.

I had 8 sister-in-laws and 8 blood aunts. I had 8 uncles in the Civil War.

I had 8 great-uncles, I had 18 uncles in all.

I started to the Civil War with 8 in my company.

I moved to Gastonia NC in 1888. 8 Children had been born in my family.

I have been a resident of Gastonia NC 38 years.

The first time I saw the ocean I was 48 years old.

I have a Christmas present 38 years old.

I was standing on the summit of Spencer's Mountain 8 hours before the nineteenth century passed out.

I voted for the removal of Gaston County Court House from Dallas to Gastonia in 1908.

The first Republican ticket I voted was for Garfield for President of the United States and George McKee for Sheriff of Gaston County, this was in 1880.

I voted no more Republican tickets until 48 years afterwards.

I was 80 years old when I voted the Republican ticket for the second time in my life.

I quit drinking coffee on May 8, 1908.

The first cotton mill built in my county, Gaston, was in 1848, it ran for 68 years regular without stopping before it was destroyed by high water.

The first railroad built through my county was in 1858.

My first trip on a train was in 1868. I rode a distance of 18 miles.

I have been 800 miles from home. I have been in 8 states.

I am glad to say I live in the best country in the world which is composed of 48 states.

The father of my country, George Washington, was president 8 years.

The Washington Monument was started under construction in 1848.

I visited Mt. Vernon and went through George Washington's home in 1918, 8 years ago.

I live 8 blocks from the city square.

I live at 408 Willow Street.

My favorite verse in the Bible is Revelations 1–18, "I am he that liveth, and was dead; and behold, I am alive for ever more, Amen; and have the keys of hell and death." On this hangs my soul. What does your soul hang on?

These are facts and are correct to December 28th, 1926.

281 From her, I understand in the marrow: The line "A pity beyond all telling is hid in the heart of love" is from W. B. Yeats's poem "The Pity of Love."

ABOUT THE AUTHOR

In addition to her bestselling Tuscany memoirs, *Under the Tuscan Sun, Bella Tuscany,* and *Every Day in Tuscany,* FRANCES MAYES is the author of the travel memoir *A Year in the World; The Tuscan Sun Cookbook;* illustrated books *In Tuscany* and *Bringing Tuscany Home* (with Edward Mayes); a novel, *Swan;* a text for readers, *The Discovery of Poetry;* and five books of poetry. Her books have been translated into more than fifty languages. She divides her time between Italy and North Carolina.

Visit Frances at francesmayesbooks.com.